# COLLECTED POEMS AND PLAYS OF
## RABINDRANATH TAGORE

For Patrick

with whom I share
a love for beautiful
words and beautiful ideas.

Marilyn.

Christmas 1993

# COLLECTED
# POEMS AND PLAYS
## *of*
# RABINDRANATH
# TAGORE

**M**
**PAPERMAC**

*First Edition* 1936
*Reprinted* 1939, 1950, 1952, 1958, 1961, 1962, 1967, 1973, 1977, 1979,
1981, 1983, 1985, 1988

MACMILLAN LONDON LIMITED
*4 Little Essex Street London WC2R 3LF
and Basingstoke
Associated companies in Auckland, Delhi, Dublin, Gaborone,
Hamburg, Harare, Hong Kong, Johannesburg, Kuala Lumpur,
Lagos, Manzini, Melbourne, Mexico City, Nairobi, New York,
Singapore and Tokyo*

*Papermac edition 1989*

ISBN 0–333–52197–8

*Printed in Hong Kong*

# CONTENTS

# GITANJALI

# GITANJALI

## I

THOU hast made me endless, such is thy pleasure. This frail vessel thou emptiest again and again, and fillest it ever with fresh life.

This little flute of a reed thou hast carried over hills and dales, and hast breathed through it melodies eternally new.

At the immortal touch of thy hands my little heart loses its limits in joy and gives birth to utterance ineffable.

Thy infinite gifts come to me only on these very small hands of mine. Ages pass, and still thou pourest, and still there is room to fill.

## II

WHEN thou commandest me to sing, it seems that my heart would break with pride; and I look to thy face, and tears come to my eyes.

All that is harsh and dissonant in my life melts into one sweet harmony—and my adoration spreads wings like a glad bird on its flight across the sea.

I know thou takest pleasure in my singing. I know that only as a singer I come before thy presence.

I touch by the edge of the far-spreading wing of my song thy feet which I could never aspire to reach.

Drunk with the joy of singing I forget myself and call thee friend who art my lord.

### III

I KNOW not how thou singest, my master! I ever listen in silent amazement.

The light of thy music illumines the world. The life-breath of thy music runs from sky to sky. The holy stream of thy music breaks through all stony obstacles and rushes on.

My heart longs to join in thy song, but vainly struggles for a voice. I would speak, but speech breaks not into song, and I cry out baffled. Ah, thou hast made my heart captive in the endless meshes of thy music, my master!

### IV

LIFE of my life, I shall ever try to keep my body pure, knowing that thy living touch is upon all my limbs.

I shall ever try to keep all untruths out from my thoughts, knowing that thou art that truth which has kindled the light of reason in my mind.

I shall ever try to drive all evils away from my heart and keep my love in flower, knowing that thou hast thy seat in the inmost shrine of my heart.

And it shall be my endeavour to reveal thee in my actions, knowing it is thy power gives me strength to act.

### V

I ASK for a moment's indulgence to sit by thy side. The works that I have in hand I will finish afterwards.

Away from the sight of thy face my heart knows no rest nor respite, and my work becomes an endless toil in a shoreless sea of toil.

To-day the summer has come at my window with its

sighs and murmurs; and the bees are plying their
minstrelsy at the court of the flowering grove.

Now it is time to sit quiet, face to face with thee,
and to sing dedication of life in this silent and overflowing leisure.

### VI

PLUCK this little flower and take it. Delay not! I fear
lest it droop and drop into the dust.

It may not find a place in thy garland, but honour it
with a touch of pain from thy hand and pluck it. I fear
lest the day end before I am aware, and the time of
offering go by.

Though its colour be not deep and its smell be faint,
use this flower in thy service and pluck it while there
is time.

### VII

MY song has put off her adornments. She has no pride
of dress and decoration. Ornaments would mar our
union; they would come between thee and me; their
jingling would drown thy whispers.

My poet's vanity dies in shame before thy sight. O
master poet, I have sat down at thy feet. Only let me
make my life simple and straight, like a flute of reed
for thee to fill with music.

### VIII

THE child who is decked with prince's robes and who
has jewelled chains round his neck loses all pleasure in
his play; his dress hampers him at every step.

In fear that it may be frayed, or stained with dust he
keeps himself from the world, and is afraid even to
move.

Mother, it is no gain, thy bondage of finery, if it keep one shut off from the healthful dust of the earth, if it rob one of the right of entrance to the great fair of common human life.

## IX

O FOOL, to try to carry thyself upon thy own shoulders! O beggar, to come to beg at thy own door!

Leave all thy burdens on his hands who can bear all, and never look behind in regret.

Thy desire at once puts out the light from the lamp it touches with its breath. It is unholy—take not thy gifts through its unclean hands. Accept only what is offered by sacred love.

## X

HERE is thy footstool and there rest thy feet where live the poorest, and lowliest, and lost.

When I try to bow to thee, my obeisance cannot reach down to the depth where thy feet rest among the poorest, and lowliest, and lost.

Pride can never approach to where thou walkest in the clothes of the humble among the poorest, and lowliest, and lost.

My heart can never find its way to where thou keepest company with the companionless among the poorest, the lowliest, and the lost.

## XI

LEAVE this chanting and singing and telling of beads! Whom dost thou worship in this lonely dark corner of a temple with doors all shut? Open thine eyes and see thy God is not before thee!

He is there where the tiller is tilling the hard ground and where the pathmaker is breaking stones. He is with them in sun and in shower, and his garment is covered with dust. Put off thy holy mantle and even like him come down on the dusty soil!

Deliverance? Where is this deliverance to be found? Our master himself has joyfully taken upon him the bonds of creation; he is bound with us all for ever.

Come out of thy meditations and leave aside thy flowers and incense! What harm is there if thy clothes become tattered and stained? Meet him and stand by him in toil and in sweat of thy brow.

## XII

THE time that my journey takes is long and the way of it long.

I came out on the chariot of the first gleam of light, and pursued my voyage through the wildernesses of worlds leaving my track on many a star and planet.

It is the most distant course that comes nearest to thyself, and that training is the most intricate which leads to the utter simplicity of a tune.

The traveller has to knock at every alien door to come to his own, and one has to wander through all the outer worlds to reach the innermost shrine at the end.

My eyes strayed far and wide before I shut them and said, "Here art thou!"

The question and the cry, "Oh, where?" melt into tears of a thousand streams and deluge the world with the flood of the assurance, "I am!"

## XIII

THE song that I came to sing remains unsung to this day.

I have spent my days in stringing and in unstringing my instrument.

The time has not come true, the words have not been rightly set; only there is the agony of wishing in my heart.

The blossom has not opened; only the wind is sighing by.

I have not seen his face, nor have I listened to his voice; only I have heard his gentle footsteps from the road before my house.

The livelong day has passed in spreading his seat on the floor; but the lamp has not been lit and I cannot ask him into my house.

I live in the hope of meeting with him; but this meeting is not yet.

## XIV

MY desires are many and my cry is pitiful, but ever didst thou save me by hard refusals; and this strong mercy has been wrought into my life through and through.

Day by day thou art making me worthy of the simple, great gifts that thou gavest to me unasked—this sky and the light, this body and the life and the mind—saving me from perils of overmuch desire.

There are times when I languidly linger and times when I awaken and hurry in search of my goal; but cruelly thou hidest thyself from before me.

Day by day thou art making me worthy of thy full

acceptance by refusing me ever and anon, saving me from perils of weak, uncertain desire.

## XV

I AM here to sing thee songs. In this hall of thine I have a corner seat.

In thy world I have no work to do; my useless life can only break out in tunes without a purpose.

When the hour strikes for thy silent worship at the dark temple of midnight, command me, my master, to stand before thee to sing.

When in the morning air the golden harp is tuned, honour me, commanding my presence.

## XVI

I HAVE had my invitation to this world's festival, and thus my life has been blessed. My eyes have seen and my ears have heard.

It was my part at this feast to play upon my instrument, and I have done all I could.

Now, I ask, has the time come at last when I may go in and see thy face and offer thee my silent salutation?

## XVII

I AM only waiting for love to give myself up at last into his hands. That is why it is so late and why I have been guilty of such omissions.

They come with their laws and their codes to bind me fast; but I evade them ever, for I am only waiting for love to give myself up at last into his hands.

People blame me and call me heedless; I doubt not they are right in their blame.

The market day is over and work is all done for the

busy. Those who came to call me in vain have gone back in anger. I am only waiting for love to give myself up at last into his hands.

## XVIII

CLOUDS heap upon clouds and it darkens. Ah, love, why dost thou let me wait outside at the door all alone?

In the busy moments of the noontide work I am with the crowd, but on this dark lonely day it is only for thee that I hope.

If thou showest me not thy face, if thou leavest me wholly aside, I know not how I am to pass these long, rainy hours.

I keep gazing on the far-away gloom of the sky, and my heart wanders wailing with the restless wind.

## XIX

IF thou speakest not I will fill my heart with thy silence and endure it. I will keep still and wait like the night with starry vigil and its head bent low with patience.

The morning will surely come, the darkness will vanish, and thy voice pour down in golden streams breaking through the sky.

Then thy words will take wing in songs from every one of my birds' nests, and thy melodies will break forth in flowers in all my forest groves.

## XX

ON the day when the lotus bloomed, alas, my mind was straying, and I knew it not. My basket was empty and the flower remained unheeded.

Only now and again a sadness fell upon me, and I started up from my dream and felt a sweet trace of a strange fragrance in the south wind.

That vague sweetness made my heart ache with longing and it seemed to me that it was the eager breath of the summer seeking for its completion.

I knew not then that it was so near, that it was mine, and that this perfect sweetness had blossomed in the depth of my own heart.

## XXI

I must launch out my boat. The languid hours pass by on the shore—Alas for me!

The spring has done its flowering and taken leave. And now with the burden of faded futile flowers I wait and linger.

The waves have become clamorous, and upon the bank in the shady lane the yellow leaves flutter and fall.

What emptiness do you gaze upon! Do you not feel a thrill passing through the air with the notes of the far-away song floating from the other shore?

## XXII

In the deep shadows of the rainy July, with secret steps, thou walkest, silent as night, eluding all watchers.

To-day the morning has closed its eyes, heedless of the insistent calls of the loud east wind, and a thick veil has been drawn over the ever-wakeful blue sky.

The woodlands have hushed their songs, and doors are all shut at every house. Thou art the solitary wayfarer in this deserted street. Oh, my only friend, my best beloved, the gates are open in my house—do not pass by like a dream.

## XXIII

ART thou abroad on this stormy night on thy journey of love, my friend? The sky groans like one in despair.

I have no sleep to-night. Ever and again I open my door and look out on the darkness, my friend!

I can see nothing before me. I wonder where lies thy path!

By what dim shore of the ink-black river, by what far edge of the frowning forest, through what mazy depth of gloom art thou threading thy course to come to me, my friend?

## XXIV

IF the day is done, if birds sing no more, if the wind has flagged tired, then draw the veil of darkness thick upon me, even as thou hast wrapt the earth with the coverlet of sleep and tenderly closed the petals of the drooping lotus at dusk.

From the traveller, whose sack of provisions is empty before the voyage is ended, whose garment is torn and dust-laden, whose strength is exhausted, remove shame and poverty, and renew his life like a flower under the cover of thy kindly night.

## XXV

IN the night of weariness let me give myself up to sleep without struggle, resting my trust upon thee.

Let me not force my flagging spirit into a poor preparation for thy worship.

It is thou who drawest the veil of night upon the tired eyes of the day to renew its sight in a fresher gladness of awakening.

## XXVI

HE came and sat by my side but I woke not. What a cursed sleep it was, O miserable me!

He came when the night was still; he had his harp in his hands, and my dreams became resonant with its melodies.

Alas, why are my nights all thus lost? Ah, why do I ever miss his sight whose breath touches my sleep?

## XXVII

LIGHT, oh, where is the light? Kindle it with the burning fire of desire!

There is the lamp but never a flicker of a flame,— is such thy fate, my heart? Ah, death were better by far for thee!

Misery knocks at thy door, and her message is that thy lord is wakeful, and he calls thee to the love-tryst through the darkness of night.

The sky is overcast with clouds and the rain is ceaseless. I know not what this is that stirs in me,—I know not its meaning.

A moment's flash of lightning drags down a deeper gloom on my sight, and my heart gropes for the path to where the music of the night calls me.

Light, oh, where is the light? Kindle it with the burning fire of desire! It thunders and the wind rushes screaming through the void. The night is black as a black stone. Let not the hours pass by in the dark. Kindle the lamp of love with thy life.

## XXVIII

OBSTINATE are the trammels, but my heart aches when I try to break them.

Freedom is all I want, but to hope for it I feel ashamed.

I am certain that priceless wealth is in thee, and that thou art my best friend, but I have not the heart to sweep away the tinsel that fills my room.

The shroud that covers me is a shroud of dust and death; I hate it, yet hug it in love.

My debts are large, my failures great, my shame secret and heavy; yet when I come to ask for my good, I quake in fear lest my prayer be granted.


## XXIX

HE whom I enclose with my name is weeping in this dungeon. I am ever busy building this wall all around; and as this wall goes up into the sky day by day I lose sight of my true being in its dark shadow.

I take pride in this great wall, and I plaster it with dust and sand lest a least hole should be left in this name; and for all the care I take I lose sight of my true being.


## XXX

I CAME out alone on my way to my tryst. But who is this that follows me in the silent dark?

I move aside to avoid his presence but I escape him not.

He makes the dust rise from the earth with his swagger; he adds his loud voice to every word that I utter.

He is my own little self, my lord, he knows no shame; but I am ashamed to come to thy door in his company.

"Prisoner, tell me, who was it that bound you?"

"It was my master," said the prisoner. "I thought I could outdo everybody in the world in wealth and power, and I amassed in my own treasure-house the money due to my king. When sleep overcame me I lay upon the bed that was for my lord, and on waking up I found I was a prisoner in my own treasure-house."

"Prisoner, tell me, who was it that wrought this unbreakable chain?"

"It was I," said the prisoner, "who forged this chain very carefully. I thought my invincible power would hold the world captive leaving me in a freedom undisturbed. Thus night and day I worked at the chain with huge fires and cruel hard strokes. When at last the work was done and the links were complete and unbreakable, I found that it held me in its grip."

## XXXII

By all means they try to hold me secure who love me in this world. But it is otherwise with thy love which is greater than theirs, and thou keepest me free.

Lest I forget them they never venture to leave me alone. But day passes by after day and thou art not seen.

If I call not thee in my prayers, if I keep not thee in my heart, thy love for me still waits for my love.

## XXXIII

When it was day they came into my house and said, "We shall only take the smallest room here."

They said, "We shall help you in the worship of your God and humbly accept only our own share of his

grace"; and then they took their seat in a corner and
they sat quiet and meek.

But in the darkness of night I find they break into
my sacred shrine, strong and turbulent, and snatch
with unholy greed the offerings from God's altar.

## XXXIV

LET only that little be left of me whereby I may name
thee my all.

Let only that little be left of my will whereby I may
feel thee on every side, and come to thee in everything,
and offer to thee my love every moment.

Let only that little be left of me whereby I may
never hide thee.

Let only that little of my fetters be left whereby I am
bound with thy will, and thy purpose is carried out in
my life—and that is the fetter of thy love.

## XXXV

WHERE the mind is without fear and the head is held
high;

Where knowledge is free;

Where the world has not been broken up into fragments by narrow domestic walls;

Where words come out from the depth of truth;

Where tireless striving stretches its arms towards
perfection;

Where the clear stream of reason has not lost its way
into the dreary desert sand of dead habit;

Where the mind is led forward by thee into ever-
widening thought and action—

Into that heaven of freedom, my Father, let my
country awake.

THIS is my prayer to thee, my lord—strike, strike at the root of penury in my heart.

Give me the strength lightly to bear my joys and sorrows.

Give me the strength to make my love fruitful in service.

Give me the strength never to disown the poor or bend my knees before insolent might.

Give me the strength to raise my mind high above daily trifles.

And give me the strength to surrender my strength to thy will with love.

XXXVII

I THOUGHT that my voyage had come to its end at the last limit of my power,—that the path before me was closed, that provisions were exhausted and the time come to take shelter in a silent obscurity.

But I find that thy will knows no end in me. And when old words die out on the tongue, new melodies break forth from the heart; and where the old tracks are lost, new country is revealed with its wonders.

XXXVIII

THAT I want thee, only thee—let my heart repeat without end. All desires that distract me, day and night, are false and empty to the core.

As the night keeps hidden in its gloom the petition for light, even thus in the depth of my unconsciousness rings the cry—"I want thee, only thee".

As the storm still seeks its end in peace when it

strikes against peace with all its might, even thus my
rebellion strikes against thy love and still its cry is—
"I want thee, only thee".

XXXIX

WHEN the heart is hard and parched up, come upon
me with a shower of mercy.

When grace is lost from life, come with a burst of
song.

When tumultuous work raises its din on all sides
shutting me out from beyond, come to me, my lord of
silence, with thy peace and rest.

When my beggarly heart sits crouched, shut up in a
corner, break open the door, my king, and come with
the ceremony of a king.

When desire blinds the mind with delusion and dust,
O thou holy one, thou wakeful, come with thy light
and thy thunder.

XL

THE rain has held back for days and days, my God, in
my arid heart. The horizon is fiercely naked—not the
thinnest cover of a soft cloud, not the vaguest hint of a
distant cool shower.

Send thy angry storm, dark with death, if it is thy
wish, and with lashes of lightning startle the sky from
end to end.

But call back, my lord, call back this pervading
silent heat, still and keen and cruel, burning the heart
with dire despair.

Let the cloud of grace bend low from above like the
tearful look of the mother on the day of the father's
wrath.

18

WHERE dost thou stand behind them all, my lover, hiding thyself in the shadows? They push thee and pass thee by on the dusty road, taking thee for naught. I wait here weary hours spreading my offerings for thee, while passers-by come and take my flowers, one by one, and my basket is nearly empty.

The morning time is past, and the noon. In the shade of evening my eyes are drowsy with sleep. Men going home glance at me and smile and fill me with shame. I sit like a beggar maid, drawing my skirt over my face, and when they ask me what it is I want, I drop my eyes and answer them not.

Oh, how, indeed, could I tell them that for thee I wait, and that thou hast promised to come? How could I utter for shame that I keep for my dowry this poverty? Ah, I hug this pride in the secret of my heart.

I sit on the grass and gaze upon the sky and dream of the sudden splendour of thy coming—all the lights ablaze, golden pennons flying over thy car, and they at the roadside standing agape, when they see thee come down from thy seat to raise me from the dust, and set at thy side this ragged beggar girl a-tremble with shame and pride, like a creeper in a summer breeze.

But time glides on and still no sound of the wheels of thy chariot. Many a procession passes by with noise and shouts and glamour of glory. Is it only thou who wouldst stand in the shadow silent and behind them all? And only I who would wait and weep and wear out my heart in vain longing?

EARLY in the day it was whispered that we should sail in a boat, only thou and I, and never a soul in the world would know of this our pilgrimage to no country and to no end.

In that shoreless ocean, at thy silently listening smile my songs would swell in melodies, free as waves, free from all bondage of words.

Is the time not come yet? Are there works still to do? Lo, the evening has come down upon the shore and in the fading light the seabirds come flying to their nests.

Who knows when the chains will be off, and the boat, like the last glimmer of sunset, vanish into the night?

## XLIII

THE day was when I did not keep myself in readiness for thee; and entering my heart unbidden even as one of the common crowd, unknown to me, my king, thou didst press the signet of eternity upon many a fleeting moment of my life.

And to-day when by chance I light upon them and see thy signature, I find they have lain scattered in the dust mixed with the memory of joys and sorrows of my trivial days forgotten.

Thou didst not turn in contempt from my childish play among dust, and the steps that I heard in my play-room are the same that are echoing from star to star.

## XLIV

THIS is my delight, thus to wait and watch at the way-side where shadow chases light and the rain comes in the wake of the summer.

Messengers, with tidings from unknown skies, greet me and speed along the road. My heart is glad within, and the breath of the passing breeze is sweet.

From dawn till dusk I sit here before my door, and I know that of a sudden the happy moment will arrive when I shall see.

In the meanwhile I smile and I sing all alone. In the meanwhile the air is filling with the perfume of promise.

### XLV

HAVE you not heard his silent steps? He comes, comes, ever comes.

Every moment and every age, every day and every night he comes, comes, ever comes.

Many a song have I sung in many a mood of mind, but all their notes have always proclaimed, "He comes, comes, ever comes."

In the fragrant days of sunny April through the forest path he comes, comes, ever comes.

In the rainy gloom of July nights on the thundering chariot of clouds he comes, comes, ever comes.

In sorrow after sorrow it is his steps that press upon my heart, and it is the golden touch of his feet that makes my joy to shine.

### XLVI

I KNOW not from what distant time thou art ever coming nearer to meet me. Thy sun and stars can never keep thee hidden from me for aye.

In many a morning and eve thy footsteps have been heard and thy messenger has come within my heart and called me in secret.

I know not why to-day my life is all astir, and a feeling of tremulous joy is passing through my heart.

It is as if the time were come to wind up my work, and I feel in the air a faint smell of thy sweet presence.

## XLVII

THE night is nearly spent waiting for him in vain. I fear lest in the morning he suddenly come to my door when I have fallen asleep wearied out. Oh, friends, leave the way open to him—forbid him not.

If the sound of his steps does not wake me, do not try to rouse me, I pray. I wish not to be called from my sleep by the clamorous choir of birds, by the riot of wind at the festival of morning light. Let me sleep undisturbed even if my lord comes of a sudden to my door.

Ah, my sleep, precious sleep, which only waits for his touch to vanish. Ah, my closed eyes that would open their lids only to the light of his smile when he stands before me like a dream emerging from darkness of sleep.

Let him appear before my sight as the first of all lights and all forms. The first thrill of joy to my awakened soul, let it come from his glance. And let my return to myself be immediate return to him.

## XLVIII

THE morning sea of silence broke into ripples of bird songs; and the flowers were all merry by the roadside; and the wealth of gold was scattered through the rift of the clouds while we busily went on our way and paid no heed.

We sang no glad songs nor played; we went not to

the village for barter; we spoke not a word nor smiled; we lingered not on the way. We quickened our pace more and more as the time sped by.

The sun rose to the mid sky and doves cooed in the shade. Withered leaves danced and whirled in the hot air of noon. The shepherd boy drowsed and dreamed in the shadow of the banyan tree, and I laid myself down by the water and stretched my tired limbs on the grass.

My companions laughed at me in scorn; they held their heads high and hurried on; they never looked back nor rested; they vanished in the distant blue haze. They crossed many meadows and hills, and passed through strange, far-away countries. All honour to you, heroic host of the interminable path! Mockery and reproach pricked me to rise, but found no response in me. I gave myself up for lost in the depth of a glad humiliation—in the shadow of a dim delight.

The repose of the sun-embroidered green gloom slowly spread over my heart. I forgot for what I had travelled, and I surrendered my mind without struggle to the maze of shadows and songs.

At last, when I woke from my slumber and opened my eyes, I saw thee standing by me, flooding my sleep with thy smile. How I had feared that the path was long and wearisome, and the struggle to reach thee was hard!

XLIX

YOU came down from your throne and stood at my cottage door.

I was singing all alone in a corner, and the melody caught your ear. You came down and stood at my cottage door.

23

Masters are many in your hall, and songs are sung there at all hours. But the simple carol of this novice struck at your love. One plaintive little strain mingled with the great music of the world, and with a flower for a prize you came down and stopped at my cottage door.

L

I HAD gone a-begging from door to door in the village path, when thy golden chariot appeared in the distance like a gorgeous dream and I wondered who was this King of all kings!

My hopes rose high and methought my evil days were at an end, and I stood waiting for alms to be given unasked and for wealth scattered on all sides in the dust.

The chariot stopped where I stood. Thy glance fell on me and thou camest down with a smile. I felt that the luck of my life had come at last. Then of a sudden thou didst hold out thy right hand and say, "What hast thou to give to me?"

Ah, what a kingly jest was it to open thy palm to a beggar to beg! I was confused and stood undecided, and then from my wallet I slowly took out the least little grain of corn and gave it to thee.

But how great my surprise when at the day's end I emptied my bag on the floor to find a least little grain of gold among the poor heap! I bitterly wept and wished that I had had the heart to give thee my all.

LI

THE night darkened. Our day's works had been done. We thought that the last guest had arrived for the night and the doors in the village were all shut. Only some said the King was to come. We laughed and said, "No, it cannot be!"

It seemed there were knocks at the door and we said it was nothing but the wind. We put out the lamps and lay down to sleep. Only some said, "It is the messenger!" We laughed and said, "No, it must be the wind!"

There came a sound in the dead of the night. We sleepily thought it was the distant thunder. The earth shook, the walls rocked, and it troubled us in our sleep. Only some said it was the sound of wheels. We said in a drowsy murmur, "No, it must be the rumbling of clouds!"

The night was still dark when the drum sounded. The voice came, "Wake up! delay not!" We pressed our hands on our hearts and shuddered with fear. Some said, "Lo, there is the King's flag!" We stood up on our feet and cried "There is no time for delay!"

The King has come—but where are lights, where are wreaths? Where is the throne to seat him? Oh, shame! Oh utter shame! Where is the hall, the decorations? Some one has said, "Vain is this cry! Greet him with empty hands, lead him into thy rooms all bare!"

Open the doors, let the conch-shells be sounded! In the depth of the night has come the King of our dark, dreary house. The thunder roars in the sky. The darkness shudders with lightning. Bring out thy tattered piece of mat and spread it in the courtyard. With the storm has come of a sudden our King of the fearful night.

## LII

I THOUGHT I should ask of thee—but I dared not—the rose wreath thou hadst on thy neck. Thus I waited for the morning, when thou didst depart, to find a few fragments on the bed. And like a beggar I searched in the dawn only for a stray petal or two.

Ah me, what is it I find? What token left of thy love? It is no flower, no spices, no vase of perfumed water. It is thy mighty sword, flashing as a flame, heavy as a bolt of thunder. The young light of morning comes through the window and spreads itself upon thy bed. The morning bird twitters and asks, "Woman, what hast thou got?" No, it is no flower, nor spices, nor vase of perfumed water—it is thy dreadful sword.

I sit and muse in wonder, what gift is this of thine. I can find no place where to hide it. I am ashamed to wear it, frail as I am, and it hurts me when I press it to my bosom. Yet shall I bear in my heart this honour of the burden of pain, this gift of thine.

From now there shall be no fear left for me in this world, and thou shalt be victorious in all my strife. Thou hast left death for my companion and I shall crown him with my life. Thy sword is with me to cut asunder my bonds, and there shall be no fear left for me in the world.

From now I leave off all petty decorations. Lord of my heart, no more shall there be for me waiting and weeping in corners, no more coyness and sweetness of demeanour. Thou hast given me thy sword for adornment. No more doll's decorations for me!

LIII

BEAUTIFUL is thy wristlet, decked with stars and cunningly wrought in myriad-coloured jewels. But more beautiful to me thy sword with its curve of lightning like the outspread wings of the divine bird of

Vishnu, perfectly poised in the angry red light of the sunset.

It quivers like the one last response of life in ecstasy of pain at the final stroke of death; it shines like the pure flame of being burning up earthly sense with one fierce flash.

Beautiful is thy wristlet, decked with starry gems; but thy sword, O lord of thunder, is wrought with uttermost beauty, terrible to behold or to think of.

## LIV

I ASKED nothing from thee; I uttered not my name to thine ear. When thou took'st thy leave I stood silent. I was alone by the well where the shadow of the tree fell aslant, and the women had gone home with their brown earthen pitchers full to the brim. They called me and shouted, "Come with us, the morning is wearing on to noon." But I languidly lingered awhile lost in the midst of vague musings.

I heard not thy steps as thou camest. Thine eyes were sad when they fell on me; thy voice was tired as thou spokest low—"Ah, I am a thirsty traveller." I started up from my day-dreams and poured water from my jar on thy joined palms. The leaves rustled overhead; the cuckoo sang from the unseen dark, and perfume of *babla* flowers came from the bend of the road.

I stood speechless with shame when my name thou didst ask. Indeed, what had I done for thee to keep me in remembrance? But the memory that I could give water to thee to allay thy thirst will cling to my heart and enfold it in sweetness. The morning hour is late, the bird sings in weary notes, *neem* leaves rustle overhead and I sit and think and think.

Languor is upon your heart and the slumber is still on your eyes.

Has not the word come to you that the flower is reigning in splendour among thorns? Wake, oh, awaken! Let not the time pass in vain!

At the end of the stony path, in the country of virgin solitude, my friend is sitting all alone. Deceive him not. Wake, oh, awaken!

What if the sky pants and trembles with the heat of the midday sun—what if the burning sand spreads its mantle of thirst—

Is there no joy in the deep of your heart? At every footfall of yours, will not the harp of the road break out in sweet music of pain?

## LVI

Thus it is that thy joy in me is so full. Thus it is that thou hast come down to me. O thou lord of all heavens, where would be thy love if I were not?

Thou hast taken me as thy partner of all this wealth. In my heart is the endless play of thy delight. In my life thy will is ever taking shape.

And for this, thou who art the King of kings hast decked thyself in beauty to captivate my heart. And for this thy love loses itself in the love of thy lover, and there art thou seen in the perfect union of two.

## LVII

Light, my light, the world-filling light, the eye-kissing light, heart-sweetening light!

Ah, the light dances, my darling, at the centre of my

life; the light strikes, my darling, the chords of my love; the sky opens, the wind runs wild, laughter passes over the earth.

The butterflies spread their sails on the sea of light. Lilies and jasmines surge up on the crest of the waves of light.

The light is shattered into gold on every cloud, my darling, and it scatters gems in profusion.

Mirth spreads from leaf to leaf, my darling, and gladness without measure. The heaven's river has drowned its banks and the flood of joy is abroad.

### LVIII

LET all the strains of joy mingle in my last song—the joy that makes the earth flow over in the riotous excess of the grass, the joy that sets the twin brothers, life and death, dancing over the wide world, the joy that sweeps in with the tempest, shaking and waking all life with laughter, the joy that sits still with its tears on the open red lotus of pain, and the joy that throws everything it has upon the dust, and knows not a word.

### LIX

YES, I know, this is nothing but thy love, O beloved of my heart—this golden light that dances upon the leaves, these idle clouds sailing across the sky, this passing breeze leaving its coolness upon my forehead.

The morning light has flooded my eyes—this is thy message to my heart. Thy face is bent from above, thy eyes look down on my eyes, and my heart has touched thy feet.

THOU hast made me known to friends whom I knew not. Thou hast given me seats in homes not my own. Thou hast brought the distant near and made a brother of the stranger.

I am uneasy at heart when I have to leave my accustomed shelter; I forget that there abides the old in the new, and that there also thou abidest.

Through birth and death, in this world or in others, wherever thou leadest me it is thou, the same, the one companion of my endless life who ever linkest my heart with bonds of joy to the unfamiliar.

When one knows thee, then alien there is none, then no door is shut. Oh, grant me my prayer that I may never lose the bliss of the touch of the one in the play of the many.

## LXIV

ON the slope of the desolate river among tall grasses I asked her, "Maiden, where do you go, shading your lamp with your mantle? My house is all dark and lonesome,—lend me your light!" She raised her dark eyes for a moment and looked at my face through the dusk. "I have come to the river," she said, "to float my lamp on the stream when the daylight wanes in the west." I stood alone among tall grasses and watched the timid flame of her lamp uselessly drifting in the tide.

In the silence of gathering night I asked her, "Maiden, your lights are all lit—then where do you go with your lamp? My house is all dark and lonesome,— lend me your light." She raised her dark eyes on my face and stood for a moment doubtful. "I have come," she said at last, "to dedicate my lamp to the sky." I stood and watched her light uselessly burning in the void.

In the moonless gloom of midnight I asked her, "Maiden, what is your quest, holding the lamp near your heart? My house is all dark and lonesome,—lend me your light." She stopped for a minute and thought and gazed at my face in the dark. "I have brought my light," she said, "to join the carnival of lamps." I stood and watched her little lamp uselessly lost among lights.

LXV

WHAT divine drink wouldst thou have, my God, from this overflowing cup of my life?

My poet, is it thy delight to see thy creation through my eyes and to stand at the portals of my ears silently to listen to thine own eternal harmony?

Thy world is weaving words in my mind and thy joy is adding music to them. Thou givest thyself to me in love and then feelest thine own entire sweetness in me.

LXVI

SHE who ever had remained in the depth of my being, in the twilight of gleams and of glimpses; she who never opened her veils in the morning light, will be my last gift to thee, my God, folded in my final song.

Words have wooed yet failed to win her; persuasion has stretched to her its eager arms in vain.

I have roamed from country to country keeping her in the core of my heart, and around her have risen and fallen the growth and decay of my life.

Over my thoughts and actions, my slumbers and dreams, she reigned yet dwelled alone and apart.

Many a man knocked at my door and asked for her and turned away in despair.

There was none in the world who ever saw her face to face, and she remained in her loneliness waiting for thy recognition.

## LXVII

THOU art the sky and thou art the nest as well.

O thou beautiful, there in the nest it is thy love that encloses the soul with colours and sounds and odours.

There comes the morning with the golden basket in her right hand bearing the wreath of beauty, silently to crown the earth.

And there comes the evening over the lonely meadows deserted by herds, through trackless paths, carrying cool draughts of peace in her golden pitcher from the western ocean of rest.

But there, where spreads the infinite sky for the soul to take her flight in, reigns the stainless white radiance. There is no day nor night, nor form nor colour, and never, never a word.

## LXVIII

THY sunbeam comes upon this earth of mine with arms outstretched and stands at my door the livelong day to carry back to thy feet clouds made of my tears and sighs and songs.

With fond delight thou wrappest about thy starry breast that mantle of misty cloud, turning it into numberless shapes and folds and colouring it with hues everchanging.

It is so light and so fleeting, tender and tearful and dark, that is why thou lovest it, O thou spotless and serene. And that is why it may cover thy awful white light with its pathetic shadows.

### LXIX

THE same stream of life that runs through my veins night and day runs through the world and dances in rhythmic measures.

It is the same life that shoots in joy through the dust of the earth in numberless blades of grass and breaks into tumultuous waves of leaves and flowers.

It is the same life that is rocked in the ocean-cradle of birth and of death, in ebb and in flow.

I feel my limbs are made glorious by the touch of this world of life. And my pride is from the life-throb of ages dancing in my blood this moment.

### LXX

Is it beyond thee to be glad with the gladness of this rhythm? to be tossed and lost and broken in the whirl of this fearful joy?

All things rush on, they stop not, they look not behind, no power can hold them back, they rush on.

Keeping steps with that restless, rapid music, seasons come dancing and pass away—colours, tunes, and perfumes pour in endless cascades in the abounding joy that scatters and gives up and dies every moment.

### LXXI

THAT I should make much of myself and turn it on all sides, thus casting coloured shadows on thy radiance —such is thy *maya*.

Thou settest a barrier in thine own being and then

callest thy severed self in myriad notes. This thy self-separation has taken body in me.

The poignant song is echoed through all the sky in many-coloured tears and smiles, alarms and hopes; waves rise up and sink again, dreams break and form. In me is thy own defeat of self.

This screen that thou hast raised is painted with innumerable figures with the brush of the night and the day. Behind it thy seat is woven in wondrous mysteries of curves, casting away all barren lines of straightness.

The great pageant of thee and me has overspread the sky. With the tune of thee and me all the air is vibrant, and all ages pass with the hiding and seeking of thee and me.

## LXXII

HE it is, the innermost one, who awakens my being with his deep hidden touches.

He it is who puts his enchantment upon these eyes and joyfully plays on the chords of my heart in varied cadence of pleasure and pain.

He it is who weaves the web of this *maya* in evanescent hues of gold and silver, blue and green, and lets peep out through the folds his feet, at whose touch I forget myself.

Days come and ages pass, and it is ever he who moves my heart in many a name, in many a guise, in many a rapture of joy and of sorrow.

## LXXIII

DELIVERANCE is not for me in renunciation. I feel the embrace of freedom in a thousand bonds of delight.

Thou ever pourest for me the fresh draught of thy

wine of various colours and fragrance, filling this earthen vessel to the brim.

My world will light its hundred different lamps with thy flame and place them before the altar of thy temple.

No, I will never shut the doors of my senses. The delights of sight and hearing and touch will bear thy delight.

Yes, all my illusions will burn into illumination of joy, and all my desires ripen into fruits of love.

### LXXIV

THE day is no more, the shadow is upon the earth. It is time that I go to the stream to fill my pitcher.

The evening air is eager with the sad music of the water. Ah, it calls me out into the dusk. In the lonely lane there is no passer-by, the wind is up, the ripples are rampant in the river.

I know not if I shall come back home. I know not whom I shall chance to meet. There at the fording in the little boat the unknown man plays upon his lute.

### LXXV

THY gifts to us mortals fulfil all our needs and yet run back to thee undiminished.

The river has its everyday work to do and hastens through fields and hamlets; yet its incessant stream winds towards the washing of thy feet.

The flower sweetens the air with its perfume; yet its last service is to offer itself to thee.

Thy worship does not impoverish the world.

From the words of the poet men take what meanings please them; yet their last meaning points to thee.

DAY after day, O lord of my life, shall I stand before thee face to face. With folded hands, O lord of all worlds, shall I stand before thee face to face.

Under thy great sky in solitude and silence, with humble heart shall I stand before thee face to face.

In this laborious world of thine, tumultuous with toil and with struggle, among hurrying crowds shall I stand before thee face to face.

And when my work shall be done in this world, O King of kings, alone and speechless shall I stand before thee face to face.

## LXXVII

I KNOW thee as my God and stand apart—I do not know thee as my own and come closer. I know thee as my father and bow before thy feet—I do not grasp thy hand as my friend's.

I stand not where thou comest down and ownest thyself as mine, there to clasp thee to my heart and take thee as my comrade.

Thou art the Brother amongst my brothers, but I heed them not, I divide not my earnings with them, thus sharing my all with thee.

In pleasure and in pain I stand not by the side of men, and thus stand by thee. I shrink to give up my life, and thus do not plunge into the great waters of life.

## LXXVIII

WHEN the creation was new and all the stars shone in their first splendour, the gods held their assembly in the sky and sang, "Oh, the picture of perfection! the joy unalloyed!"

But one cried of a sudden—"It seems that somewhere there is a break in the chain of light and one of the stars has been lost."

The golden string of their harp snapped, their song stopped, and they cried in dismay—"Yes, that lost star was the best, she was the glory of all heavens!"

From that day the search is unceasing for her, and the cry goes on from one to the other that in her the world has lost its one joy!

Only in the deepest silence of night the stars smile and whisper among themselves—"Vain is this seeking! Unbroken perfection is over all!"

## LXXIX

If it is not my portion to meet thee in this my life then let me ever feel that I have missed thy sight—let me not forget for a moment, let me carry the pangs of this sorrow in my dreams and in my wakeful hours.

As my days pass in the crowded market of this world and my hands grow full with the daily profits, let me ever feel that I have gained nothing—let me not forget for a moment, let me carry the pangs of this sorrow in my dreams and in my wakeful hours.

When I sit by the roadside, tired and panting, when I spread my bed low in the dust, let me ever feel that the long journey is still before me—let me not forget for a moment, let me carry the pangs of this sorrow in my dreams and in my wakeful hours.

When my rooms have been decked out and the flutes sound and the laughter there is loud, let me ever feel that I have not invited thee to my house—let me not forget for a moment, let me carry the pangs of this sorrow in my dreams and in my wakeful hours.

## LXXX

I AM like a remnant of a cloud of autumn uselessly roaming in the sky, O my sun ever-glorious! Thy touch has not yet melted my vapour, making me one with thy light, and thus I count months and years separated from thee.

If this be thy wish and if this be thy play, then take this fleeting emptiness of mine, paint it with colours, gild it with gold, float it on the wanton wind and spread it in varied wonders.

And again when it shall be thy wish to end this play at night, I shall melt and vanish away in the dark, or it may be in a smile of the white morning, in a coolness of purity transparent.

## LXXXI

ON many an idle day have I grieved over lost time. But it is never lost, my lord. Thou hast taken every moment of my life in thine own hands.

Hidden in the heart of things thou art nourishing seeds into sprouts, buds into blossoms, and ripening flowers into fruitfulness.

I was tired and sleeping on my idle bed and imagined all work had ceased. In the morning I woke up and found my garden full with wonders of flowers.

## LXXXII

TIME is endless in thy hands, my lord. There is none to count thy minutes.

Days and nights pass and ages bloom and fade like flowers. Thou knowest how to wait.

Thy centuries follow each other perfecting a small wild flower.

We have no time to lose, and having no time we must scramble for our chances. We are too poor to be late.

And thus it is that time goes by while I give it to every querulous man who claims it, and thine altar is empty of all offerings to the last.

At the end of the day I hasten in fear lest thy gate be shut; but I find that yet there is time.


### LXXXIII

MOTHER, I shall weave a chain of pearls for thy neck with my tears of sorrow.

The stars have wrought their anklets of light to deck thy feet, but mine will hang upon thy breast.

Wealth and fame come from thee and it is for thee to give or to withhold them. But this my sorrow is absolutely mine own, and when I bring it to thee as my offering thou rewardest me with thy grace.


### LXXXIV

IT is the pang of separation that spreads throughout the world and gives birth to shapes innumerable in the infinite sky.

It is this sorrow of separation that gazes in silence all night from star to star and becomes lyric among rustling leaves in rainy darkness of July.

It is this overspreading pain that deepens into loves and desires, into sufferings and joys in human homes; and this it is that ever melts and flows in songs through my poet's heart.

## LXXXV

WHEN the warriors came out first from their master's hall, where had they hid their power? Where were their armour and their arms?

They looked poor and helpless, and the arrows were showered upon them on the day they came out from their master's hall.

When the warriors marched back again to their master's hall, where did they hide their power?

They had dropped the sword and dropped the bow and the arrow; peace was on their foreheads, and they had left the fruits of their life behind them on the day they marched back again to their master's hall.

## LXXXVI

DEATH, thy servant, is at my door. He has crossed the unknown sea and brought thy call to my home.

The night is dark and my heart is fearful—yet I will take up the lamp, open my gates and bow to him my welcome. It is thy messenger who stands at my door.

I will worship him with folded hands, and with tears. I will worship him placing at his feet the treasure of my heart.

He will go back with his errand done, leaving a dark shadow on my morning; and in my desolate home only my forlorn self will remain as my last offering to thee.

## LXXXVII

IN desperate hope I go and search for her in all the corners of my room; I find her not.

My house is small and what once has gone from it can never be regained.

But infinite is thy mansion, my lord, and seeking her I have come to thy door.

I stand under the golden canopy of thine evening sky and I lift my eager eyes to thy face.

I have come to the brink of eternity from which nothing can vanish—no hope, no happiness, no vision of a face seen through tears.

Oh, dip my emptied life into that ocean, plunge it into the deepest fullness. Let me for once feel that lost sweet touch in the allness of the universe.

## LXXXVIII

DEITY of the ruined temple! The broken strings of *Vina* sing no more your praise. The bells in the evening proclaim not your time of worship. The air is still and silent about you.

In your desolate dwelling comes the vagrant spring breeze. It brings the tidings of flowers—the flowers that for your worship are offered no more.

Your worshipper of old wanders ever longing for favour still refused. In the eventide, when fires and shadows mingle with the gloom of dust, he wearily comes back to the ruined temple with hunger in his heart.

Many a festival day comes to you in silence, deity of the ruined temple. Many a night of worship goes away with lamp unlit.

Many new images are built by masters of cunning art and carried to the holy stream of oblivion when their time is come.

Only the deity of the ruined temple remains un-worshipped in deathless neglect.

## LXXXIX

No more noisy, loud words from me—such is my master's will. Henceforth I deal in whispers. The speech of my heart will be carried on in murmurings of a song.

Men hasten to the King's market. All the buyers and sellers are there. But I have my untimely lèave in the middle of the day, in the thick of work.

Let then the flowers come out in my garden, though it is not their time; and let the midday bees strike up their lazy hum.

Full many an hour have I spent in the strife of the good and the evil, but now it is the pleasure of my playmate of the empty days to draw my heart on to him; and I know not why is this sudden call to what useless inconsequence!

## XC

ON the day when death will knock at thy door what wilt thou offer to him?

Oh, I will set before my guest the full vessel of my life—I will never let him go with empty hands.

All the sweet vintage of all my autumn days and summer nights, all the earnings and gleanings of my busy life will I place before him at the close of my days when death will knock at my door.

## XCI

O THOU the last fulfilment of life, Death, my death, come and whisper to me!

Day after day have I kept watch for thee; for thee have I borne the joys and pangs of life.

All that I am, that I have, that I hope, and all my

love have ever flowed towards thee in depth of secrecy. One final glance from thine eyes and my life will be ever thine own.

The flowers have been woven and the garland is ready for the bridegroom. After the wedding the bride shall leave her home and meet her lord alone in the solitude of night.

XCII

I KNOW that the day will come when my sight of this earth shall be lost, and life will take its leave in silence, drawing the last curtain over my eyes.

Yet stars will watch at night, and morning rise as before, and hours heave like sea waves casting up pleasures and pains.

When I think of this end of my moments, the barrier of the moments breaks and I see by the light of death thy world with its careless treasures. Rare is its lowliest seat, rare is its meanest of lives.

Things that I longed for in vain and things that I got —let them pass. Let me but truly possess the things that I ever spurned and overlooked.

XCIII

I HAVE got my leave. Bid me farewell, my brothers! I bow to you all and take my departure.

Here I give back the keys of my door—and I give up all claims to my house. I only ask for last kind words from you.

We were neighbours for long, but I received more than I could give. Now the day has dawned and the lamp that lit my dark corner is out. A summons has come and I am ready for my journey.

AT this time of my parting, wish me good luck, my friends! The sky is flushed with the dawn and my path lies beautiful.

Ask not what I have with me to take there. I start on my journey with empty hands and expectant heart.

I shall put on my wedding garland. Mine is not the red-brown dress of the traveller, and though there are dangers on the way I have no fear in my mind.

The evening star will come out when my voyage is done and the plaintive notes of the twilight melodies be struck up from the King's gateway.

## XCV

I WAS not aware of the moment when I first crossed the threshold of this life.

What was the power that made me open out into this vast mystery like a bud in the forest at midnight?

When in the morning I looked upon the light I felt in a moment that I was no stranger in this world, that the inscrutable without name and form had taken me in its arms in the form of my own mother.

Even so, in death the same unknown will appear as ever known to me. And because I love this life, I know I shall love death as well.

The child cries out when from the right breast the mother takes it away, in the very next moment to find in the left one its consolation.

## XCVI

WHEN I go from hence let this be my parting word, that what I have seen is unsurpassable.

I have tasted of the hidden honey of this lotus that expands on the ocean of light, and thus am I blessed— let this be my parting word.

In this playhouse of infinite forms I have had my play and here have I caught sight of him that is formless.

My whole body and my limbs have thrilled with his touch who is beyond touch; and if the end comes here, let it come—let this be my parting word.


## XCVII

WHEN my play was with thee I never questioned who thou wert. I knew nor shyness nor fear, my life was boisterous.

In the early morning thou wouldst call me from my sleep like my own comrade and lead me running from glade to glade.

On those days I never cared to know the meaning of songs thou sangest to me. Only my voice took up the tunes, and my heart danced in their cadence.

Now, when the playtime is over, what is this sudden sight that is come upon me? The world with eyes bent upon thy feet stands in awe with all its silent stars.


## XCVIII

I WILL deck thee with trophies, garlands of my defeat. It is never in my power to escape unconquered.

I surely know my pride will go to the wall, my life will burst its bonds in exceeding pain, and my empty heart will sob out in music like a hollow reed, and the stone will melt in tears.

I surely know the hundred petals of a lotus will not

remain closed for ever and the secret recess of its honey will be bared.

From the blue sky an eye shall gaze upon me and summon me in silence. Nothing will be left for me, nothing whatever, and utter death shall I receive at thy feet.

## XCIX

WHEN I give up the helm I know that the time has come for thee to take it. What there is to do will be instantly done. Vain is this struggle.

Then take away your hands and silently put up with your defeat, my heart, and think it your good fortune to sit perfectly still where you are placed.

These my lamps are blown out at every little puff of wind, and trying to light them I forget all else again and again.

But I shall be wise this time and wait in the dark, spreading my mat on the floor; and whenever it is thy pleasure, my lord, come silently and take thy seat here.

## C

I DIVE down into the depth of the ocean of forms, hoping to gain the perfect pearl of the formless.

No more sailing from harbour to harbour with this my weather-beaten boat. The days are long past when my sport was to be tossed on waves.

And now I am eager to die into the deathless.

Into the audience hall by the fathomless abyss where swells up the music of toneless strings I shall take this harp of my life.

I shall tune it to the notes of for ever, and, when it

has sobbed out its last utterance, lay down my silent harp at the feet of the silent.

## CI

EVER in my life have I sought thee with my songs. It was they who led me from door to door, and with them have I felt about me, searching and touching my world.

It was my songs that taught me all the lessons I ever learnt; they showed me secret paths, they brought before my sight many a star on the horizon of my heart.

They guided me all the day long to the mysteries of the country of pleasure and pain, and, at last, to what palace gate have they brought me in the evening at the end of my journey?

## CII

I BOASTED among men that I had known you. They see your pictures in all works of mine. They come and ask me, "Who is he?" I know not how to answer them. I say, "Indeed, I cannot tell." They blame me and they go away in scorn. And you sit there smiling.

I put my tales of you into lasting songs. The secret gushes out from my heart. They come and ask me, "Tell me all your meanings." I know not how to answer them. I say, "Ah, who knows what they mean!" They smile and go away in utter scorn. And you sit there smiling.

## CIII

IN one salutation to thee, my God, let all my senses spread out and touch this world at thy feet.

Like a rain-cloud of July hung low with its burden of unshed showers let all my mind bend down at thy door in one salutation to thee.

Let all my songs gather together their diverse strains into a single current and flow to a sea of silence in one salutation to thee.

Like a flock of homesick cranes flying night and day back to their mountain nests let all my life take its voyage to its eternal home in one salutation to thee.

# THE CRESCENT MOON

# THE CRESCENT MOON

## THE HOME

I PACED alone on the road across the field while the sunset was hiding its last gold like a miser.

The daylight sank deeper and deeper into the darkness, and the widowed land, whose harvest had been reaped, lay silent.

Suddenly a boy's shrill voice rose into the sky. He traversed the dark unseen, leaving the track of his song across the hush of the evening.

His village home lay there at the end of the waste land, beyond the sugar-cane field, hidden among the shadows of the banana and the slender areca palm, the coconut and the dark green jack-fruit trees.

I stopped for a moment in my lonely way under the starlight, and saw spread before me the darkened earth surrounding with her arms countless homes furnished with cradles and beds, mothers' hearts and evening lamps, and young lives glad with a gladness that knows nothing of its value for the world.

## ON THE SEASHORE

ON the seashore of endless worlds children meet.

The infinite sky is motionless overhead and the restless water is boisterous. On the seashore of endless worlds the children meet with shouts and dances.

51

They build their houses with sand, and they play with empty shells. With withered leaves they weave their boats and smilingly float them on the vast deep. Children have their play on the seashore of worlds.

They know not how to swim, they know not how to cast nets. Pearl-fishers dive for pearls, merchants sail in their ships, while children gather pebbles and scatter them again. They seek not for hidden treasures, they know not how to cast nets.

The sea surges up with laughter, and pale gleams the smile of the sea-beach. Death-dealing waves sing meaningless ballads to the children, even like a mother while rocking her baby's cradle. The sea plays with children, and pale gleams the smile of the sea-beach.

On the seashore of endless worlds children meet. Tempest roams in the pathless sky, ships are wrecked in the trackless water, death is abroad and children play. On the seashore of endless worlds is the great meeting of children.

## THE SOURCE

THE sleep that flits on baby's eyes—does anybody know from where it comes? Yes, there is a rumour that it has its dwelling where, in the fairy village among shadows of the forest dimly lit with glow-worms, there hang two shy buds of enchantment. From there it comes to kiss baby's eyes.

The smile that flickers on baby's lips when he sleeps
—does anybody know where it was born? Yes, there is a
rumour that a young pale beam of a crescent moon
touched the edge of a vanishing autumn cloud, and
there the smile was first born in the dream of a dew-
washed morning—the smile that flickers on baby's lips
when he sleeps.

The sweet, soft freshness that blooms on baby's limbs
—does anybody know where it was hidden so long? Yes,
when the mother was a young girl it lay pervading her
heart in tender and silent mystery of love—the sweet,
soft freshness that has bloomed on baby's limbs.


## BABY'S WAY

IF baby only wanted to, he could fly up to heaven this
moment.

It is not for nothing that he does not leave us.

He loves to rest his head on mother's bosom, and
cannot ever bear to lose sight of her.


Baby knows all manner of wise words, though few on
earth can understand their meaning.

It is not for nothing that he never wants to speak.

The one thing he wants is to learn mother's words
from mother's lips. That is why he looks so innocent.


Baby had a heap of gold and pearls, yet he came like
a beggar on to this earth.

It is not for nothing he came in such a disguise.

This dear little naked mendicant pretends to be

utterly helpless, so that he may beg for mother's wealth of love.

Baby was so free from every tie in the land of the tiny crescent moon.
It was not for nothing he gave up his freedom.
He knows that there is room for endless joy in mother's little corner of a heart, and it is sweeter far than liberty to be caught and pressed in her dear arms.

Baby never knew how to cry. He dwelt in the land of perfect bliss.
It is not for nothing he has chosen to shed tears.
Though with the smile of his dear face he draws mother's yearning heart to him, yet his little cries over tiny troubles weave the double bond of pity and love.


## THE UNHEEDED PAGEANT

AH, who was it coloured that little frock, my child, and covered your sweet limbs with that little red tunic?
You have come out in the morning to play in the courtyard, tottering and tumbling as you run.
But who was it coloured that little frock, my child?

What is it makes you laugh, my little life-bud?
Mother smiles at you standing on the threshold.
She claps her hands and her bracelets jingle, and you dance with your bamboo stick in your hand like a tiny little shepherd.
But what is it makes you laugh, my little life-bud?

O beggar, what do you beg for, clinging to your mother's neck with both your hands?

O greedy heart, shall I pluck the world like a fruit from the sky to place it on your little rosy palm?

O beggar, what are you begging for?

The wind carries away in glee the tinkling of your anklet bells.

The sun smiles and watches your toilet.

The sky watches over you when you sleep in your mother's arms, and the morning comes tiptoe to your bed and kisses your eyes.

The wind carries away in glee the tinkling of your anklet bells.

The fairy mistress of dreams is coming towards you, flying through the twilight sky.

The world-mother keeps her seat by you in your mother's heart.

He who plays his music to the stars is standing at your window with his flute.

And the fairy mistress of dreams is coming towards you, flying through the twilight sky.


## SLEEP-STEALER

WHO stole sleep from baby's eyes? I must know.

Clasping her pitcher to her waist mother went to fetch water from the village near by.

It was noon. The children's playtime was over; the ducks in the pond were silent.

The shepherd boy lay asleep under the shadow of the banyan tree.

The crane stood grave and still in the swamp near the mango grove.

In the meanwhile the Sleep-stealer came and, snatching sleep from baby's eyes, flew away.

When mother came back she found baby travelling the room over on all fours.

Who stole sleep from our baby's eyes? I must know. I must find her and chain her up.

I must look into that dark cave, where, through boulders and scowling stones, trickles a tiny stream.

I must search in the drowsy shade of the *bakula* grove, where pigeons coo in their corner, and fairies' anklets tinkle in the stillness of starry nights.

In the evening I will peep into the whispering silence of the bamboo forest, where fireflies squander their light, and will ask every creature I meet, "Can anybody tell me where the Sleep-stealer lives?"

Who stole sleep from baby's eyes? I must know.

Shouldn't I give her a good lesson if I could only catch her!

I would raid her nest and see where she hoards all her stolen sleep.

I would plunder it all, and carry it home.

I would bind her two wings securely, set her on the bank of the river, and then let her play at fishing with a reed among the rushes and water-lilies.

When the marketing is over in the evening, and the village children sit in their mothers' laps, then the night birds will mockingly din her ears with:

"Whose sleep will you steal now?"

# THE BEGINNING

"Where have I come from, where did you pick me up?" the baby asked its mother.

She answered, half crying, half laughing, and clasping the baby to her breast,—

"You were hidden in my heart as its desire, my darling.

You were in the dolls of my childhood's games; and when with clay I made the image of my god every morning, I made and unmade you then.

You were enshrined with our household deity, in his worship I worshipped you.

In all my hopes and my loves, in my life, in the life of my mother you have lived.

In the lap of the deathless Spirit who rules our home you have been nursed for ages.

When in girlhood my heart was opening its petals, you hovered as a fragrance about it.

Your tender softness bloomed in my youthful limbs, like a glow in the sky before the sunrise.

Heaven's first darling, twin-born with the morning light, you have floated down the stream of the world's life, and at last you have stranded on my heart.

As I gaze on your face, mystery overwhelms me; you who belong to all have become mine.

For fear of losing you I hold you tight to my breast. What magic has snared the world's treasure in these slender arms of mine?"

## BABY'S WORLD

I wish I could take a quiet corner in the heart of my baby's very own world.

I know it has stars that talk to him, and a sky that stoops down to his face to amuse him with its silly clouds and rainbows.

Those who make believe to be dumb, and look as if they never could move, come creeping to his window with their stories and with trays crowded with bright toys.

I wish I could travel by the road that crosses baby's mind, and out beyond all bounds;

Where messengers run errands for no cause between the kingdoms of kings of no history;

Where Reason makes kites of her laws and flies them, and Truth sets Fact free from its fetters.

## WHEN AND WHY

When I bring you coloured toys, my child, I understand why there is such a play of colours on clouds, on water, and why flowers are painted in tints—when I give coloured toys to you, my child.

When I sing to make you dance, I truly know why there is music in leaves, and why waves send their chorus of voices to the heart of the listening earth—when I sing to make you dance.

When I bring sweet things to your greedy hands, I know why there is honey in the cup of the flower, and why fruits are secretly filled with sweet juice—when I bring sweet things to your greedy hands.

When I kiss your face to make you smile, my darling, I surely understand what pleasure streams from the sky in morning light, and what delight the summer breeze brings to my body—when I kiss you to make you smile.


## DEFAMATION

WHY are those tears in your eyes, my child?

How horrid of them to be always scolding you for nothing!

You have stained your fingers and face with ink while writing—is that why they call you dirty?

O, fie! Would they dare to call the full moon dirty because it has smudged its face with ink?

For every little trifle they blame you, my child. They are ready to find fault for nothing.

You tore your clothes while playing—is that why they call you untidy?

O, fie! What would they call an autumn morning that smiles through its ragged clouds?

Take no heed of what they say to you, my child.

They make a long list of your misdeeds.

Everybody knows how you love sweet things—is that why they call you greedy?

O, fie! What then would they call us who love you?


## THE JUDGE

SAY of him what you please, but I know my child's failings.

I do not love him because he is good, but because he is my little child.

How should you know how dear he can be when you try to weigh his merits against his faults?

When I must punish him he becomes all the more a part of my being.

When I cause his tears to come my heart weeps with him.

I alone have a right to blame and punish, for he only may chastise who loves.


## PLAYTHINGS

CHILD, how happy you are sitting in the dust, playing with a broken twig all the morning!

I smile at your play with that little bit of a broken twig.

I am busy with my accounts, adding up figures by the hour.

Perhaps you glance at me and think, "What a stupid game to spoil your morning with!"

Child, I have forgotten the art of being absorbed in sticks and mud-pies.

I seek out costly playthings, and gather lumps of gold and silver.

With whatever you find you create your glad games. I spend both my time and my strength over things I can never obtain.

In my frail canoe I struggle to cross the sea of desire, and forget that I too am playing a game.

## THE ASTRONOMER

I ONLY said, "When in the evening the round full moon gets entangled among the branches of that *Kadam* tree, couldn't somebody catch it?"

But dādā [1] laughed at me and said, "Baby, you are the silliest child I have ever known. The moon is ever so far from us, how could anybody catch it?"

I said, "Dādā, how foolish you are! When mother looks out of her window and smiles down at us playing, would you call her far away?"

Still dādā said, "You are a stupid child! But, baby, where could you find a net big enough to catch the moon with?"

I said, "Surely you could catch it with your hands."

But dādā laughed and said, "You are the silliest child I have known. If it came nearer, you would see how big the moon is."

I said, "Dādā, what nonsense they teach at your school! When mother bends her face down to kiss us, does her face look very big?"

But still dādā says, "You are a stupid child."


## CLOUDS AND WAVES

MOTHER, the folk who live up in the clouds call out to me—

"We play from the time we wake till the day ends.

We play with the golden dawn, we play with the silver moon."

I ask, "But how am I to get up to you?"

They answer, "Come to the edge of the earth, lift

---

[1] Elder brother.

up your hands to the sky, and you will be taken up into the clouds."

"My mother is waiting for me at home," I say. "How can I leave her and come?"

Then they smile and float away.

But I know a nicer game than that, mother.

I shall be the cloud and you the moon.

I shall cover you with both my hands, and our house-top will be the blue sky.

The folk who live in the waves call out to me—

"We sing from morning till night; on and on we travel and know not where we pass."

I ask, "But how am I to join you?"

They tell me, "Come to the edge of the shore and stand with your eyes tight shut, and you will be carried out upon the waves."

I say, "My mother always wants me at home in the evening—how can I leave her and go?"

Then they smile, dance and pass by.

But I know a better game than that.

I will be the waves and you will be a strange shore.

I shall roll on and on and on, and break upon your lap with laughter.

And no one in the world will know where we both are.

### THE *CHAMPA* FLOWER

SUPPOSING I became a *champa* flower, just for fun, and grew on a branch high up that tree, and shook in the wind with laughter and danced upon the newly budded leaves, would you know me, mother?

62

You would call, "Baby, where are you?" and I should laugh to myself and keep quite quiet.

I should slyly open my petals and watch you at your work.

When after your bath, with wet hair spread on your shoulders, you walked through the shadow of the *champa* tree to the little court where you say your prayers, you would notice the scent of the flower, but not know that it came from me.

When after the midday meal you sat at the window reading *Ramayana*, and the tree's shadow fell over your hair and your lap, I should fling my wee little shadow on to the page of your book, just where you were reading.

But would you guess that it was the tiny shadow of your little child?

When in the evening you went to the cowshed with the lighted lamp in your hand, I should suddenly drop on to the earth again and be your own baby once more, and beg you to tell me a story.

"Where have you been, you naughty child?"

"I won't tell you, mother." That's what you and I would say then.


## FAIRYLAND

IF people came to know where my king's palace is, it would vanish into the air.

The walls are of white silver and the roof of shining gold.

The queen lives in a palace with seven courtyards, and she wears a jewel that cost all the wealth of seven kingdoms.

But let me tell you, mother, in a whisper, where my king's palace is.

It is at the corner of our terrace where the pot of the *tulsi* plant stands.

The princess lies sleeping on the far-away shore of the seven impassable seas.

There is none in the world who can find her but myself.

She has bracelets on her arms and pearl drops in her ears; her hair sweeps down upon the floor.

She will wake when I touch her with my magic wand, and jewels will fall from her lips when she smiles.

But let me whisper in your ear, mother; she is there in the corner of our terrace where the pot of the *tulsi* plant stands.

When it is time for you to go to the river for your bath, step up to that terrace on the roof.

I sit in the corner where the shadows of the walls meet together.

Only puss is allowed to come with me, for she knows where the barber in the story lives.

But let me whisper, mother, in your ear where the barber in the story lives.

It is at the corner of the terrace where the pot of the *tulsi* plant stands.


## THE LAND OF THE EXILE

MOTHER, the light has grown grey in the sky; I do not know what the time is.

There is no fun in my play, so I have come to you. It is Saturday, our holiday.

Leave off your work, mother; sit here by the window and tell me where the desert of Tepāntar in the fairy tale is.

The shadow of the rains has covered the day from end to end.

The fierce lightning is scratching the sky with its nails.

When the clouds rumble and it thunders, I love to be afraid in my heart and cling to you.

When the heavy rain patters for hours on the bamboo leaves, and our windows shake and rattle at the gusts of wind, I like to sit alone in the room, mother, with you, and hear you talk about the desert of Tepāntar in the fairy tale.

Where is it, mother, on the shore of what sea, at the foot of what hills, in the kingdom of what king?

There are no hedges there to mark the fields, no footpath across it by which the villagers reach their village in the evening, or the woman who gathers dry sticks in the forest can bring her load to the market. With patches of yellow grass in the sand and only one tree where the pair of wise old birds have their nest, lies the desert of Tepāntar.

I can imagine how, on just such a cloudy day, the young son of the king is riding alone on a grey horse through the desert, in search of the princess who lies imprisoned in the giant's palace across that unknown water.

When the haze of the rain comes down in the distant sky, and lightning starts up like a sudden fit of pain, does he remember his unhappy mother, abandoned by the king, sweeping the cow-stall and wiping her eyes, while he rides through the desert of Tepāntar in the fairy tale?

See, mother, it is almost dark before the day is over, and there are no travellers yonder on the village road.

The shepherd boy has gone home early from the pasture, and men have left their fields to sit on mats under the eaves of their huts, watching the scowling clouds.

Mother, I have left all my books on the shelf—do not ask me to do my lessons now.

When I grow up and am big like my father, I shall learn all that must be learnt.

But just for to-day, tell me, mother, where the desert of Tepāntar in the fairy tale is.

## THE RAINY DAY

SULLEN clouds are gathering fast over the black fringe of the forest.

O child, do not go out!

The palm trees in a row by the lake are smiting their heads against the dismal sky; the crows with their draggled wings are silent on the tamarind branches, and the eastern bank of the river is haunted by a deepening gloom.

Our cow is lowing loud, tied at the fence.

O child, wait here till I bring her into the stall.

66

Men have crowded into the flooded field to catch the fishes as they escape from the overflowing ponds; the rain-water is running in rills through the narrow lanes like a laughing boy who has run away from his mother to tease her.

Listen, someone is shouting for the boatman at the ford.
O child, the daylight is dim, and the crossing at the ferry is closed.
The sky seems to ride fast upon the madly rushing rain; the water in the river is loud and impatient; women have hastened home early from the Ganges with their filled pitchers.

The evening lamps must be made ready.
O child, do not go out!
The road to the market is desolate, the lane to the river is slippery. The wind is roaring and struggling among the bamboo branches like a wild beast tangled in a net.

## PAPER BOATS

DAY by day I float my paper boats one by one down the running stream.

In big black letters I write my name on them and the name of the village where I live.

I hope that someone in some strange land will find them and know who I am.

I load my little boats with *shiuli* flowers from our garden, and hope that these blooms of the dawn will be carried safely to land in the night.

I launch my paper boats and look up into the sky and see the little clouds setting their white bulging sails.

I know not what playmate of mine in the sky sends them down the air to race with my boats!

When night comes I bury my face in my arms and dream that my paper boats float on and on under the midnight stars.

The fairies of sleep are sailing in them, and the lading is their baskets full of dreams.

## THE SAILOR

THE boat of the boatman Madhu is moored at the wharf of Rajgunj.

It is uselessly laden with jute, and has been lying there idle for ever so long.

If he would only lend me his boat, I should man her with a hundred oars, and hoist sails, five or six or seven.

I should never steer her to stupid markets.

I should sail the seven seas and the thirteen rivers of fairyland.

But, mother, you won't weep for me in a corner.

I am not going into the forest like Ramachandra to come back only after fourteen years.

I shall become the prince of the story, and fill my boat with whatever I like.

I shall take my friend Ashu with me. We shall sail merrily across the seven seas and the thirteen rivers of fairyland.

We shall set sail in the early morning light.

When at noontide you are bathing at the pond, we shall be in the land of a strange king.

We shall pass the ford of Tirpurni, and leave behind us the desert of Tepāntar.

When we come back it will be getting dark, and I shall tell you of all that we have seen.

I shall cross the seven seas and the thirteen rivers of fairyland.

## THE FURTHER BANK

I LONG to go over there to the further bank of the river,

Where those boats are tied to the bamboo poles in a line;

Where men cross over in their boats in the morning with ploughs on their shoulders to till their far-away fields;

Where the cowherds make their lowing cattle swim across to the riverside pasture;

Whence they all come back home in the evening, leaving the jackals to howl in the island overgrown with weeds.

Mother, if you don't mind, I should like to become the boatman of the ferry when I am grown up.

They say there are strange pools hidden behind that high bank,

Where flocks of wild ducks come when the rains are over, and thick reeds grow round the margins where water-birds lay their eggs;

Where snipes with their dancing tails stamp their tiny footprints upon the clean soft mud;

Where in the evening the tall grasses crested with

white flowers invite the moonbeam to float upon their waves.

Mother, if you don't mind, I should like to become the boatman of the ferryboat when I am grown up.

I shall cross and cross back from bank to bank, and all the boys and girls of the village will wonder at me while they are bathing.

When the sun climbs the mid sky and morning wears on to noon, I shall come running to you, saying, "Mother, I am hungry!"

When the day is done and the shadows cower under the trees, I shall come back in the dusk.

I shall never go away from you into the town to work like father.

Mother, if you don't mind, I should like to become the boatman of the ferryboat when I am grown up.


## THE FLOWER-SCHOOL

WHEN storm-clouds rumble in the sky and June showers come down,

The moist east wind comes marching over the heath to blow its bagpipes among the bamboos.

Then crowds of flowers come out of a sudden, from nobody knows where, and dance upon the grass in wild glee.

Mother, I really think the flowers go to school underground.

They do their lessons with doors shut, and if they want to come out to play before it is time, their master makes them stand in a corner.

When the rains come they have their holidays.
Branches clash together in the forest, and the leaves
rustle in the wild wind, the thunder-clouds clap their
giant hands and the flower children rush out in dresses
of pink and yellow and white.

Do you know, mother, their home is in the sky,
where the stars are.
Haven't you seen how eager they are to get there?
Don't you know why they are in such a hurry?
Of course, I can guess to whom they raise their
arms: they have their mother as I have my own.


## THE MERCHANT

IMAGINE, mother, that you are to stay at home and I
am to travel into strange lands.
Imagine that my boat is ready at the landing fully
laden.
Now think well, mother, before you say what I shall
bring for you when I come back.

Mother, do you want heaps and heaps of gold?
There, by the banks of golden streams, fields are full
of golden harvest.
And in the shade of the forest path the golden
*champa* flowers drop on the ground.
I will gather them all for you in many hundred
baskets.

Mother, do you want pearls big as the raindrops of
autumn?
I shall cross to the pearl island shore.

There in the early morning light pearls tremble on the meadow flowers, pearls drop on the grass, and pearls are scattered on the sand in spray by the wild sea-waves.

My brother shall have a pair of horses with wings to fly among the clouds.

For father I shall bring a magic pen that, without his knowing, will write of itself.

For you, mother, I must have the casket and jewel that cost seven kings their kingdoms.

## SYMPATHY

IF I were only a little puppy, not your baby, mother dear, would you say "No" to me if I tried to eat from your dish?

Would you drive me off, saying to me, "Get away, you naughty little puppy"?

Then go, mother, go! I will never come to you when you call me, and never let you feed me any more.

If I were only a little green parrot, and not your baby, mother dear, would you keep me chained lest I should fly away?

Would you shake your finger at me and say, "What an ungrateful wretch of a bird! It is gnawing at its chain day and night"?

Then go, mother, go! I will run away into the woods; I will never let you take me in your arms again.

## VOCATION

WHEN the gong sounds ten in the morning and I walk to school by our lane,

Every day I meet the hawker crying, "Bangles, crystal bangles!"

There is nothing to hurry him on, there is no road he must take, no place he must go to, no time when he must come home.

I wish I were a hawker, spending my day in the road, crying, "Bangles, crystal bangles!"

When at four in the afternoon I come back from the school,

I can see through the gate of that house the gardener digging the ground.

He does what he likes with his spade, he soils his clothes with dust, nobody takes him to task if he gets baked in the sun or gets wet.

I wish I were a gardener digging away at the garden with nobody to stop me from digging.

Just as it gets dark in the evening and my mother sends me to bed,

I can see through my open window the watchman walking up and down.

The lane is dark and lonely, and the street-lamp stands like a giant with one red eye in its head.

The watchman swings his lantern and walks with his shadow at his side, and never once goes to bed in his life.

I wish I were a watchman walking the streets all night, chasing the shadows with my lantern.

# SUPERIOR

MOTHER, your baby is silly! She is so absurdly childish!

She does not know the difference between the lights in the streets and the stars.

When we play at eating with pebbles, she thinks they are real food, and tries to put them into her mouth.

When I open a book before her and ask her to learn her a, b, c, she tears the leaves with her hands and roars for joy at nothing; this is your baby's way of doing her lesson.

When I shake my head at her in anger and scold her and call her naughty, she laughs and thinks it great fun.

Everybody knows that father is away, but if in play I call aloud "Father," she looks about her in excitement and thinks that father is near.

When I hold my class with the donkeys that our washerman brings to carry away the clothes and I warn her that I am the schoolmaster, she will scream for no reason and call me dādā.[1]

Your baby wants to catch the moon. She is so funny; she calls Ganesh [2] Gānush.

Mother, your baby is silly! She is so absurdly childish!


# THE LITTLE BIG MAN

I AM small because I am a little child. I shall be big when I am as old as my father is.

[1] Elder brother.
[2] Ganesh, a common name in India, also that of the god with the elephant's head.

74

My teacher will come and say, "It is late, bring your slate and your books."

I shall tell him, " Do you not know I am as big as father? And I must not have lessons any more."

My master will wonder and say, "He can leave his books if he likes, for he is grown up."

I shall dress myself and walk to the fair where the crowd is thick.

My uncle will come rushing up to me and say, "You will get lost, my boy; let me carry you."

I shall answer, "Can't you see, uncle, I am as big as father? I must go to the fair alone."

Uncle will say, "Yes, he can go wherever he likes, for he is grown up."

Mother will come from her bath when I am giving money to my nurse, for I shall know how to open the box with my key.

Mother will say, "What are you about, naughty child?"

I shall tell her, "Mother, don't you know, I am as big as father, and I must give silver to my nurse."

Mother will say to herself, "He can give money to whom he likes, for he is grown up."

In the holiday time in October father will come home and, thinking that I am still a baby, will bring for me from the town little shoes and small silken frocks.

I shall say, "Father, give them to my dādā, for I am as big as you are."

Father will think and say, "He can buy his own clothes if he likes, for he is grown up."

## TWELVE O'CLOCK

MOTHER, I do want to leave off my lessons now. I have been at my book all the morning.

You say it is only twelve o'clock. Suppose it isn't any later; can't you ever think it is afternoon when it is only twelve o'clock?

I can easily imagine now that the sun has reached the edge of that rice-field, and the old fisher-woman is gathering herbs for her supper by the side of the pond.

I can just shut my eyes and think that the shadows are growing darker under the *madar* tree, and the water in the pond looks shiny black.

If twelve o'clock can come in the night, why can't the night come when it is twelve o'clock?


## AUTHORSHIP

YOU say that father writes a lot of books, but what he writes I don't understand.

He was reading to you all the evening, but could you really make out what he meant?

What nice stories, mother, you can tell us! Why can't father write like that, I wonder?

Did he never hear from his own mother stories of giants and fairies and princesses?

Has he forgotten them all?

Often when he gets late for his bath you have to go and call him an hundred times.

You wait and keep his dishes warm for him, but he goes on writing and forgets.

Father always plays at making books.

If ever I go to play in father's room, you come and call me, "What a naughty child!"

If I make the slightest noise you say, "Don't you see that father's at his work?"

What's the fun of always writing and writing?

When I take up father's pen or pencil and write upon his book just as he does,—a, b, c, d, e, f, g, h, i,—why do you get cross with me then, mother?

You never say a word when father writes.

When my father wastes such heaps of paper, mother, you don't seem to mind at all.

But if I take only one sheet to make a boat with, you say, "Child, how troublesome you are!"

What do you think of father's spoiling sheets and sheets of paper with black marks all over on both sides?

## THE WICKED POSTMAN

WHY do you sit there on the floor so quiet and silent, tell me, mother dear?

The rain is coming in through the open window, making you all wet, and you don't mind it.

Do you hear the gong striking four? It is time for my brother to come home from school.

What has happened to you that you look so strange?

Haven't you got a letter from father to-day?

I saw the postman bringing letters in his bag for almost everybody in the town.

Only, father's letters he keeps to read himself. I am sure the postman is a wicked man.

But don't be unhappy about that, mother dear.

To-morrow is market day in the next village. You ask your maid to buy some pens and papers.

I myself will write all father's letters; you will not find a single mistake.

I shall write from A right up to K.

But, mother, why do you smile?

You don't believe that I can write as nicely as father does!

But I shall rule my paper carefully, and write all the letters beautifully big.

When I finish my writing do you think I shall be so foolish as father and drop it into the horrid postman's bag?

I shall bring it to you myself without waiting, and letter by letter help you to read my writing.

I know the postman does not like to give you the really nice letters.


## THE HERO

MOTHER, let us imagine we are travelling, and passing through a strange and dangerous country.

You are riding in a palanquin and I am trotting by you on a red horse.

It is evening and the sun goes down. The waste of Joradighi lies wan and grey before us. The land is desolate and barren.

You are frightened and thinking—"I know not where we have come to."

I say to you, "Mother, do not be afraid."

The meadow is prickly with spiky grass, and through it runs a narrow broken path.

There are no cattle to be seen in the wide field; they have gone to their village stalls.

It grows dark and dim on the land and sky, and we cannot tell where we are going.

Suddenly you call me and ask me in a whisper, "What light is that near the bank?"

Just then there bursts out a fearful yell, and figures come running towards us.

You sit crouched in your palanquin and repeat the names of the gods in prayer.

The bearers, shaking in terror, hide themselves in the thorny bush.

I shout to you, "Don't be afraid, mother. I am here."

With long sticks in their hands and hair all wild about their heads, they come nearer and nearer.

I shout, "Have a care, you villains! One step more and you are dead men."

They give another terrible yell and rush forward.

You clutch my hand and say, "Dear boy, for heaven's sake, keep away from them."

I say, "Mother, just you watch me."

Then I spur my horse for a wild gallop, and my sword and buckler clash against each other.

The fight becomes so fearful, mother, that it would give you a cold shudder could you see it from your palanquin.

Many of them fly, and a great number are cut to pieces.

I know you are thinking, sitting all by yourself, that your boy must be dead by this time.

But I come to you all stained with blood, and say, "Mother, the fight is over now."

You come out and kiss me, pressing me to your heart, and you say to yourself,

"I don't know what I should do if I hadn't my boy to escort me."

A thousand useless things happen day after day, and why couldn't such a thing come true by chance?

It would be like a story in a book.

My brother would say, "Is it possible? I always thought he was so delicate!"

Our village people would all say in amazement, "Was it not lucky that the boy was with his mother?"


## THE END

IT is time for me to go, mother; I am going.

When in the paling darkness of the lonely dawn you stretch out your arms for your baby in the bed, I shall say, "Baby is not there!"—mother, I am going.

I shall become a delicate draught of air and caress you; and I shall be ripples in the water when you bathe, and kiss you and kiss you again.

In the gusty night when the rain patters on the leaves you will hear my whisper in your bed, and my laughter will flash with the lightning through the open window into your room.

If you lie awake, thinking of your baby till late into the night, I shall sing to you from the stars, "Sleep, mother, sleep."

On the straying moonbeams I shall steal over your bed, and lie upon your bosom while you sleep.

I shall become a dream, and through the little opening of your eyelids I shall slip into the depths of your sleep; and when you wake up and look round startled, like a twinkling firefly I shall flit out into the darkness.

When, on the great festival of *puja*, the neighbours' children come and play about the house, I shall melt into the music of the flute and throb in your heart all day.

Dear auntie will come with *puja*-presents and will ask, "Where is our baby, sister?" Mother, you will tell her softly, "He is in the pupils of my eyes, he is in my body and in my soul."

## THE RECALL

THE night was dark when she went away, and they slept.

The night is dark now, and I call for her, "Come back, my darling; the world is asleep; and no one would know, if you came for a moment while stars are gazing at stars."

She went away when the trees were in bud and the spring was young.

Now the flowers are in high bloom and I call, "Come back, my darling. The children gather and scatter flowers in reckless sport. And if you come and take one little blossom no one will miss it."

Those that used to play are playing still, so spend-thrift is life.

I listen to their chatter and call, "Come back, my

darling, for mother's heart is full to the brim with love, and if you come to snatch only one little kiss from her no one will grudge it."


## THE FIRST JASMINES

AH, these jasmines, these white jasmines!

I seem to remember the first day when I filled my hands with these jasmines, these white jasmines.

I have loved the sunlight, the sky and the green earth;

I have heard the liquid murmur of the river through the darkness of midnight;

Autumn sunsets have come to me at the bend of a road in the lonely waste, like a bride raising her veil to accept her lover.

Yet my memory is still sweet with the first white jasmines that I held in my hands when I was a child.

Many a glad day has come in my life, and I have laughed with merrymakers on festival nights.

On grey mornings of rain I have crooned many an idle song.

I have worn round my neck the evening wreath of *bakulas* woven by the hand of love.

Yet my heart is sweet with the memory of the first fresh jasmines that filled my hands when I was a child.


## THE BANYAN TREE

O YOU shaggy-headed banyan tree standing on the bank of the pond, have you forgotten the little child, like the birds that have nested in your branches and left you?

Do you not remember how he sat at the window and wondered at the tangle of your roots that plunged underground?

The women would come to fill their jars in the pond, and your huge black shadow would wriggle on the water like sleep struggling to wake up.

Sunlight danced on the ripples like restless tiny shuttles weaving golden tapestry.

Two ducks swam by the weedy margin above their shadows, and the child would sit still and think.

He longed to be the wind and blow through your rustling branches, to be your shadow and lengthen with the day on the water, to be a bird and perch on your topmost twig, and to float like those ducks among the weeds and shadows.


## BENEDICTION

BLESS this little heart, this white soul that has won the kiss of heaven for our earth.

He loves the light of the sun, he loves the sight of his mother's face.

He has not learned to despise the dust, and to hanker after gold.

Clasp him to your heart and bless him.

He has come into this land of an hundred cross-roads.

I know not how he chose you from the crowd, came to your door, and grasped your hand to ask his way.

He will follow you, laughing and talking, and not a doubt in his heart.

Keep his trust, lead him straight and bless him.

Lay your hand on his head, and pray that though the waves underneath grow threatening, yet the breath from above may come and fill his sails and waft him to the haven of peace.

Forget him not in your hurry, let him come to your heart and bless him.

## THE GIFT

I WANT to give you something, my child, for we are drifting in the stream of the world.

Our lives will be carried apart, and our love forgotten.

But I am not so foolish as to hope that I could buy your heart with my gifts.

Young is your life, your path long, and you drink the love we bring you at one draught and turn and run away from us.

You have your play and your playmates. What harm is there if you have no time or thought for us!

We, indeed, have leisure enough in old age to count the days that are past, to cherish in our hearts what our hands have lost for ever.

The river runs swift with a song, breaking through all barriers. But the mountain stays and remembers, and follows her with his love.

## MY SONG

THIS song of mine will wind its music around you, my child, like the fond arms of love.

This song of mine will touch your forehead like a kiss of blessing.

When you are alone it will sit by your side and whisper in your ear, when you are in the crowd it will fence you about with aloofness.

My song will be like a pair of wings to your dreams, it will transport your heart to the verge of the unknown.

It will be like the faithful star overhead when dark night is over your road.

My song will sit in the pupils of your eyes, and will carry your sight into the heart of things.

And when my voice is silent in death, my song will speak in your living heart.


## THE CHILD-ANGEL

THEY clamour and fight, they doubt and despair, they know no end to their wranglings.

Let your life come amongst them like a flame of light, my child, unflickering and pure, and delight them into silence.

They are cruel in their greed and their envy, their words are like hidden knives thirsting for blood.

Go and stand amidst their scowling hearts, my child, and let your gentle eyes fall upon them like the forgiving peace of the evening over the strife of the day.

Let them see your face, my child, and thus know the meaning of all things; let them love you and thus love each other.

Come and take your seat in the bosom of the limitless, my child. At sunrise open and raise your heart like a blossoming flower, and at sunset bend your head and in silence complete the worship of the day.

# THE LAST BARGAIN

"COME and hire me," I cried, while in the morning I was walking on the stone-paved road.

Sword in hand, the King came in his chariot.

He held my hand and said, "I will hire you with my power."

But his power counted for naught, and he went away in his chariot.

In the heat of the midday the houses stood with shut doors.

I wandered along the crooked lane.

An old man came out with his bag of gold.

He pondered and said, "I will hire you with my money."

He weighed his coins one by one, but I turned away.

It was evening. The garden hedge was all aflower.

The fair maid came out and said, "I will hire you with a smile."

Her smile paled and melted into tears, and she went back alone into the dark.

The sun glistened on the sand, and the sea waves broke waywardly.

A child sat playing with shells.

He raised his head and seemed to know me, and said, "I hire you with nothing."

From thenceforward that bargain struck in child's play made me a free man.

# THE GARDENER

# THE GARDENER

## I

*Servant.* Have mercy upon your servant, my queen!

*Queen.* The assembly is over and my servants are all gone. Why do you come at this late hour?

*Servant.* When you have finished with others, that is my time.

I come to ask what remains for your last servant to do.

*Queen.* What can you expect when it is too late?

*Servant.* Make me the gardener of your flower garden.

*Queen.* What folly is this?

*Servant.* I will give up my other work.

I throw my swords and lances down in the dust. Do not send me to distant courts; do not bid me undertake new conquests. But make me the gardener of your flower garden.

*Queen.* What will your duties be?

*Servant.* The service of your idle days.

I will keep fresh the grassy path where you walk in the morning, where your feet will be greeted with praise at every step by the flowers eager for death.

I will swing you in a swing among the branches of the *saptaparna*, where the early evening moon will struggle to kiss your skirt through the leaves.

I will replenish with scented oil the lamp that burns by your bedside, and decorate your footstool with sandal and saffron paste in wondrous designs.

*Queen.* What will you have for your reward?

*Servant.* To be allowed to hold your little fists like tender lotus-buds and slip flower-chains over your wrists; to tinge the soles of your feet with the red juice of *ashoka* petals and kiss away the speck of dust that may chance to linger there.

*Queen.* Your prayers are granted, my servant, you will be the gardener of my flower garden.


## II

"Ah, poet, the evening draws near; your hair is turning grey.

"Do you in your lonely musing hear the message of the hereafter?"

"It is evening," the poet said, "and I am listening because some one may call from the village, late though it be.

"I watch if young straying hearts meet together, and two pairs of eager eyes beg for music to break their silence and speak for them.

"Who is there to weave their passionate songs, if I sit on the shore of life and contemplate death and the beyond?

"The early evening star disappears.

"The glow of a funeral pyre slowly dies by the silent river.

"Jackals cry in chorus from the courtyard of the deserted house in the light of the worn-out moon.

"If some wanderer, leaving home, come here to watch the night and with bowed head listen to the murmur of the darkness, who is there to whisper the secrets of life into his ears if I, shutting my doors, should try to free myself from mortal bonds?

"It is a trifle that my hair is turning grey.

"I am ever as young or as old as the youngest and the oldest of this village.

"Some have smiles, sweet and simple, and some a sly twinkle in their eyes.

"Some have tears that well up in the daylight, and others tears that are hidden in the gloom.

"They all have need for me, and I have no time to brood over the after-life.

"I am of an age with each, what matter if my hair turns grey?"

### III

In the morning I cast my net into the sea.

I dragged up from the dark abyss things of strange aspect and strange beauty—some shone like a smile, some glistened like tears, and some were flushed like the cheeks of a bride.

When with the day's burden I went home, my love was sitting in the garden idly tearing the leaves of a flower.

I hesitated for a moment, and then placed at her feet all that I had dragged up, and stood silent.

She glanced at them and said, "What strange things are these? I know not of what use they are!"

I bowed my head in shame and thought, "I have not fought for these, I did not buy them in the market; they are not fit gifts for her."

Then the whole night through I flung them one by one into the street.

In the morning travellers came; they picked them up and carried them into far countries.

## IV

AH me, why did they build my house by the road to the market town?

They moor their laden boats near my trees.
They come and go and wander at their will.
I sit and watch them; my time wears on.
Turn them away I cannot. And thus my days pass by.

Night and day their steps sound by my door.
Vainly I cry, "I do not know you."
Some of them are known to my fingers, some to my nostrils, the blood in my veins seems to know them, and some are known to my dreams.
Turn them away I cannot. I call them and say, "Come to my house whoever chooses. Yes, come."

In the morning the bell rings in the temple.
They come with their baskets in their hands.
Their feet are rosy-red. The early light of dawn is on their faces.
Turn them away I cannot. I call them and I say, "Come to my garden to gather flowers. Come hither."

In the midday the gong sounds at the palace gate.
I know not why they leave their work and linger near my hedge.
The flowers in their hair are pale and faded; the notes are languid in their flutes.
Turn them away I cannot. I call them and say, "The shade is cool under my trees. Come, friends."

At night the crickets chirp in the woods.

Who is it that comes slowly to my door and gently knocks?

I vaguely see the face, not a word is spoken, the stillness of the sky is all around.

Turn away my silent guest I cannot. I look at the face through the dark, and hours of dreams pass by.

## V

I AM restless. I am athirst for far-away things.

My soul goes out in a longing to touch the skirt of the dim distance.

O Great Beyond, O the keen call of thy flute!

I forget, I ever forget, that I have no wings to fly, that I am bound in this spot evermore.

I am eager and wakeful, I am a stranger in a strange land.

Thy breath comes to me whispering an impossible hope.

Thy tongue is known to my heart as its very own.

O Far-to-seek, O the keen call of thy flute!

I forget, I ever forget, that I know not the way, that I have not the winged horse.

I am listless, I am a wanderer in my heart.

In the sunny haze of the languid hours, what vast vision of thine takes shape in the blue of the sky!

O Farthest End, O the keen call of thy flute!

I forget, I ever forget, that the gates are shut everywhere in the house where I dwell alone!

## VI

THE tame bird was in a cage, the free bird was in the forest.

93

They met when the time came, it was a decree of fate.

The free bird cries, "O my love, let us fly to the wood."

The cage bird whispers, "Come hither, let us both live in the cage."

Says the free bird, "Among bars, where is there room to spread one's wings?"

"Alas," cries the cage bird, "I should not know where to sit perched in the sky."

The free bird cries, "My darling, sing the songs of the woodlands."

The cage bird says, "Sit by my side, I'll teach you the speech of the learned."

The forest bird cries, "No, ah no! songs can never be taught."

The cage bird says, "Alas for me, I know not the songs of the woodlands."

Their love is intense with longing, but they never can fly wing to wing.

Through the bars of the cage they look, and vain is their wish to know each other.

They flutter their wings in yearning, and sing, "Come closer, my love!"

The free bird cries, "It cannot be, I fear the closed doors of the cage."

The cage bird whispers, "Alas, my wings are powerless and dead."

## VII

O MOTHER, the young Prince is to pass by our door,—how can I attend to my work this morning?

Show me how to braid up my hair; tell me what garment to put on.

Why do you look at me amazed, mother?
I know well he will not glance up once at my
window; I know he will pass out of my sight in the
twinkling of an eye; only the vanishing strain of the
flute will come sobbing to me from afar.
But the young Prince will pass by our door, and I
will put on my best for the moment.

O mother, the young Prince did pass by our door,
and the morning sun flashed from his chariot.
I swept aside the veil from my face, I tore the ruby
chain from my neck and flung it in his path.
Why do you look at me amazed, mother?
I know well he did not pick up my chain; I know it
was crushed under his wheels leaving a red stain upon the
dust, and no one knows what my gift was nor to whom.
But the young Prince did pass by our door, and I
flung the jewel from my breast before his path.

## VIII

WHEN the lamp went out by my bed I woke up with
the early birds.
I sat at my open window with a fresh wreath on my
loose hair.
The young traveller came along the road in the rosy
mist of the morning.
A pearl chain was on his neck, and the sun's rays
fell on his crown. He stopped before my door and asked
me with an eager cry, "Where is she?"
For very shame I could not say, "She is I, young
traveller, she is I."

It was dusk and the lamp was not lit.
I was listlessly braiding my hair.

95

The young traveller came on his chariot in the glow of the setting sun.

His horses were foaming at the mouth, and there was dust on his garment.

He alighted at my door and asked in a tired voice, "Where is she?"

For very shame I could not say, "She is I, weary traveller, she is I."

It is an April night. The lamp is burning in my room. The breeze of the south comes gently. The noisy parrot sleeps in its cage.

My bodice is of the colour of the peacock's throat, and my mantle is green as young grass.

I sit upon the floor at the window watching the deserted street.

Through the dark night I keep humming, "She is I, despairing traveller, she is I."

## IX

WHEN I go alone at night to my love-tryst, birds do not sing, the wind does not stir, the houses on both sides of the street stand silent.

It is my own anklets that grow loud at every step and I am ashamed.

When I sit on my balcony and listen for his footsteps, leaves do not rustle on the trees, and the water is still in the river like the sword on the knees of a sentry fallen asleep.

It is my own heart that beats wildly—I do not know how to quiet it.

When my love comes and sits by my side, when my

body trembles and my eyelids droop, the night darkens, the wind blows out the lamp, and the clouds draw veils over the stars.

It is the jewel at my own breast that shines and gives light. I do not know how to hide it.

x

LET your work be, bride. Listen, the guest has come.

Do you hear, he is gently shaking the chain which fastens the door?

See that your anklets make no loud noise, and that your step is not over-hurried at meeting him.

Let your work be, bride, the guest has come in the evening.

No, it is not the ghostly wind, bride, do not be frightened.

It is the full moon on a night of April; shadows are pale in the courtyard; the sky overhead is bright.

Draw your veil over your face if you must, carry the lamp to the door if you fear.

No, it is not the ghostly wind, bride, do not be frightened.

Have no word with him if you are shy; stand aside by the door when you meet him.

If he asks you questions, and if you wish to, you can lower your eyes in silence.

Do not let your bracelets jingle when, lamp in hand, you lead him in.

Have no word with him if you are shy.

Have you not finished your work yet, bride? Listen, the guest has come.

Have you not lit the lamp in the cowshed?

97

Have you not got ready the offering-basket for the evening service?

Have you not put the red lucky mark at the parting of your hair, and done your toilet for the night?

O bride, do you hear, the guest has come?

Let your work be!

## XI

COME as you are; do not loiter over your toilet.

If your braided hair has loosened, if the parting of your hair be not straight, if the ribbons of your bodice be not fastened, do not mind.

Come as you are; do not loiter over your toilet.

Come, with quick steps over the grass.

If the raddle come from your feet because of the dew, if the rings of bells upon your feet slacken, if pearls drop out of your chain, do not mind.

Come, with quick steps over the grass.

Do you see the clouds wrapping the sky?

Flocks of cranes fly up from the further river-bank and fitful gusts of wind rush over the heath.

The anxious cattle run to their stalls in the village.

Do you see the clouds wrapping the sky?

In vain you light your toilet lamp—it flickers and goes out in the wind.

Who can know that your eyelids have not been touched with lampblack? For your eyes are darker than rain-clouds.

In vain you light your toilet lamp—it goes out.

Come as you are; do not loiter over your toilet.

If the wreath is not woven, who cares; if the wrist-chain has not been linked, let it be.

The sky is overcast with clouds—it is late.

Come as you are; do not loiter over your toilet.

XII

If you would be busy and fill your pitcher, come, O come to my lake.

The water will cling round your feet and babble its secret.

The shadow of the coming rain is on the sands, and the clouds hang low upon the blue lines of the trees like the heavy hair above your eyebrows.

I know well the rhythm of your steps, they are beating in my heart.

Come, O come to my lake, if you must fill your pitcher.

If you would be idle and sit listless and let your pitcher float on the water, come, O come to my lake.

The grassy slope is green, and the wild flowers beyond number.

Your thoughts will stray out of your dark eyes like birds from their nests.

Your veil will drop to your feet.

Come, O come to my lake, if you must sit idle.

If you would leave off your play and dive in the water, come, O come to my lake.

Let your blue mantle lie on the shore; the blue water will cover you and hide you.

The waves will stand a-tiptoe to kiss your neck and whisper in your ears.

Come, O come to my lake, if you would dive in the water.

If you must be mad and leap to your death, come, O come to my lake.

It is cool and fathomlessly deep.

It is dark like a sleep that is dreamless.

There in its depths nights and days are one, and songs are silence.

Come, O come to my lake, if you would plunge to your death.

## XIII

I ASKED nothing, only stood at the edge of the wood behind the tree.

Languor was still upon the eyes of the dawn, and the dew in the air.

The lazy smell of the damp grass hung in the thin mist above the earth.

Under the banyan tree you were milking the cow with your hands, tender and fresh as butter.

And I was standing still.

I did not say a word. It was the bird that sang unseen from the thicket.

The mango tree was shedding its flowers upon the village road, and the bees came humming one by one.

On the side of the pond the gate of Shiva's temple was opened and the worshipper had begun his chants.

With the vessel on your lap you were milking the cow.

I stood with my empty can.

I did not come near you.

The sky woke with the sound of the gong at the temple.

The dust was raised in the road from the hoofs of the driven cattle.

With the gurgling pitchers at their hips, women came from the river.

Your bracelets were jingling, and foam brimming over the jar.

The morning wore on and I did not come near you.

## XIV

I WAS walking by the road, I do not know why, when the noonday was past and bamboo branches rustled in the wind.

The prone shadows with their outstretched arms clung to the feet of the hurrying light.

The *koels* were weary of their songs.

I was walking by the road, I do not know why.

The hut by the side of the water is shaded by an overhanging tree.

Some one was busy with her work, and her bangles made music in the corner.

I stood before this hut, I know not why.

The narrow winding road crosses many a mustard field, and many a mango forest.

It passes by the temple of the village and the market at the river landing-place.

I stopped by this hut, I do not know why.

Years ago it was a day of breezy March when the murmur of the spring was languorous, and mango blossoms were dropping on the dust.

The rippling water leapt and licked the brass vessel that stood on the landing-step.

I think of that day of breezy March, I do not know why.

Shadows are deepening and cattle returning to their folds.
The light is grey upon the lonely meadows, and the villagers are waiting for the ferry at the bank.
I slowly return upon my steps, I do not know why.

## XV

I RUN as a musk-deer runs in the shadow of the forest mad with his own perfume.
The night is the night of mid-May, the breeze is the breeze of the south.
I lose my way and I wander, I seek what I cannot get, I get what I do not seek.

From my heart comes out and dances the image of my own desire.
The gleaming vision flits on.
I try to clasp it firmly, it eludes me and leads me astray.
I seek what I cannot get, I get what I do not seek.

## XVI

HANDS cling to hands and eyes linger on eyes: thus begins the record of our hearts.
It is the moonlit night of March; the sweet smell of *henna* is in the air; my flute lies on the earth neglected and your garland of flowers is unfinished.
This love between you and me is simple as a song.

Your veil of the saffron colour makes my eyes drunk.

The jasmine wreath that you wove me thrills to my heart like praise.

It is a game of giving and withholding, revealing and screening again; some smiles and some little shyness, and some sweet useless struggles.

This love between you and me is simple as a song.

No mystery beyond the present; no striving for the impossible; no shadow behind the charm; no groping in the depth of the dark.

This love between you and me is simple as a song.

We do not stray out of all words into the ever silent; we do not raise our hands to the void for things beyond hope.

It is enough what we give and we get.

We have not crushed the joy to the utmost to wring from it the wine of pain.

This love between you and me is simple as a song.

## XVII

THE yellow bird sings in their tree and makes my heart dance with gladness.

We both live in the same village, and that is our one piece of joy.

Her pair of pet lambs come to graze in the shade of our garden trees.

If they stray into our barley field, I take them up in my arms.

The name of our village is Khanjanā, and Anjana they call our river.

My name is known to all the village, and her name is Ranjana.

Only one field lies between us.

Bees that have hived in our grove go to seek honey in theirs.

Flowers launched from their landing-stairs come floating by the stream where we bathe.

Baskets of dried *kusm* flowers come from their fields to our market.

The name of our village is **Kha**njanā, and Anjanā they call our river.

My name is known to all the village, and her name is Ranjanā.

The lane that winds to their house is fragrant in the spring with mango flowers.

When their linseed is ripe for harvest the hemp is in bloom in our field.

The stars that smile on their cottage send us the same twinkling look.

The rain that floods their tank makes glad our *kadam* forest.

The name of our village is Khanjanā, and Anjanā they call our river.

My name is known to all the village, and her name is Ranjanā.

### XVIII

WHEN the two sisters go to fetch water, they come to this spot and they smile.

They must be aware of somebody who stands behind the trees whenever they go to fetch water.

The two sisters whisper to each other when they pass this spot.

They must have guessed the secret of that somebody

who stands behind the trees whenever they go to fetch water.

Their pitchers lurch suddenly, and water spills when they reach this spot.

They must have found out that somebody's heart is beating who stands behind the trees whenever they go to fetch water.

The two sisters glance at each other when they come to this spot, and they smile.

There is a laughter in their swift-stepping feet, which makes confusion in somebody's mind who stands behind the trees whenever they go to fetch water.

### XIX

You walked by the riverside path with the full pitcher upon your hip.

Why did you swiftly turn your face and peep at me through your fluttering veil?

That gleaming look from the dark came upon me like a breeze that sends a shiver through the rippling water and sweeps away to the shadowy shore.

It came to me like the bird of the evening that hurriedly flies across the lampless room from the one open window to the other, and disappears in the night.

You are hidden as a star behind the hills, and I am a passer-by upon the road.

But why did you stop for a moment and glance at my face through your veil while you walked by the river-side path with the full pitcher upon your hip?

## XX

DAY after day he comes and goes away.

Go, and give him a flower from my hair, my friend.
If he asks who was it that sent it, I entreat you do not
tell him my name—for he only comes and goes away.

He sits on the dust under the tree.
Spread there a seat with flowers and leaves, my
friend.
His eyes are sad, and they bring sadness to my heart.
He does not speak what he has in mind; he only comes
and goes away.

## XXI

WHY did he choose to come to my door, the wandering
youth, when the day dawned?
As I come in and out I pass by him every time, and
my eyes are caught by his face.
I know not if I should speak to him or keep silent.
Why did he choose to come to my door?

The cloudy nights in July are dark; the sky is soft
blue in the autumn; the spring days are restless with the
south wind.
He weaves his songs with fresh tunes every time.
I turn from my work and my eyes fill with the mist.
Why did he choose to come to my door?

## XXII

WHEN she passed by me with quick steps, the end of
her skirt touched me.
From the unknown island of a heart came a sudden
warm breath of spring.

106

A flutter of a flitting touch brushed me and vanished in a moment, like a torn flower-petal blown in the breeze.

It fell upon my heart like a sigh of her body and whisper of her heart.

## XXIII

WHY do you sit there and jingle your bracelets in mere idle sport?

Fill your pitcher. It is time for you to come home.

Why do you stir the water with your hands and fitfully glance at the road for some one in mere idle sport?

Fill your pitcher and come home.

The morning hours pass by—the dark water flows on.

The waves are laughing and whispering to each other in mere idle sport.

The wandering clouds have gathered at the edge of the sky on yonder rise of the land.

They linger and look at your face and smile in mere idle sport.

Fill your pitcher and come home.

## XXIV

Do not keep to yourself the secret of your heart, my friend!

Say it to me, only to me, in secret.

You who smile so gently, softly whisper, my heart will hear it, not my ears.

The night is deep, the house is silent, the birds' nests are shrouded with sleep.

Speak to me through hesitating tears, through falter-
ing smiles, through sweet shame and pain, the secret of
your heart!

XXV

"COME to us, youth, tell us truly why there is madness
in your eyes?"

"I know not what wine of wild poppy I have drunk,
that there is this madness in my eyes."

"Ah, shame!"

"Well, some are wise and some foolish, some are
watchful and some careless. There are eyes that smile
and eyes that weep—and madness is in my eyes."

"Youth, why do you stand so still under the shadow
of the tree?"

"My feet are languid with the burden of my heart,
and I stand still in the shadow."

"Ah, shame!"

"Well, some march on their way and some linger,
some are free and some are fettered—and my feet are
languid with the burden of my heart."

XXVI

"WHAT comes from your willing hands I take. I beg
for nothing more."

"Yes, yes, I know you, modest mendicant, you ask
for all that one has."

"If there be a stray flower for me I will wear it in my
heart."

"But if there be thorns?"

"I will endure them."

108

"Yes, yes, I know you, modest mendicant, you ask for all that one has."

"If but once you should raise your loving eyes to my face it would make my life sweet beyond death."

"But if there be only cruel glances?"

"I will keep them piercing my heart."

"Yes, yes, I know you, modest mendicant, you ask for all that one has."

## XXVII

"TRUST love even if it brings sorrow. Do not close up your heart."

"Ah, no, my friend, your words are dark, I cannot understand them."

"The heart is only for giving away with a tear and a song, my love."

"Ah, no, my friend, your words are dark, I cannot understand them."

"Pleasure is frail like a dewdrop, while it laughs it dies. But sorrow is strong and abiding. Let sorrowful love wake in your eyes."

"Ah, no, my friend, your words are dark, I cannot understand them."

"The lotus blooms in the sight of the sun, and loses all that it has. It would not remain in bud in the eternal winter mist."

"Ah, no, my friend, your words are dark, I cannot understand them."

## XXVIII

YOUR questioning eyes are sad. They seek to know my meaning as the moon would fathom the sea.

I have bared my life before your eyes from end to end, with nothing hidden or held back. That is why you know me not.

If it were only a gem, I could break it into a hundred pieces and string them into a chain to put on your neck.

If it were only a flower, round and small and sweet, I could pluck it from its stem to set it in your hair.

But it is a heart, my beloved. Where are its shores and its bottom?

You know not the limits of this kingdom, still you are its queen.

If it were only a moment of pleasure it would flower in an easy smile, and you could see it and read it in a moment.

If it were merely a pain it would melt in limpid tears, reflecting its inmost secret without a word.

But it is love, my beloved.

Its pleasure and pain are boundless, and endless its wants and wealth.

It is as near to you as your life, but you can never wholly know it.


### XXIX

SPEAK to me, my love! Tell me in words what you sang.

The night is dark. The stars are lost in clouds. The wind is sighing through the leaves.

I will let loose my hair. My blue cloak will cling round me like night. I will clasp your head to my bosom; and there in the sweet loneliness murmur on your heart. I will shut my eyes and listen. I will not look in your face.

When your words are ended, we will sit still and silent. Only the trees will whisper in the dark.

The night will pale. The day will dawn. We shall look at each other's eyes and go on our different paths.

Speak to me, my love! Tell me in words what you sang.

### XXX

YOU are the evening cloud floating in the sky of my dreams.

I paint you and fashion you ever with my love longings.

You are my own, my own, Dweller in my endless dreams!

Your feet are rosy-red with the glow of my heart's desire, Gleaner of my sunset songs!

Your lips are bitter-sweet with the taste of my wine of pain.

You are my own, my own, Dweller in my lonesome dreams!

With the shadow of my passion have I darkened your eyes, Haunter of the depth of my gaze!

I have caught you and wrapt you, my love, in the net of my music.

You are my own, my own, Dweller in my deathless dreams!

### XXXI

MY heart, the bird of the wilderness, has found its sky in your eyes.

They are the cradle of the morning, they are the kingdom of the stars.

My songs are lost in their depths.

Let me but soar in that sky, in its lonely immensity.

Let me but cleave its clouds and spread wings in its sunshine.

XXXII

TELL me if this be all true, my lover, tell me if this be true.

When these eyes flash their lightning the dark clouds in your breast make stormy answer.

Is it true that my lips are sweet like the opening bud of the first conscious love?

Do the memories of vanished months of May linger in my limbs?

Does the earth, like a harp, shiver into songs with the touch of my feet?

Is it then true that the dewdrops fall from the eyes of night when I am seen, and the morning light is glad when it wraps my body round?

Is it true, is it true, that your love travelled alone through ages and worlds in search of me?

That when you found me at last, your age-long desire found utter peace in my gentle speech and my eyes and lips and flowing hair?

Is it then true that the mystery of the Infinite is written on this little forehead of mine?

Tell me, my lover, if all this be true.

XXXIII

I LOVE you, beloved. Forgive me my love.

Like a bird losing its way I am caught.

When my heart was shaken it lost its veil and was naked. Cover it with pity, beloved, and forgive me my love.

If you cannot love me, beloved, forgive me my pain.
Do not look askance at me from afar.
I will steal back to my corner and sit in the dark.
With both hands I will cover my naked shame.
Turn your face from me, beloved, and forgive me my
pain

If you love me, beloved, forgive me my joy.
When my heart is borne away by the flood of happiness, do not smile at my perilous abandonment.
When I sit on my throne and rule you with my tyranny of love, when like a goddess I grant you my favour, bear with my pride, beloved, and forgive me my joy.

### XXXIV

Do not go, my love, without asking my leave.
I have watched all night, and now my eyes are heavy with sleep.
I fear lest I lose you when I am sleeping.
Do not go, my love, without asking my leave.

I start up and stretch my hands to touch you. I ask myself, "Is it a dream?"
Could I but entangle your feet with my heart and hold them fast to my breast!
Do not go, my love, without asking my leave.

### XXXV

Lest I should know you too easily, you play with me.
You blind me with flashes of laughter to hide your tears.
I know, I know your art,
You never say the word you would.

Lest I should not prize you, you elude me in a thousand ways.

Lest I should confuse you with the crowd, you stand aside.

I know, I know your art,
You never walk the path you would.

Your claim is more than that of others, that is why you are silent.

With playful carelessness you avoid my gifts.

I know, I know your art,
You never will take what you would.

### XXXVI

HE whispered, "My love, raise your eyes."

I sharply chid him, and said "Go!" But he did not stir.

He stood before me and held both my hands. I said, "Leave me!" But he did not go.

He brought his face near my ear. I glanced at him and said, "What a shame!" But he did not move.

His lips touched my cheek. I trembled and said, "You dare too much." But he had no shame.

He put a flower in my hair. I said, "It is useless!" But he stood unmoved.

He took the garland from my neck and went away. I weep and ask my heart, "Why does he not come back?"

### XXXVII

WOULD you put your wreath of fresh flowers on my neck, fair one?

But you must know that the one wreath that I had woven is for the many, for those who are seen in glimpses, or dwell in lands unexplored, or live in poets' songs.

It is too late to ask my heart in return for yours.

There was a time when my life was like a bud, all its perfume was stored in its core.

Now it is squandered far and wide.

Who knows the enchantment that can gather and shut it up again?

My heart is not mine to give to one only, it is given to the many.

## XXXVIII

My love, once upon a time your poet launched a great epic in his mind.

Alas, I was not careful, and it struck your ringing anklets and came to grief.

It broke up into scraps of songs and lay scattered at your feet.

All my cargo of the stories of old wars was tossed by the laughing waves and soaked in tears and sank.

You must make this loss good to me, my love.

If my claims to immortal fame after death are shattered, make me immortal while I live.

And I will not mourn for my loss nor blame you.

## XXXIX

I try to weave a wreath all the morning, but the flowers slip and they drop out.

You sit there watching me in secret through the corner of your prying eyes.

Ask those eyes, darkly planning mischief, whose fault
it was.

I try to sing a song, but in vain.
A hidden smile trembles on your lips; ask of it the
reason of my failure.
Let your smiling lips say on oath how my voice lost
itself in silence like a drunken bee in the lotus.

It is evening, and the time for the flowers to close
their petals.
Give me leave to sit by your side, and bid my lips
to do the work that can be done in silence and in the
dim light of stars.

## XL

AN unbelieving smile flits on your eyes when I come to
you to take my leave.
I have done it so often that you think I will soon
return.
To tell you the truth I have the same doubt in my
mind.
For the spring days come again time after time; the
full moon takes leave and comes on another visit, the
flowers come again and blush upon their branches year
after year, and it is likely that I take my leave only to
come to you again.
But keep the illusion awhile; do not send it away
with ungentle haste.
When I say I leave you for all time, accept it as true,
and let a mist of tears for one moment deepen the dark
rim of your eyes.
Then smile as archly as you like when I come again.

I LONG to speak the deepest words I have to say to you; but I dare not, for fear you should laugh.

That is why I laugh at myself and shatter my secret in jest.

I make light of my pain, afraid you should do so.

I long to tell you the truest words I have to say to you; but I dare not, being afraid that you would not believe them.

That is why I disguise them in untruth, saying the contrary of what I mean.

I make my pain appear absurd, afraid that you should do so.

I long to use the most precious words I have for you; but I dare not, fearing I should not be paid with like value.

That is why I give you hard names and boast of my callous strength.

I hurt you, for fear you should never know any pain.

I long to sit silent by you; but I dare not lest my heart come out at my lips.

That is why I prattle and chatter lightly and hide my heart behind words.

I rudely handle my pain, for fear you should do so.

I long to go away from your side; but I dare not, for fear my cowardice should become known to you.

That is why I hold my head high and carelessly come into your presence.

Constant thrusts from your eyes keep my pain fresh for ever.

O MAD, superbly drunk;

If you kick open your doors and play the fool in public;

If you empty your bag in a night, and snap your fingers at prudence;

If you walk in curious paths and play with useless things;

Reck not rhyme or reason;

If unfurling your sails before the storm you snap the rudder in two,

Then I will follow you, comrade, and be drunken and go to the dogs.

I have wasted my days and nights in the company of steady wise neighbours.

Much knowing has turned my hair grey, and much watching has made my sight dim.

For years I have gathered and heaped up scraps and fragments of things:

Crush them and dance upon them, and scatter them all to the winds.

For I know 'tis the height of wisdom to be drunken and go to the dogs.

Let all crooked scruples vanish, let me hopelessly lose my way.

Let a gust of wild giddiness come and sweep me away from my anchors.

The world is peopled with worthies, and workers, useful and clever.

There are men who are easily first, and men who come decently after.

Let them be happy and prosper, and let me be foolishly futile.

For I know 'tis the end of all works to be drunken
and go to the dogs.

I swear to surrender this moment all claims to the
ranks of the decent.

I let go my pride of learning and judgment of right
and of wrong.

I'll shatter memory's vessel, scattering the last drop
of tears.

With the foam of the berry-red wine I will bathe and
brighten my laughter.

The badge of the civil and staid I'll tear into shreds
for the nonce.

I'll take the holy vow to be worthless, to be drunken
and go to the dogs.

## XLIII

No, my friends, I shall never be an ascetic, whatever
you may say.

I shall never be an ascetic if she does not take the vow
with me.

It is my firm resolve that if I cannot find a shady
shelter and a companion for my penance, I shall never
turn ascetic.

No, my friends, I shall never leave my hearth and
home, and retire into the forest solitude, if rings no
merry laughter in its echoing shade and if the end of no
saffron mantle flutters in the wind; if its silence is not
deepened by soft whispers.

I shall never be an ascetic.

REVEREND sir, forgive this pair of sinners. Spring winds to-day are blowing in wild eddies, driving dust and dead leaves away, and with them your lessons are all lost.

Do not say, father, that life is a vanity.

For we have made truce with death for once, and only for a few fragrant hours we two have been made immortal.

Even if the King's army came and fiercely fell upon us we should sadly shake our heads and say, "Brothers, you are disturbing us. If you must have this noisy game, go and clatter your arms elsewhere. Since only for a few fleeting moments we have been made immortal."

If friendly people came and flocked around us, we should humbly bow to them and say, "This extravagant good fortune is an embarrassment to us. Room is scarce in the infinite sky where we dwell. For in the spring-time flowers come in crowds, and the busy wings of bees jostle each other. Our little heaven, where dwell only we two immortals, is too absurdly narrow."

### XLV

To the guests that must go bid God-speed and brush away all traces of their steps.

Take to your bosom with a smile what is easy and simple and near.

To-day is the festival of phantoms that know not when they die.

Let your laughter be but a meaningless mirth like twinkles of light on the ripples.

Let your life lightly dance on the edges of Time like dew on the tip of a leaf.

Strike in chords from your harp fitful momentary rhythms.

## XLVI

YOU left me and went on your way.

I thought I should mourn for you and set your solitary image in my heart wrought in a golden song.

But ah, my evil fortune, time is short.

Youth wanes year after year; the spring days are fugitive; the frail flowers die for nothing, and the wise man warns me that life is but a dewdrop on the lotus leaf.

Should I neglect all this to gaze after one who has turned her back on me?

That would be rude and foolish, for time is short.

Then, come, my rainy nights with pattering feet; smile, my golden autumn; come, careless April, scattering your kisses abroad.

You come, and you, and you also?

My loves, you know we are mortals. Is it wise to break one's heart for the one who takes her heart away? For time is short.

It is sweet to sit in a corner to muse and write in rhymes that you are all my world.

It is heroic to hug one's sorrow and determine not to be consoled.

But a fresh face peeps across my door and raises its eyes to my eyes.

I cannot but wipe away my tears and change the tune of my song.

For time is short.

XLVII

IF you would have it so, I will end my singing.

If it sets your heart aflutter, I will take away my eyes from your face.

If it suddenly startles you in your walk, I will step aside and take another path.

If it confuses you in your flower-weaving, I will shun your lonely garden.

If it makes the water wanton and wild, I will not row my boat by your bank.

XLVIII

FREE me from the bonds of your sweetness, my love! No more of this wine of kisses.

This mist of heavy incense stifles my heart.

Open the doors, make room for the morning light.

I am lost in you, wrapped in the folds of your caresses.

Free me from your spells, and give me back the manhood to offer you my freed heart.

XLIX

I HOLD her hands and press her to my breast.

I try to fill my arms with her loveliness, to plunder her sweet smile with kisses, to drink her dark glances with my eyes.

Ah, but where is it? Who can strain the blue from the sky?

122

I try to grasp the beauty; it eludes me, leaving only
the body in my hands.

Baffled and weary I come back.

How can the body touch the flower which only the
spirit may touch?

L

LOVE, my heart longs day and night for the meeting
with you—for the meeting that is like all-devouring
death.

Sweep me away like a storm; take everything I have;
break open my sleep and plunder my dreams. Rob me
of my world.

In that devastation, in the utter nakedness of spirit,
let us become one in beauty.

Alas for my vain desire! Where is this hope for union
except in thee, my God?

LI

THEN finish the last song and let us leave.

Forget this night when the night is no more.

Whom do I try to clasp in my arms? Dreams can
never be made captive.

My eager hands press emptiness to my heart and it
bruises my breast.

LII

WHY did the lamp go out?

I shaded it with my cloak to save it from the wind,
that is why the lamp went out.

Why did the flower fade?

I pressed it to my heart with anxious love, that is
why the flower faded.

123

Why did the stream dry up?
I put a dam across it to have it for my use, that is why the stream dried up.

Why did the harp-string break?
I tried to force a note that was beyond its power, that is why the harp-string is broken.

### LIII

WHY do you put me to shame with a look?
I have not come as a beggar.
Only for a passing hour I stood at the end of your courtyard outside the garden hedge.
Why do you put me to shame with a look?

Not a rose did I gather from your garden, not a fruit did I pluck.
I humbly took my shelter under the wayside shade where every strange traveller may stand.
Not a rose did I pluck.

Yes, my feet were tired, and the shower of rain came down.
The winds cried out among the swaying bamboo branches.
The clouds ran across the sky as though in the flight from defeat.
My feet were tired.

I know not what you thought of me or for whom you were waiting at your door.
Flashes of lightning dazzled your watching eyes.

How could I know that you could see me where I stood in the dark?

I know not what you thought of me.

The day is ended, and the rain has ceased for a moment.

I leave the shadow of the tree at the end of your garden and this seat on the grass.

It has darkened; shut your door; I go my way.

The day is ended.

### LIV

WHERE do you hurry with your basket this late evening when the marketing is over?

They all have come home with their burdens; the moon peeps from above the village trees.

The echoes of the voices calling for the ferry run across the dark water to the distant swamp where wild ducks sleep.

Where do you hurry with your basket when the marketing is over?

Sleep has laid her fingers upon the eyes of the earth.

The nests of the crows have become silent, and the murmurs of the bamboo leaves are silent.

The labourers home from their fields spread their mats in the courtyards.

Where do you hurry with your basket when the marketing is over?

### LV

IT was midday when you went away.

The sun was strong in the sky.

I had done my work and sat alone on my balcony when you went away.

Fitful gusts came winnowing through the smells of many distant fields.

The doves cooed tireless in the shade, and a bee strayed in my room humming the news of many distant fields.

The village slept in the noonday heat. The road lay deserted.

In sudden fits the rustling of the leaves rose and died.

I gazed at the sky and wove in the blue the letters of a name I had known, while the village slept in the noonday heat.

I had forgotten to braid my hair. The languid breeze played with it upon my cheek.

The river ran unruffled under the shady bank.

The lazy white clouds did not move.

I had forgotten to braid my hair.

It was midday when you went away.

The dust of the road was hot and the fields panting.

The doves cooed among the dense leaves.

I was alone in my balcony when you went away.

## LVI

I WAS one among many women busy with the obscure daily tasks of the household.

Why did you single me out and bring me away from the cool shelter of our common life?

126

Love unexpressed is sacred. It shines like gems in the gloom of the hidden heart. In the light of the curious day it looks pitifully dark.

Ah, you broke through the cover of my heart and dragged my trembling love into the open place, destroying for ever the shady corner where it hid its nest.

The other women are the same as ever.

No one has peeped into their inmost being, and they themselves know not their own secret.

Lightly they smile, and weep, chatter, and work. Daily they go to the temple, light their lamps, and fetch water from the river.

I hoped my love would be saved from the shivering shame of the shelterless, but you turn your face away.

Yes, your path lies open before you, but you have cut off my return, and left me stripped naked before the world with its lidless eyes staring night and day.

## LVII

I PLUCKED your flower, O world!

I pressed it to my heart and the thorn pricked.

When the day waned and it darkened, I found that the flower had faded, but the pain remained.

More flowers will come to you with perfume and pride, O world!

But my time for flower-gathering is over, and through the dark night I have not my rose, only the pain remains.

## LVIII

ONE morning in the flower garden a blind girl came to offer me a flower-chain in the cover of a lotus leaf.

I put it round my neck, and tears came to my eyes.

I kissed her and said, "You are blind even as the flowers are.

"You yourself know not how beautiful is your gift."

## LIX

O WOMAN, you are not merely the handiwork of God, but also of men; these are ever endowing you with beauty from their hearts.

Poets are weaving for you a web with threads of golden imagery; painters are giving your form ever new immortality.

The sea gives its pearls, the mines their gold, the summer gardens their flowers to deck you, to cover you, to make you more precious.

The desire of men's hearts has shed its glory over your youth.

You are one-half woman and one-half dream.

## LX

AMIDST the rush and roar of life, O Beauty, carved in stone, you stand mute and still, alone and aloof.

Great Time sits enamoured at your feet and murmurs: "Speak, speak to me, my love; speak, my bride!"

But your speech is shut up in stone, O Immovable Beauty!

## LXI

PEACE, my heart, let the time for the parting be sweet.

Let it not be a death but completeness.

Let love melt into memory and pain into songs.

Let the flight through the sky end in the folding of the wings over the nest.

Let the last touch of your hands be gentle like the flower of the night.

Stand still, O Beautiful End, for a moment, and say your last words in silence.

I bow to you and hold up my lamp to light you on your way.

## LXII

In the dusky path of a dream I went to seek the love who was mine in a former life.

Her house stood at the end of a desolate street.

In the evening breeze her pet peacock sat drowsing on its perch, and the pigeons were silent in their corner.

She set her lamp down by the portal and stood before me.

She raised her large eyes to my face and mutely asked, "Are you well, my friend?"

I tried to answer, but our language had been lost and forgotten.

I thought and thought; our names would not come to my mind.

Tears shone in her eyes. She held up her right hand to me. I took it and stood silent.

Our lamp had flickered in the evening breeze and died.

TRAVELLER, must you go?

The night is still and the darkness swoons upon the forest.

The lamps are bright in our balcony, the flowers all fresh, and the youthful eyes still awake.

Is the time for your parting come?

Traveller, must you go?

We have not bound your feet with our entreating arms.

Your doors are open. Your horse stands saddled at the gate.

If we have tried to bar your passage it was but with our songs.

Did we ever try to hold you back it was but with our eyes.

Traveller, we are helpless to keep you. We have only our tears.

What quenchless fire glows in your eyes?

What restless fever runs in your blood?

What call from the dark urges you?

What awful incantation have you read among the stars in the sky, that with a sealed secret message the night entered your heart, silent and strange?

If you do not care for merry meetings, if you must have peace, weary heart, we shall put our lamps out and silence our harps.

We shall sit still in the dark in the rustle of leaves, and the tired moon will shed pale rays on your window.

O traveller, what sleepless spirit has touched you from the heart of the midnight?

## LXIV

I SPENT my day on the scorching hot dust of the road.

Now, in the cool of the evening, I knock at the door of the inn. It is deserted and in ruins.

A grim *ashath* tree spreads its hungry clutching roots through the gaping fissures of the walls.

Days have been when wayfarers came here to wash their weary feet.

They spread their mats in the courtyard in the dim light of the early moon, and sat and talked of strange lands.

They woke refreshed in the morning when birds made them glad, and friendly flowers nodded their heads at them from the wayside.

But no lighted lamp awaited me when I came here.

The black smudges of smoke left by many a forgotten evening lamp stare, like blind eyes, from the wall.

Fireflies flit in the bush near the dried-up pond, and bamboo branches fling their shadows on the grass-grown path.

I am the guest of no one at the end of my day.

The long night is before me, and I am tired.

## LXV

Is that your call again?

The evening has come. Weariness clings round me like the arms of entreating love.

Do you call me?

I had given all my day to you, cruel mistress, must you also rob me of my night?

Somewhere there is an end to everything, and the loneness of the dark is one's own.

Must your voice cut through it and smite me?

Has the evening no music of sleep at your gate?
Do the silent-winged stars never climb the sky above your pitiless tower?
Do the flowers never drop on the dust in soft death in your garden?

Must you call me, you unquiet one?
Then let the sad eyes of love vainly watch and weep.
Let the lamp burn in the lonely house.
Let the ferry-boat take the weary labourers to their home.
I leave behind my dreams and I hasten to your call.

## LXVI

A WANDERING madman was seeking the touchstone, with matted locks, tawny and dust-laden, and body worn to a shadow, his lips tight-pressed, like the shut-up doors of his heart, his burning eyes like the lamp of a glow-worm seeking its mate.

Before him the endless ocean roared.
The garrulous waves ceaselessly talked of hidden treasures, mocking the ignorance that knew not their meaning.
Maybe he now had no hope remaining, yet he would not rest, for the search had become his life,—
Just as the ocean for ever lifts its arms to the sky for the unattainable—

Just as the stars go in circles, yet seeking a goal that can never be reached—

Even so on the lonely shore the madman with dusty tawny locks still roamed in search of the touchstone.

One day a village boy came up and asked, "Tell me, where did you come at this golden chain about your waist?"

The madman started—the chain that once was iron was verily gold; it was not a dream, but he did not know when it had changed.

He struck his forehead wildly—where, O where had he without knowing it achieved success?

It had grown into a habit, to pick up pebbles and touch the chain, and to throw them away without looking to see if a change had come; thus the madman found and lost the touchstone.

The sun was sinking low in the west, the sky was of gold.

The madman returned on his footsteps to seek anew the lost treasure, with his strength gone, his body bent, and his heart in the dust, like a tree uprooted.

### LXVII

THOUGH the evening comes with slow steps and has signalled for all songs to cease;

Though your companions have gone to their rest and you are tired;

Though fear broods in the dark and the face of the sky is veiled;

Yet, bird, O my bird, listen to me, do not close your wings.

That is not the gloom of the leaves of the forest, that is the sea swelling like a dark black snake.

That is not the dance of the flowering jasmine, that is flashing foam.

Ah, where is the sunny green shore, where is your nest?

Bird, O my bird, listen to me, do not close your wings.

The lone night lies along your path, the dawn sleeps behind the shadowy hills.

The stars hold their breath counting the hours, the feeble moon swims the deep night.

Bird, O my bird, listen to me, do not close your wings.

There is no hope, no fear for you.

There is no word, no whisper, no cry.

There is no home, no bed of rest.

There is only your own pair of wings and the pathless sky.

Bird, O my bird, listen to me, do not close your wings.

### LXVIII

NONE lives for ever, brother, and nothing lasts for long. Keep that in mind and rejoice.

Our life is not the one old burden, our path is not the one long journey.

One sole poet has not to sing one aged song.

The flower fades and dies; but he who wears the flower has not to mourn for it for ever.

Brother, keep that in mind and rejoice.

There must come a full pause to weave perfection into music.

Life droops toward its sunset to be drowned in the golden shadows.

Love must be called from its play to drink sorrow and be borne to the heaven of tears.

Brother, keep that in mind and rejoice.

We hasten to gather our flowers lest they are plundered by the passing winds.

It quickens our blood and brightens our eyes to snatch kisses that would vanish if we delayed.

Our life is eager, our desires are keen, for time tolls the bell of parting.

Brother, keep that in mind and rejoice.

There is not time for us to clasp a thing and crush it and fling it away to the dust.

The hours trip rapidly away, hiding their dreams in their skirts.

Our life is short; it yields but a few days for love.

Were it for work and drudgery it would be endlessly long.

Brother, keep that in mind and rejoice.

Beauty is sweet to us, because she dances to the same fleeting tune with our lives.

Knowledge is precious to us, because we shall never have time to complete it.

All is done and finished in the eternal Heaven.

But earth's flowers of illusion are kept eternally fresh by death.

Brother, keep that in mind and rejoice.

I HUNT for the golden stag.

You may smile, my friends, but I pursue the vision that eludes me.

I run across hills and dales, I wander through nameless lands, because I am hunting for the golden stag.

You come and buy in the market and go back to your homes laden with goods, but the spell of the homeless winds has touched me I know not when and where.

I have no care in my heart; all my belongings I have left far behind me.

I run across hills and dales, I wander through nameless lands—because I am hunting for the golden stag.

## LXX

I REMEMBER a day in my childhood I floated a paper boat in the ditch.

It was a wet day of July; I was alone and happy over my play.

I floated my paper boat in the ditch.

Suddenly the storm-clouds thickened, winds came in gusts, and rain poured in torrents.

Rills of muddy water rushed and swelled the stream and sunk my boat.

Bitterly I thought in my mind that the storm came on purpose to spoil my happiness; all its malice was against me.

The cloudy day of July is long to-day, and I have been musing over all those games in life wherein I was loser.

I was blaming my fate for the many tricks it played on me, when suddenly I remembered the paper boat that sank in the ditch.

## LXXI

THE day is not yet done, the fair is not over, the fair on the river-bank.

I had feared that my time had been squandered and my last penny lost.

But no, my brother, I have still something left. My fate has not cheated me of everything.

The selling and buying are over.

All the dues on both sides have been gathered in, and it is time for me to go home.

But, gatekeeper, do you ask for your toll?

Do not fear, I have still something left. My fate has not cheated me of everything.

The lull in the wind threatens storm, and the lowering clouds in the west bode no good.

The hushed water waits for the wind.

I hurry to cross the river before the night overtakes me.

O ferryman, you want your fee!

Yes, brother, I have still something left. My fate has not cheated me of everything.

In the wayside under the tree sits the beggar. Alas, he looks at my face with a timid hope!

He thinks I am rich with the day's profit.

Yes, brother, I have still something left. My fate has not cheated me of everything.

The night grows dark and the road lonely. Fireflies gleam among the leaves.

Who are you that follow me with stealthy silent steps?

Ah, I know, it is your desire to rob me of all my gains. I will not disappoint you!

For I still have something left, and my fate has not cheated me of everything.

At midnight I reach home. My hands are empty.

You are waiting with anxious eyes at my door, sleepless and silent.

Like a timorous bird you fly to my breast with eager love.

Ay, ay, my God, much remains still. My fate has not cheated me of everything.


## LXXII

WITH days of hard travail I raised a temple. It had no doors or windows, its walls were thickly built with massive stones.

I forgot all else, I shunned all the world, I gazed in rapt contemplation at the image I had set upon the altar.

It was always night inside, and lit by the lamps of perfumed oil.

The ceaseless smoke of incense wound my heart in its heavy coils.

Sleepless, I carved on the walls fantastic figures in

mazy bewildering lines—winged horses, flowers with human faces, women with limbs like serpents.

No passage was left anywhere through which could enter the song of birds, the murmur of leaves, or hum of the busy village.

The only sound that echoed in its dark dome was that of incantations which I chanted.

My mind became keen and still like a pointed flame, my senses swooned in ecstasy.

I knew not how time passed till the thunderstone had struck the temple, and a pain stung me through the heart.

The lamp looked pale and ashamed; the carvings on the walls, like chained dreams, stared meaningless in the light as they would fain hide themselves.

I looked at the image on the altar. I saw it smiling and alive with the living touch of God. The night I had imprisoned had spread its wings and vanished.


## LXXIII

INFINITE wealth is not yours, my patient and dusky mother dust!

You toil to fill the mouths of your children, but food is scarce.

The gift of gladness that you have for us is never perfect.

The toys that you make for your children are fragile.

You cannot satisfy all our hungry hopes, but should I desert you for that?

Your smile which is shadowed with pain is sweet to my eyes.

Your love which knows not fulfilment is dear to my heart.

From your breast you have fed us with life but not immortality, that is why your eyes are ever wakeful.

For ages you are working with colour and song, yet your heaven is not built, but only its sad suggestion.

Over your creations of beauty there is the mist of tears.

I will pour my songs into your mute heart, and my love into your love.

I will worship you with labour.

I have seen your tender face and I love your mournful dust, Mother Earth.


## LXXIV

IN the world's audience hall the simple blade of grass sits on the same carpet with the sunbeam and the stars of midnight.

Thus my songs share their seats in the heart of the world with the music of the clouds and forests.

But, you man of riches, your wealth has no part in the simple grandeur of the sun's glad gold and the mellow gleam of the musing moon.

The blessing of the all-embracing sky is not shed upon it.

And when death appears, it pales and withers and crumbles into dust.


## LXXV

AT midnight the would-be ascetic announced:

"This is the time to give up my home and seek for God. Ah, who has held me so long in delusion here?"

God whispered, "I," but the ears of the man were stopped.

With a baby asleep at her breast lay his wife, peacefully sleeping on one side of the bed.

The man said, "Who are ye that have fooled me so long?"

The voice said again, "They are God," but he heard it not.

The baby cried out in its dream, nestling close to its mother.

God commanded, "Stop, fool, leave not thy home," but still he heard not.

God sighed and complained, "Why does my servant wander to seek me, forsaking me?"


## LXXVI

THE fair was on before the temple. It had rained from the early morning and the day came to its end.

Brighter than all the gladness of the crowd was the bright smile of a girl who bought for a farthing a whistle of palm leaf.

The shrill joy of that whistle floated above all laughter and noise.

An endless throng of people came and jostled together. The road was muddy, the river in flood, the field under water in ceaseless rain.

Greater than all the troubles of the crowd was a little boy's trouble—he had not a farthing to buy a painted stick.

His wistful eyes gazing at the shop made this whole meeting of men so pitiful.

## LXXVII

THE workman and his wife from the west country are busy digging to make bricks for the kiln.

Their little daughter goes to the landing-place by the river; there she has no end of scouring and scrubbing of pots and pans.

Her little brother, with shaven head and brown, naked, mud-covered limbs, follows after her and waits patiently on the high bank at her bidding.

She goes back home with the full pitcher poised on her head, the shining brass pot in her left hand, holding the child with her right—she the tiny servant of her mother, grave with the weight of the household cares.

One day I saw this naked boy sitting with legs outstretched.

In the water his sister sat rubbing a drinking-pot with a handful of earth, turning it round and round.

Near by a soft-haired lamb stood grazing along the bank.

It came close to where the boy sat and suddenly bleated aloud, and the child started up and screamed.

His sister left off cleaning her pot and ran up.

She took up her brother in one arm and the lamb in the other, and dividing her caresses between them bound in one bond of affection the offspring of beast and man.

## LXXVIII

IT was in May. The sultry noon seemed endlessly long. The dry earth gaped with thirst in the heat.

When I heard from the riverside a voice calling, "Come, my darling!"

I shut my book and opened the window to look out.

I saw a big buffalo with mud-stained hide standing near the river with placid, patient eyes; and a youth, knee-deep in water, calling it to its bath.

I smiled amused and felt a touch of sweetness in my heart.

## LXXIX

I OFTEN wonder where lie hidden the boundaries of recognition between man and the beast whose heart knows no spoken language.

Through what primal paradise in a remote morning of creation ran the simple path by which their hearts visited each other?

Those marks of their constant tread have not been effaced though their kinship has been long forgotten.

Yet suddenly in some wordless music the dim memory wakes up and the beast gazes into the man's face with a tender trust, and the man looks down into its eyes with amused affection.

It seems that the two friends meet masked, and vaguely know each other through the disguise.

## LXXX

WITH a glance of your eyes you could plunder all the wealth of songs struck from poets' harps, fair woman!

But for their praises you have no ear, therefore I come to praise you.

You could humble at your feet the proudest heads in the world.

But it is your loved ones, unknown to fame, whom you choose to worship, therefore I worship you.

The perfection of your arms would add glory to kingly splendour with their touch.

But you use them to sweep away the dust, and to make clean your humble home, therefore I am filled with awe.

## LXXXI

WHY do you whisper so faintly in my ears, O Death, my Death?

When the flowers droop in the evening and cattle come back to their stalls, you stealthily come to my side and speak words that I do not understand.

Is this how you must woo and win me, with the opiate of drowsy murmur and cold kisses, O Death, my Death?

Will there be no proud ceremony for our wedding?
Will you not tie up with a wreath your tawny coiled locks?

Is there none to carry your banner before you, and will not the night be on fire with your red torch-lights, O Death, my Death?

Come with your conch-shells sounding, come in the sleepless night.

Dress me with a crimson mantle, grasp my hand and take me.

Let your chariot be ready at my door with your horses neighing impatiently.

Raise my veil and look at my face proudly, O Death, my Death!

## LXXXII

WE are to play the game of death to-night, my bride and I.

The night is black, the clouds in the sky are capricious, and the waves are raving at sea.

We have left our bed of dreams, flung open the door and come out, my bride and I.

We sit upon a swing, and the storm-winds give us a wild push from behind.

My bride starts up with fear and delight, she trembles and clings to my breast.

Long have I served her tenderly.

I made for her a bed of flowers and I closed the doors to shut out the rude light from her eyes.

I kissed her gently on her lips and whispered softly in her ears till she half swooned in languor.

She was lost in the endless mist of vague sweetness.

She answered not to my touch, my songs failed to arouse her.

To-night has come to us the call of the storm from the wild.

My bride has shivered and stood up, she has clasped my hand and come out.

Her hair is flying in the wind, her veil is fluttering, her garland rustles over her breast.

The push of death has swung her into life.

We are face to face and heart to heart, my bride and I.

### LXXXIII

SHE dwelt on the hillside by the edge of a maize-field, near the spring that flows in laughing rills through the solemn shadows of ancient trees. The women came there to fill their jars, and travellers would sit there to rest and talk. She worked and dreamed daily to the tune of the bubbling stream.

One evening the stranger came down from the cloud-hidden peak; his locks were tangled like drowsy snakes.

We asked in wonder, "Who are you?" He answered not but sat by the garrulous stream and silently gazed at the hut where she dwelt. Our hearts quaked in fear and we came back home when it was night.

Next morning when the women came to fetch water at the spring by the deodar trees, they found the doors open in her hut, but her voice was gone and where was her smiling face? The empty jar lay on the floor and her lamp had burnt itself out in the corner. No one knew where she had fled to before it was morning—and the stranger had gone.

In the month of May the sun grew strong and the snow melted, and we sat by the spring and wept. We wondered in our mind, "Is there a spring in the land where she has gone and where she can fill her vessel in these hot thirsty days?" And we asked each other in dismay, "Is there a land beyond these hills where we live?"

It was a summer night; the breeze blew from the south; and I sat in her deserted room where the lamp stood still unlit. When suddenly from before my eyes the hills vanished like curtains drawn aside. "Ah, it is she who comes. How are you, my child? Are you happy? But where can you shelter under this open sky? And, alas! our spring is not here to allay your thirst."

"Here is the same sky," she said, "only free from the fencing hills,—this is the same stream grown into a river,—the same earth widened into a plain." "Everything is here," I sighed, "only we are not." She smiled sadly and said, "You are in my heart." I woke up and heard the babbling of the stream and the rustling of the deodars at night.

## LXXXIV

OVER the green and yellow rice-fields sweep the shadows of the autumn clouds followed by the swift-chasing sun.

The bees forget to sip their honey; drunken with light they foolishly hover and hum.

The ducks in the islands of the river clamour in joy for mere nothing.

Let none go back home, brothers, this morning, let none go to work.

Let us take the blue sky by storm and plunder space as we run.

Laughter floats in the air like foam on the flood.

Brothers, let us squander our morning in futile songs.

## LXXXV

WHO are you, reader, reading my poems an hundred years hence?

I cannot send you one single flower from this wealth of the spring, one single streak of gold from yonder clouds.

Open your doors and look abroad.

From your blossoming garden gather fragrant memories of the vanished flowers of an hundred years before.

In the joy of your heart may you feel the living joy that sang one spring morning, sending its glad voice across an hundred years.

# CHITRA

THIS lyrical drama is based on the following story from the *Mahabharata*.

In the course of his wanderings, in fulfilment of a vow of penance, Arjuna came to Manipur. There he saw Chitrāngadā, the beautiful daughter of Chitravāhana, the king of the country. Smitten with her charms, he asked the king for the hand of his daughter in marriage. Chitravāhana asked him who he was, and learning that he was Arjuna the Pandava, told him that Prabhanjana, one of his ancestors in the kingly line of Manipur, had long been childless. In order to obtain an heir, he performed severe penances. Pleased with these austerities, the god Shiva gave him this boon, that he and his successors should each have one child. It so happened that the promised child had invariably been a son. He, Chitravāhana, was the first to have only a daughter Chitrāngadā to perpetuate the race. He had, therefore, always treated her as a son and had made her his heir. Continuing, the king said:

"The one son that will be born to her must be the perpetuator of my race. That son will be the price that I shall demand for this marriage. You can take her, if you like, on this condition."

Arjuna promised and took Chitrāngadā to wife, and lived in her father's capital for three years. When a son was born to them, he embraced her with affection, and taking leave of her and her father, set out again on his travels.

# THE CHARACTERS

GODS:

MADANA (Eros)

VASANTA (Lycoris)

MORTALS:

CHITRA, daughter of the King of Manipur

ARJUNA, a prince of the house of the Kurus. He is of the Kshatriya or "warrior" caste, and during the action is living as a Hermit retired in the forest

VILLAGERS from an outlying district of Manipur

NOTE.—The dramatic poem "Chitra" has been performed in India without scenery—the actors being surrounded by the audience. Proposals for its production here having been made to the author, he went through this translation and provided stage directions, but wished these omitted if it were printed as a book.

# CHITRA

## SCENE I

*Chitra.* Art thou the god with the five darts, the Lord of Love?

*Madana.* I am he who was the first born in the heart of the Creator. I bind in bonds of pain and bliss the lives of men and women!

*Chitra.* I know, I know what that pain is and those bonds.—And who art thou, my lord?

*Vasanta.* I am his friend—Vasanta—the King of the Seasons. Death and decrepitude would wear the world to the bone but that I follow them and constantly attack them. I am Eternal Youth.

*Chitra.* I bow to thee, Lord Vasanta.

*Madana.* But what stern vow is thine, fair stranger? Why dost thou wither thy fresh youth with penance and mortification? Such a sacrifice is not fit for the worship of love. Who art thou and what is thy prayer?

*Chitra.* I am Chitra, the daughter of the kingly house of Manipur. With godlike grace Lord Shiva promised to my royal grandsire an unbroken line of male descent. Nevertheless, the divine word proved power-less to change the spark of life in my mother's womb—so invincible was my nature, woman though I be.

*Madana.* I know, that is why thy father brings thee up as his son. He has taught thee the use of the bow and all the duties of a king.

*Chitra.* Yes, that is why I am dressed in man's attire

153

and have left the seclusion of a woman's chamber. I know no feminine wiles for winning hearts. My hands are strong to bend the bow, but I have never learnt Cupid's archery, the play of eyes.

*Madana.* That requires no schooling, fair one. The eye does its work untaught, and he knows how well, who is struck in the heart.

*Chitra.* One day in search of game I roved alone to the forest on the bank of the Purna river. Tying my horse to a tree-trunk I entered a dense thicket on the track of a deer. I found a narrow sinuous path meandering through the dusk of the entangled boughs, the foliage vibrated with the chirping of crickets, when of a sudden I came upon a man lying on a bed of dried leaves, across my path. I asked him haughtily to move aside, but he heeded not. Then with the sharp end of my bow I pricked him in contempt. Instantly he leapt up with straight, tall limbs, like a sudden tongue of fire from a heap of ashes. An amused smile flickered round the corners of his mouth, perhaps at the sight of my boyish countenance. Then for the first time in my life I felt myself a woman, and knew that a man was before me.

*Madana.* At the auspicious hour I teach the man and the woman this supreme lesson to know themselves. What happened after that?

*Chitra.* With fear and wonder I asked him, "Who are you?" "I am Arjuna," he said, "of the great Kuru clan." I stood petrified like a statue, and forgot to do him obeisance. Was this indeed Arjuna, the one great idol of my dreams? Yes, I had long ago heard how he had vowed a twelve-years' celibacy. Many a day my young ambition had spurred me on to break my lance with him, to challenge him in disguise to single combat, and prove my skill in arms against him. Ah, foolish heart, whither fled thy presumption? Could I but exchange my youth with all its aspirations for the clod of earth under his feet, I should deem it a most precious grace. I know not in what whirlpool of thought I was lost, when suddenly I saw him vanish through the trees. O foolish woman, neither didst thou greet him, nor speak a word, nor beg forgiveness, but stoodest like a barbarian boor while he contemptuously walked away! . . . Next morning I laid aside my man's clothing. I donned bracelets, anklets, waist-chain, and a gown of purple-red silk. The unaccustomed dress clung about my shrinking shame; but I hastened on my quest, and found Arjuna in the forest temple of Shiva.

*Madana.* Tell me the story to the end. I am the heart-born god, and I understand the mystery of these impulses.

*Chitra.* Only vaguely can I remember what things I said, and what answer I got. Do not ask me to tell you all. Shame fell on me like a thunderbolt, yet could not break me to pieces, so utterly hard, so like a man am I. His last words as I walked home pricked my ears like red-hot needles. "I have taken the vow of celibacy. I am not fit to be thy husband!" Oh, the vow of a man! Surely thou knowest, thou god of love, that un-numbered saints and sages have surrendered the merits of their lifelong penance at the feet of a woman. I broke my bow in two and burnt my arrows in the fire. I hated my strong, lithe arm, scored by drawing the bow-string. O Love, god Love, thou hast laid low in the dust the vain pride of my manlike strength; and all my man's training lies crushed under thy feet. Now

155

teach me thy lessons; give me the power of the weak and the weapon of the unarmed hand.

*Madana.* I will be thy friend. I will bring the world-conquering Arjuna a captive before thee, to accept his rebellion's sentence at thy hand.

*Chitra.* Had I but the time needed, I could win his heart by slow degrees, and ask no help of the gods. I would stand by his side as a comrade, drive the fierce horses of his war-chariot, attend him in the pleasures of the chase, keep guard at night at the entrance of his tent, and help him in all the great duties of a Kshatriya, rescuing the weak, and meting out justice where it is due. Surely at last the day would have come for him to look at me and wonder, "What boy is this? Has one of my slaves in a former life followed me like my good deeds into this?" I am not the woman who nourishes her despair in lonely silence, feeding it with nightly tears and covering it with the daily patient smile, a widow from her birth. The flower of my desire shall never drop into the dust before it has ripened to fruit. But it is the labour of a lifetime to make one's true self known and honoured. Therefore I have come to thy door, thou world-vanquishing Love, and thou, Vasanta, youthful Lord of the Seasons, take from my young body this primal injustice, an unattractive plainness. For a single day make me superbly beautiful, even as beautiful as was the sudden blooming of love in my heart. Give me but one brief day of perfect beauty, and I will answer for the days that follow.

*Madana.* Lady, I grant thy prayer.

*Vasanta.* Not for the short span of a day, but for one whole year the charm of spring blossoms shall nestle round thy limbs.

*Arjuna.* Was I dreaming or was what I saw by the lake truly there? Sitting on the mossy turf, I mused over bygone years in the sloping shadows of the evening, when slowly there came out from the folding darkness of foliage an apparition of beauty in the perfect form of a woman, and stood on a white slab of stone at the water's brink. It seemed that the heart of the earth must heave in joy under her bare white feet. Methought the vague veilings of her body should melt in ecstasy into air as the golden mist of dawn melts from off the snowy peak of the eastern hill. She bowed herself above the shining mirror of the lake and saw the reflection of her face. She started up in awe and stood still; then smiled, and with a careless sweep of her left arm unloosed her hair and let it trail on the earth at her feet. She bared her bosom and looked at her arms, so flawlessly modelled, and instinct with an exquisite caress. Bending her head she saw the sweet blossoming of her youth and the tender bloom and blush of her skin. She beamed with a glad surprise. So, if the white lotus-bud on opening her eyes in the morning were to arch her neck and see her shadow in the water, would she wonder at herself the livelong day. But a moment after the smile passed from her face and a shade of sadness crept into her eyes. She bound up her tresses, drew her veil over her arms, and sighing slowly, walked away like a beauteous evening fading into the night. To me the supreme fulfilment of desire seemed to have been revealed in a flash and then to have vanished. . . . But who is it that pushes the door?

(*Enter Chitra, dressed as a woman*)

157

Ah! it is she. Quiet, my heart!

Fear me not, lady! I am a Kshatriya.

*Chitra.* Honoured sir, you are my guest. I live in this temple. I know not in what way I can show you hospitality.

*Arjuna.* Fair lady, the very sight of you is indeed the highest hospitality. If you will not take it amiss I would ask you a question.

*Chitra.* You have permission.

*Arjuna.* What stern vow keeps you immured in this solitary temple, depriving all mortals of a vision of so much loveliness?

*Chitra.* I harbour a secret desire in my heart, for the fulfilment of which I offer daily prayers to Lord Shiva.

*Arjuna.* Alas, what can you desire, you who are the desire of the whole world? From the easternmost hill on whose summit the morning sun first prints his fiery foot to the end of the sunset land have I travelled. I have seen whatever is most precious, beautiful and great on the earth. My knowledge shall be yours, only say for what or for whom you seek.

*Chitra.* He whom I seek is known to all.

*Arjuna.* Indeed! Who may this favourite of the gods be, whose fame has captured your heart?

*Chitra.* Sprung from the highest of all royal houses, the greatest of all heroes is he.

*Arjuna.* Lady,. offer not such wealth of beauty as is yours on the altar of false reputation. Spurious fame spreads from tongue to tongue like the fog of the early dawn before the sun rises. Tell me who in the highest of kingly lines is the supreme hero?

*Chitra.* Hermit, you are jealous of other men's fame. Do you not know that all over the world the royal house of the Kurus is the most famous?

*Arjuna.* The house of the Kurus!

*Chitra.* And have you never heard of the greatest name of that far-famed house?

*Arjuna.* From your own lips let me hear it.

*Chitra.* Arjuna, the conqueror of the world. I have culled from the mouths of the multitude that imperishable name and hidden it with care in my maiden heart. Hermit, why do you look perturbed? Has that name only a deceitful glitter? Say so, and I will not hesitate to break this casket of my heart and throw the false gem to the dust.

*Arjuna.* Be his name and fame, his bravery and prowess false or true, for mercy's sake do not banish him from your heart—for he kneels at your feet even now.

*Chitra.* You, Arjuna!

*Arjuna.* Yes, I am he, the love-hungered guest at your door.

*Chitra.* Then it is not true that Arjuna has taken a vow of chastity for twelve long years?

*Arjuna.* But you have dissolved my vow even as the moon dissolves the night's vow of obscurity.

*Chitra.* Oh, shame upon you! What have you seen in me that makes you false to yourself? Whom do you seek in these dark eyes, in these milk-white arms, if you are ready to pay for her the price of your probity? Not my true self, I know. Surely this cannot be love, this is not man's highest homage to woman. Alas, that this frail disguise, the body, should make one blind to the light of the deathless spirit! Yes, now indeed I know, Arjuna, the fame of your heroic manhood is false.

*Arjuna.* Ah, I feel how vain is fame, the pride of prowess! Everything seems to me a dream. You alone

159

are perfect; you are the wealth of the world, the end of all poverty, the goal of all efforts, the one woman! Others there are who can be but slowly known, while to see you for a moment is to see perfect completeness once and for ever.

*Chitra.* Alas, it is not I, not I, Arjuna! It is the deceit of a god. Go, go, my hero, go! Woo not falsehood, offer not your great heart to an illusion. Go!

## SCENE III

*Chitra.* No, impossible! To face that fervent gaze that almost grasps you like clutching hands of the hungry spirit within; to feel his heart struggling to break its bounds, urging its passionate cry through the entire body—and then to send him away like a beggar—no, impossible!

(*Enter Madana and Vasanta*)

Ah, god of love, what fearful flame is this with which thou hast enveloped me? I burn, and I burn whatever I touch.

*Madana.* I desire to know what happened last night.

*Chitra.* At evening I lay down on a grassy bed strewn with the petals of spring flowers, and recollected the wonderful praise of my beauty I had heard from Arjuna—drinking drop by drop the honey that I had stored during the long day. The history of my past life like that of my former existences was forgotten. I felt like a flower, which has but a few fleeting hours to listen to all the humming flatteries and whispered murmurs of the woodlands and then must lower its eyes from the sky, bend its head and at a breath give itself up to the dust without a cry, thus ending the short story of a perfect moment that has neither past nor future.

*Vasanta.* A limitless life of glory can bloom and spend itself in a morning.

*Madana.* Like an endless meaning in the narrow span of a song.

*Chitra.* The southern breeze caressed me to sleep. From the flowering *Malati* bower overhead silent kisses dropped over my body. On my hair, my breast, my feet, each flower chose a bed to die on. I slept. And suddenly, in the depth of my sleep, I felt as if some intense eager look, like tapering fingers of flame, touched my slumbering body. I started up and saw the Hermit standing before me. The moon had moved to the west, peering through the leaves to espy this wonder of divine art wrought in a fragile human frame. The air was heavy with perfume; the silence of the night was vocal with the chirping of crickets; the reflections of the trees hung motionless in the lake; and with his staff in his hand he stood, tall and straight and still, like a forest tree. It seemed to me that I had, on opening my eyes, died to all realities of life and undergone a dream birth into a shadow land. Shame slipped to my feet like loosened clothes. I heard his call—"Beloved, my most beloved!" And all my forgotten lives united as one and responded to it. I said, "Take me, take all I am!" And I stretched out my arms to him. The moon set behind the trees. One curtain of darkness covered all. Heaven and earth, time and space, pleasure and pain, death and life merged together in an unbearable ecstasy. . . . With the first gleam of light, the first twitter of birds, I rose up and sat leaning on my left arm. He lay asleep with a vague smile about his lips like the crescent moon in the morning. The rosy-red glow of the dawn fell upon his noble forehead. I sighed and stood up. I drew together the leafy lianas to screen the streaming sun from his face. I looked about me and saw the same old earth. I remembered what I used to be, and ran and ran like a deer afraid of her own shadow, through the forest path strewn with *shephali* flowers. I found a lonely nook, and sitting down covered my face with both hands, and tried to weep and cry. But no tears came to my eyes.

*Madana.* Alas, thou daughter of mortals! I stole from the divine storehouse the fragrant wine of heaven, filled with it one earthly night to the brim, and placed it in thy hand to drink—yet still I hear this cry of anguish!

*Chitra (bitterly).* Who drank it? The rarest completion of life's desire, the first union of love was proffered to me, but was wrested from my grasp! This borrowed beauty, this falsehood that enwraps me, will slip from me taking with it the only monument of that sweet union, as the petals fall from an overblown flower; and the woman ashamed of her naked poverty will sit weeping day and night. Lord Love, this cursed appearance companions me like a demon robbing me of all the prizes of love—all the kisses for which my heart is athirst.

*Madana.* Alas, how vain thy single night had been! The barque of joy came in sight, but the waves would not let it touch the shore.

*Chitra.* Heaven came so close to my hand that I forgot for a moment that it had not reached me. But when I woke in the morning from my dream I found that my body had become my own rival. It is my hateful task to deck her every day, to send her to my beloved and see her caressed by him. O god, take back thy boon!

*Madana.* But if I take it from you how can you stand before your lover? To snatch away the cup from his lips when he has scarcely drained his first draught of pleasure, would not that be cruel? With what resentful anger he must regard thee then!

*Chitra.* That would be better far than this. I will reveal my true self to him, a nobler thing than this disguise. If he rejects it, if he spurns me and breaks my heart, I will bear even that in silence.

*Vasanta.* Listen to my advice. When with the advent of autumn the flowering season is over, then comes the triumph of fruitage. A time will come of itself when the heat-cloyed bloom of the body will droop and Arjuna will gladly accept the abiding fruitful truth in thee. O child, go back to thy mad festival.

### SCENE IV

*Chitra.* Why do you watch me like that, my warrior?

*Arjuna.* I watch how you weave that garland. Skill and grace, the twin brother and sister, are dancing playfully on your finger-tips. I am watching and thinking.

*Chitra.* What are you thinking, sir?

*Arjuna.* I am thinking that you, with this same lightness of touch and sweetness, are weaving my days of exile into an immortal wreath, to crown me when I return home.

*Chitra.* Home! But this love is not for a home!

*Arjuna.* Not for a home?

*Chitra.* No. Never talk of that. Take to your home what is abiding and strong. Leave the little wild flower where it was born; leave it beautifully to die at the day's end among all fading blossoms and decaying leaves. Do not take it to your palace hall to fling it on the stony floor which knows no pity for things that fade and are forgotten.

*Arjuna.* Is ours that kind of love?

*Chitra.* Yes, no other! Why regret it? That which was meant for idle days should never outlive them. Joy turns into pain when the door by which it should depart is shut against it. Take it and keep it as long as it lasts. Let not the satiety of your evening claim more than the desire of your morning could earn. . . . The day is done. Put this garland on. I am tired. Take me in your arms, my love. Let all vain bickerings of discontent die away at the sweet meeting of our lips.

*Arjuna.* Hush! Listen, my beloved, the sound of prayer-bells from the distant village temple steals upon the evening air across the silent trees!

## SCENE V

*Vasanta.* I cannot keep pace with thee, my friend! I am tired. It is a hard task to keep alive the fire thou hast kindled. Sleep overtakes me, and the fan drops from my hand, and cold ashes cover the glow of the fire. I start up again from my slumber and with all my might rescue the weary flame. But this can go on no longer.

*Madana.* I know, thou art as fickle as a child. Ever restless is thy play in heaven and on earth. Things that thou for days buildest up with endless detail thou dost

164

shatter in a moment without regret. But this work of ours is nearly finished. Pleasure-winged days fly fast, and the year, almost at its end, swoons in rapturous bliss.

## SCENE VI

*Arjuna.* I woke in the morning and found that my dreams had distilled a gem. I have no casket to inclose it, no king's crown whereon to fix it, no chain from which to hang it, and yet have not the heart to throw it away. My Kshatriya's right arm, idly occupied in holding it, forgets its duties.

*(Enter Chitra)*

*Chitra.* Tell me your thoughts, sir!

*Arjuna.* My mind is busy with thoughts of hunting to-day. See, how the rain pours in torrents and fiercely beats upon the hillside. The dark shadow of the clouds hangs heavily over the forest, and the swollen stream, like reckless youth, overleaps all barriers with mocking laughter. On such rainy days we five brothers would go to the Chitraka forest to chase wild beasts. Those were glad times. Our hearts danced to the drumbeat of rumbling clouds. The woods resounded with the screams of peacocks. Timid deer could not hear our approaching steps for the patter of rain and the noise of waterfalls; the leopards would leave their tracks on the wet earth, betraying their lairs. Our sport over, we dared each other to swim across turbulent streams on our way back home. The restless spirit is on me. I long to go hunting.

*Chitra.* First run down the quarry you are now following. Are you quite certain that the enchanted deer you pursue must needs be caught? No, not yet. Like a

165

dream the wild creature eludes you when it seems most nearly yours. Look how the wind is chased by the mad rain that discharges a thousand arrows after it. Yet it goes free and unconquered. Our sport is like that, my love! You give chase to the fleet-footed spirit of beauty, aiming at her every dart you have in your hands. Yet this magic deer runs ever free and untouched.

*Arjuna.* My love, have you no home where kind hearts are waiting for your return? A home which you once made sweet with your gentle service and whose light went out when you left it for this wilderness?

*Chitra.* Why these questions? Are the hours of unthinking pleasure over? Do you not know that I am no more than what you see before you? For me there is no vista beyond. The dew that hangs on the tip of a *kinsuka* petal has neither name nor destination. It offers no answer to any question. She whom you love is like that perfect bead of dew.

*Arjuna.* Has she no tie with the world? Can she be merely like a fragment of heaven dropped on the earth through the carelessness of a wanton god?

*Chitra.* Yes.

*Arjuna.* Ah, that is why I always seem about to lose you. My heart is unsatisfied, my mind knows no peace. Come closer to me, unattainable one! Surrender yourself to the bonds of name and home and parentage. Let my heart feel you on all sides and live with you in the peaceful security of love.

*Chitra.* Why this vain effort to catch and keep the tints of the clouds, the dance of the waves, the smell of the flowers?

*Arjuna.* Mistress mine, do not hope to pacify love with airy nothings. Give me something to clasp, something that can last longer than pleasure, that can endure even through suffering.

*Chitra.* Hero mine, the year is not yet full, and you are tired already! Now I know that it is Heaven's blessing that has made the flower's term of life short. Could this body of mine have drooped and died with the flowers of last spring it surely would have died with honour. Yet, its days are numbered, my love. Spare it not, press it dry of honey, for fear your beggar's heart come back to it again and again with unsated desire, like a thirsty bee when summer blossoms lie dead in the dust.

## SCENE VII

*Madana.* To-night is thy last night.

*Vasanta.* The loveliness of your body will return to-morrow to the inexhaustible stores of the spring. The ruddy tint of thy lips freed from the memory of Arjuna's kisses, will bud anew as a pair of fresh *asoka* leaves, and the soft, white glow of thy skin will be born again in a hundred fragrant jasmine flowers.

*Chitra.* O gods, grant me this prayer! To-night, in its last hour, let my beauty flash its brightest, like the final flicker of a dying flame.

*Madana.* Thou shalt have thy wish.

## SCENE VIII

*Villagers.* Who will protect us now?

*Arjuna.* Why, by what danger are you threatened?

*Villagers.* The robbers are pouring from the northern hills like a mountain flood to devastate our village.

167

*Arjuna.* Have you in this kingdom no warden?

*Villagers.* Princess Chitra was the terror of all evil-doers. While she was in this happy land we feared natural deaths, but had no other fears. Now she has gone on a pilgrimage, and none knows where to find her.

*Arjuna.* Is the warden of this country a woman?

*Villagers.* Yes, she is our father and mother in one.

[*Exeunt*

(*Enter Chitra*)

*Chitra.* Why are you sitting all alone?

*Arjuna.* I am trying to imagine what kind of woman Princess Chitra may be. I hear so many stories of her from all sorts of men.

*Chitra.* Ah, but she is not beautiful. She has no such lovely eyes as mine, dark as death. She can pierce any target she will, but not our hero's heart.

*Arjuna.* They say that in valour she is a man, and a woman in tenderness.

*Chitra.* That, indeed, is her greatest misfortune. When a woman is merely a woman; when she winds herself round and round men's hearts with her smiles and sobs and services and caressing endearments; then she is happy. Of what use to her are learning and great achievements? Could you have seen her only yesterday in the court of the Lord Shiva's temple by the forest path, you would have passed by without deigning to look at her. But have you grown so weary of woman's beauty that you seek in her for a man's strength?

With green leaves wet from the spray of the foaming waterfall, I have made our noonday bed in a cavern dark as night. There the cool of the soft green mosses thick on the black and dripping stone kisses your eyes to sleep. Let me guide you thither.

168

*Arjuna.* Not to-day, beloved.

*Chitra.* Why not to-day?

*Arjuna.* I have heard that a horde of robbers has neared the plains. Needs must I go and prepare my weapons to protect the frightened villagers.

*Chitra.* You need have no fear for them. Before she started on her pilgrimage, Princess Chitra had set strong guards at all the frontier passes.

*Arjuna.* Yet permit me for a short while to set about a Kshatriya's work. With new glory will I ennoble this idle arm, and make of it a pillow more worthy of your head.

*Chitra.* What if I refuse to let you go, if I keep you entwined in my arms? Would you rudely snatch yourself free and leave me? Go then! But you must know that the liana, once broken in two, never joins again. Go, if your thirst is quenched. But, if not, then remember that the goddess of pleasure is fickle, and waits for no man. Sit for a while, my lord! Tell me what uneasy thoughts tease you. Who occupied your mind to-day? Is it Chitra?

*Arjuna.* Yes, it is Chitra. I wonder in fulfilment of what vow she has gone on her pilgrimage. Of what could she stand in need?

*Chitra.* Her needs? Why, what has she ever had, the unfortunate creature? Her very qualities are as prison walls, shutting her woman's heart in a bare cell. She is obscured, she is unfulfilled. Her womanly love must content itself dressed in rags; beauty is denied her. She is like the spirit of a cheerless morning, sitting upon the stony mountain peak, all her light blotted out by dark clouds. Do not ask me of her life. It will never sound sweet to man's ear.

169

*Arjuna.* I am eager to learn all about her. I am like a traveller come to a strange city at midnight. Domes and towers and garden-trees look vague and shadowy, and the dull moan of the sea comes fitfully through the silence of sleep. Wistfully he waits for the morning to reveal to him all the strange wonders. Oh, tell me her story.

*Chitra.* What more is there to tell?

*Arjuna.* I seem to see her, in my mind's eye, riding on a white horse, proudly holding the reins in her left hand, and in her right a bow, and like the Goddess of Victory dispensing glad hope all round her. Like a watchful lioness she protects the litter at her dugs with a fierce love. Woman's arms, though adorned with naught but unfettered strength, are beautiful! My heart is restless, fair one, like a serpent reviving from his long winter's sleep. Come, let us both race on swift horses side by side, like twin orbs of light sweeping through space. Out from this slumbrous prison of green gloom, this dank, dense cover of perfumed intoxication, choking breath.

*Chitra.* Arjuna, tell me true, if, now at once, by some magic I could shake myself free from this voluptuous softness, this timid bloom of beauty shrinking from the rude and healthy touch of the world, and fling it from my body like borrowed clothes, would you be able to bear it? If I stand up straight and strong with the strength of a daring heart spurning the wiles and arts of twining weakness, if I hold my head high like a tall young mountain fir, no longer trailing in the dust like a liana, shall I then appeal to man's eye? No, no, you could not endure it. It is better that I should keep spread about me all the dainty playthings of fugitive

170

youth, and wait for you in patience. When it pleases you to return, I will smilingly pour out for you the wine of pleasure in the cup of this beauteous body. When you are tired and satiated with this wine, you can go to work or play; and when I grow old I will accept humbly and gratefully whatever corner is left for me. Would it please your heroic soul if the playmate of the night aspired to be the helpmeet of the day, if the left arm learnt to share the burden of the proud right arm?

*Arjuna.* I never seem to know you aright. You seem to me like a goddess hidden within a golden image. I cannot touch you, I cannot pay you my dues in return for your priceless gifts. Thus my love is incomplete. Sometimes in the enigmatic depth of your sad look, in your playful words mocking at their own meaning, I gain glimpses of a being trying to rend asunder the languorous grace of her body, to emerge in a chaste fire of pain through a vaporous veil of smiles. Illusion is the first appearance of Truth. She advances towards her lover in disguise. But a time comes when she throws off her ornaments and veils and stands clothed in naked dignity. I grope for that ultimate *you*, that bare simplicity of truth.

Why these tears, my love? Why cover your face with your hands? Have I pained you, my darling? Forget what I said. I will be content with the present. Let each separate moment of beauty come to me like a bird of mystery from its unseen nest in the dark bearing a message of music. Let me for ever sit with my hope on the brink of its realization, and thus end my days.

## SCENE IX

### (*Chitra and Arjuna*)

*Chitra* (*cloaked*). My lord, has the cup been drained to the last drop? Is this, indeed, the end? No, when all is done something still remains, and that is my last sacrifice at your feet.

I brought from the garden of heaven flowers of incomparable beauty with which to worship you, god of my heart. If the rites are over, if the flowers have faded, let me throw them out of the temple (*unveiling in her original male attire*). Now, look at your worshipper with gracious eyes.

I am not beautifully perfect as the flowers with which I worshipped. I have many flaws and blemishes. I am a traveller in the great world-path, my garments are dirty, and my feet are bleeding with thorns. Where should I achieve flower-beauty, the unsullied loveliness of a moment's life? The gift that I proudly bring you is the heart of a woman. Here have all pains and joys gathered, the hopes and fears and shames of a daughter of the dust; here love springs up struggling toward immortal life. Herein lies an imperfection which yet is noble and grand. If the flower-service is finished, my master, accept *this* as your servant for the days to come!

I am Chitra, the King's daughter. Perhaps you will remember the day when a woman came to you in the temple of Shiva, her body loaded with ornaments and finery. That shameless woman came to court you as though she were a man. You rejected her; you did well. My lord, I am that woman. She was my disguise. Then by the boon of gods I obtained for a year the most radiant form that a mortal ever wore, and wearied my hero's heart with the burden of that deceit. Most surely I am not that woman.

I am Chitra. No goddess to be worshipped, nor yet the object of common pity to be brushed aside like a moth with indifference. If you deign to keep me by your side in the path of danger and daring, if you allow me to share the great duties of your life, then you will know my true self. If your babe, whom I am nourishing in my womb, be born a son, I shall myself teach him to be a second Arjuna, and send him to you when the time comes, and then at last you will truly know me. To-day I can only offer you Chitra, the daughter of a king.

*Arjuna.* Beloved, my life is full!

# FRUIT-GATHERING

# FRUIT-GATHERING

### I

Bid me and I shall gather my fruits to bring them in full baskets into your courtyard, though some are lost and some not ripe.

For the season grows heavy with its fullness, and there is a plaintive shepherd's pipe in the shade.

Bid me and I shall set sail on the river.

The March wind is fretful, fretting the languid waves into murmurs.

The garden has yielded its all, and in the weary hour of evening the call comes from your house on the shore in the sunset.

### II

My life when young was like a flower—a flower that loosens a petal or two from her abundance and never feels the loss when the spring breeze comes to beg at her door.

Now at the end of youth my life is like a fruit, having nothing to spare, and waiting to offer herself completely with her full burden of sweetness.

.　.　.　.　.　.

### IV

I woke and found his letter with the morning.

I do not know what it says, for I cannot read.

I shall leave the wise man alone with his books, I

177

shall not trouble him, for who knows if he can read what the letter says.

Let me hold it to my forehead and press it to my heart.

When the night grows still and stars come out one by one I will spread it on my lap and stay silent.

The rustling leaves will read it aloud to me, the rushing stream will chant it, and the seven wise stars will sing it to me from the sky.

I cannot find what I seek, I cannot understand what I would learn; but this unread letter has lightened my burdens and turned my thoughts into songs.

## V

A HANDFUL of dust could hide your signal when I did not know its meaning.

Now that I am wiser I read it in all that hid it before.

It is painted in petals of flowers; waves flash it from their foam; hills hold it high on their summits.

I had my face turned from you, therefore I read the letters awry and knew not their meaning.

## VI

WHERE roads are made I lose my way.

In the wide water, in the blue sky there is no line of a track.

The pathway is hidden by the birds' wings, by the star-fires, by the flowers of the wayfaring seasons.

And I ask my heart if its blood carries the wisdom of the unseen way.

## VII

ALAS, I cannot stay in the house, and home has become no home to me, for the eternal Stranger calls, he is going along the road.

The sound of his footfall knocks at my breast; it pains me!

The wind is up, the sea is moaning.

I leave all my cares and doubts to follow the homeless tide, for the Stranger calls me, he is going along the road.

## VIII

BE ready to launch forth, my heart! and let those linger who must.

For your name has been called in the morning sky.

Wait for none!

The desire of the bud is for the night and dew, but the blown flower cries for the freedom of light.

Burst your sheath, my heart, and come forth!

## IX

WHEN I lingered among my hoarded treasure I felt like a worm that feeds in the dark upon the fruit where it was born.

I leave this prison of decay.

I care not to haunt the mouldy stillness, for I go in search of everlasting youth; I throw away all that is not one with my life nor as light as my laughter.

I run through time and, O my heart, in your chariot dances the poet who sings while he wanders.

## X

You took my hand and drew me to your side, made me sit on the high seat before all men, till I became timid, unable to stir and walk my own way; doubting and debating at every step lest I should tread upon any thorn of their disfavour.

I am freed at last!
The blow has come, the drum of insult sounded, my seat is laid low in the dust.
My paths are open before me.

My wings are full of the desire of the sky.
I go to join the shooting stars of midnight, to plunge into the profound shadow.
I am like the storm-driven cloud of summer that, having cast off its crown of gold, hangs as a sword the thunderbolt upon a chain of lightning.
In desperate joy I run upon the dusty path of the despised; I draw near to your final welcome.

The child finds its mother when it leaves her womb.
When I am parted from you, thrown out from your household, I am free to see your face.

## XI

It decks me only to mock me, this jewelled chain of mine.
It bruises me when on my neck, it strangles me when I struggle to tear it off.
It grips my throat, it chokes my singing.

Could I but offer it to your hand, my Lord, I would be saved.

Take it from me, and in exchange bind me to you with a garland, for I am ashamed to stand before you with this jewelled chain on my neck.

## XII

FAR below flowed the Jumna, swift and clear, above frowned the jutting bank.

Hills dark with the woods and scarred with the torrents were gathered around.

Govinda, the great Sikh teacher, sat on the rock reading scriptures, when Raghunath, his disciple, proud of his wealth, came and bowed to him and said, "I have brought my poor present, unworthy of your acceptance."

Thus saying he displayed before the teacher a pair of gold bangles wrought with costly stones.

The master took up one of them, twirling it round his finger, and the diamonds darted shafts of light.

Suddenly it slipped from his hand and rolled down the bank into the water.

"Alas," screamed Raghunath, and jumped into the stream.

The teacher set his eyes upon his book, and the water held and hid what it stole and went its way.

The daylight faded when Raghunath came back to the teacher tired and dripping.

He panted and said, "I can still get it back if you show me where it fell."

The teacher took up the remaining bangle and throwing it into the water said, "It is there."

## XIII

To move is to meet you every moment,

Fellow-traveller!

It is to sing to the falling of your feet.

He whom your breath touches does not glide by the shelter of the bank.

He spreads a reckless sail to the wind and rides the turbulent water.

He who throws his doors open and steps onward receives your greeting.

He does not stay to count his gain or to mourn his loss; his heart beats the drum for his march, for that is to march with you every step,

Fellow-traveller!

## XIV

My portion of the best in this world will come from your hands: such was your promise.

Therefore your light glistens in my tears.

I fear to be led by others lest I miss you waiting in some road corner to be my guide.

I walk my own wilful way till my very folly tempts you to my door.

For I have your promise that my portion of the best in this world will come from your hands.

## XV

Your speech is simple, my Master, but not theirs who talk of you.

I understand the voice of your stars and the silence of your trees.

I know that my heart would open like a flower; that my life has filled itself at a hidden fountain.

Your songs, like birds from the lonely land of snow, are winging to build their nests in my heart against the warmth of its April, and I am content to wait for the merry season.

## XVI

THEY knew the way and went to seek you along the narrow lane, but I wandered abroad into the night, for I was ignorant.

I was not schooled enough to be afraid of you in the dark, therefore I came upon your doorstep unaware.

The wise rebuked me and bade me be gone, for I had not come by the lane.

I turned away in doubt, but you held me fast, and their scolding became louder every day.

.    .    .    .    .

## XVIII

NO: it is not yours to open buds into blossoms.

Shake the bud, strike it; it is beyond your power to make it blossom.

Your touch soils it, you tear its petals to pieces and strew them in the dust.

But no colours appear, and no perfume.

Ah! it is not for you to open the bud into a blossom.

He who can open the bud does it so simply.

He gives it a glance, and the life-sap stirs through its veins.

At his breath the flower spreads its wings and flutters in the wind.

Colours flush out like heart-longings, the perfume betrays a sweet secret.

He who can open the bud does it so simply.


## XIX

Sudās, the gardener, plucked from his tank the last lotus left by the ravage of winter and went to sell it to the King at the palace gate.

There he met a traveller who said to him, "Ask your price for the last lotus,—I shall offer it to Lord Buddha."

Sudās said, "If you pay one golden *māshā* it will be yours."

The traveller paid it.

At that moment the King came out and he wished to buy the flower, for he was on his way to see Lord Buddha, and he thought, "It would be a fine thing to lay at his feet the lotus that bloomed in winter."

When the gardener said he had been offered a golden *māshā* the King offered him ten, but the traveller doubled the price.

The gardener, being greedy, imagined a greater gain from him for whose sake they were bidding. He bowed and said, "I cannot sell this lotus."

In the hushed shade of the mango grove beyond the city wall Sudās stood before Lord Buddha, on whose lips sat the silence of love and whose eyes beamed peace like the morning star of the dew-washed autumn.

Sudās looked in his face and put the lotus at his feet and bowed his head to the dust.

Buddha smiled and asked, "What is your wish, my son?"

Sudās cried, "The least touch of your feet."

## XX

MAKE me thy poet, O Night, veiled Night!

There are some who have sat speechless for ages in thy shadow; let me utter their songs.

Take me up on thy chariot without wheels: running noiselessly from world to world, thou queen in the palace of time, thou darkly beautiful!

Many a questioning mind has stealthily entered thy courtyard and roamed through thy lampless house seeking for answers.

From many a heart, pierced with the arrow of joy from the hands of the Unknown, have burst forth glad chants, shaking the darkness to its foundation.

Those wakeful souls gaze in the starlight in wonder at the treasure they have suddenly found.

Make me their poet, O Night, the poet of thy fathomless silence.

## XXI

I WILL meet one day the Life within me, the joy that hides in my life, though the days perplex my path with their idle dust.

I have known it in glimpses, and its fitful breath has come upon me making my thoughts fragrant for a while.

I will meet one day the Joy without me that dwells behind the screen of light—and will stand in the overflowing solitude where all things are seen as by their creator.

•    •    •    •    •

## XXIV

THE night is dark and your slumber is deep in the hush of my being.
Wake, O Pain of Love, for I know not how to open the door, and I stand outside.

The hours wait, the stars watch, the wind is still, the silence is heavy in my heart.
Wake, Love, wake! brim my empty cup, and with a breath of song ruffle the night.

## XXV

THE bird of the morning sings.
Whence has he word of the morning before the morning breaks, and when the dragon night still holds the sky in its cold black coils?

Tell me, bird of the morning, how, through the twofold night of the sky and the leaves, he found his way into your dream, the messenger out of the east?
The world did not believe you when you cried, "The sun is on his way, the night is no more."
O sleeper, awake!
Bare your forehead, waiting for the first blessing of light, and sing with the bird of the morning in glad faith.

## XXVI

THE beggar in me lifted his lean hands to the starless sky and cried into night's ear with his hungry voice.

His prayers were to the blind Darkness who lay like a fallen god in a desolate heaven of lost hopes.

The cry of desire eddied round a chasm of despair, a wailing bird circling its empty nest.

But when morning dropped anchor at the rim of the East, the beggar in me leapt and cried:

"Blessed am I that the deaf night denied me—that its coffer was empty."

He cried, "O Life, O Light, you are precious! and precious is the joy that at last has known you!"

## XXVII

SANĀTAN was telling his beads by the Ganges when a Brahmin in rags came to him and said, "Help me, I am poor!"

"My alms-bowl is all that is my own," said Sanātan. "I have given away everything I had."

"But my lord Shiva came to me in my dreams," said the Brahmin, "and counselled me to come to you."

Sanātan suddenly remembered he had picked up a stone without price among the pebbles on the river-bank, and thinking that some one might need it hid it in the sands.

He pointed out the spot to the Brahmin, who wondering dug up the stone.

The Brahmin sat on the earth and mused alone till the sun went down behind the trees, and cowherds went home with their cattle.

Then he rose and came slowly to Sanātan and said,

"Master, give me the least fraction of the wealth that disdains all the wealth of the world."

And he threw the precious stone into the water.

## XXVIII

TIME after time I came to your gate with raised hands, asking for more and yet more.

You gave and gave, now in slow measure, now in sudden excess.

I took some, and some things I let drop; some lay heavy on my hands; some I made into playthings and broke them when tired; till the wrecks and the hoard of your gifts grew immense, hiding you, and the ceaseless expectation wore my heart out.

Take, oh, take—has now become my cry.

Shatter all from this beggar's bowl: put out this lamp of the importunate watcher: hold my hands, raise me from the still-gathering heap of your gifts into the bare infinity of your uncrowded presence.

## XXIX

YOU have set me among those who are defeated.

I know it is not for me to win, nor to leave the game.

I shall plunge into the pool although but to sink to the bottom.

I shall play the game of my undoing.

I shall stake all I have and when I lose my last penny I shall stake myself, and then I think I shall have won through my utter defeat.

## XXX

A SMILE of mirth spread over the sky when you dressed my heart in rags and sent her forth into the road to beg.

She went from door to door, and many a time when her bowl was nearly full she was robbed.

At the end of the weary day she came to your palace gate holding up her pitiful bowl, and you came and took her hand and seated her beside you on your throne.

## XXXI

"Who among you will take up the duty of feeding the hungry?" Lord Buddha asked his followers when famine raged at Shravasti.

Ratnākar, the banker, hung his head and said, "Much more is needed than all my wealth to feed the hungry."

Jaysen, the chief of the King's army, said, "I would gladly give my life's blood, but there is not enough food in my house."

Dharmapāl, who owned broad acres of land, said with a sigh, "The drought demon has sucked my fields dry. I know not how to pay King's dues."

Then rose Supriyā, the mendicant's daughter.
She bowed to all and meekly said, "I will feed the hungry."

"How!" they cried in surprise. "How can you hope to fulfil that vow?"

"I am the poorest of you all," said Supriyā, "that is my strength. I have my coffer and my store at each of your houses."

## XXXII

My king was unknown to me, therefore when he claimed his tribute I was bold to think I would hide myself, leaving my debts unpaid.

I fled and fled behind my day's work and my night's dreams.
But his claims followed me at every breath I drew.
Thus I came to know that I am known to him and no place left which is mine.

Now I wish to lay my all before his feet, and gain the right to my place in his kingdom.

## XXXIII

When I thought I would mould you, an image from my life for men to worship, I brought my dust and desires and all my coloured delusions and dreams.
When I asked you to mould with my life an image from your heart for you to love, you brought your fire and force, and truth, loveliness and peace.

## XXXIV

"Sire," announced the servant to the King, "the saint Narottam has never deigned to enter your royal temple.
"He is singing God's praise under the trees by the open road. The temple is empty of worshippers.
"They flock round him like bees round the white lotus, leaving the golden jar of honey unheeded."

The King, vexed at heart, went to the spot where Narottam sat on the grass.

He asked him, "Father, why leave my temple of the golden dome and sit on the dust outside to preach God's love?"

"Because God is not there in your temple," said Narottam.

The King frowned and said, "Do you know, twenty millions of gold went to the making of that marvel of art, and it was consecrated to God with costly rites?"

"Yes, I know it," answered Narottam. "It was in that year when thousands of your people whose houses had been burned stood vainly asking for help at your door.

"And God said, 'The poor creature who can give no shelter to his brothers would build my house!'

"And he took his place with the shelterless under the trees by the road.

"And that golden bubble is empty of all but hot vapour of pride."

The King cried in anger, "Leave my land."

Calmly said the saint, "Yes, banish me where you have banished my God."

## XXXV

THE trumpet lies in the dust.

The wind is weary, the light is dead.

Ah, the evil day!

Come, fighters, carrying your flags, and singers, with your war-songs!

Come, pilgrims of the march, hurrying on your journey!

The trumpet lies in the dust waiting for us.

I was on my way to the temple with my evening offerings, seeking for a place of rest after the day's dusty toil: hoping my hurts would be healed and the stains in my garment washed white, when I found thy trumpet lying in the dust.

Was it not the hour for me to light my evening lamp? Had not the night sung its lullaby to the stars?

O thou blood-red rose, my poppies of sleep have paled and faded!

I was certain my wanderings were over and my debts all paid when suddenly I came upon thy trumpet lying in the dust.

Strike my drowsy heart with thy spell of youth! Let my joy in life blaze up in fire.

Let the shafts of awakening fly through the heart of night, and a thrill of dread shake blindness and palsy.

I have come to raise thy trumpet from the dust.

Sleep is no more for me—my walk shall be through showers of arrows.

Some shall run out of their houses and come to my side—some shall weep.

Some in their beds shall toss and groan in dire dreams.

For to-night thy trumpet shall be sounded.

From thee I have asked peace only to find shame.

Now I stand before thee—help me to put on my armour!

Let hard blows of trouble strike fire into my life.

Let my heart beat in pain, the drum of thy victory.

My hands shall be utterly emptied to take up thy trumpet.

## XXXVI

WHEN, mad in their mirth, they raised dust to soil thy robe, O Beautiful, it made my heart sick.

I cried to thee and said, "Take thy rod of punishment and judge them."

The morning light struck upon those eyes, red with the revel of night; the place of the white lily greeted their burning breath; the stars through the depth of the sacred dark stared at their carousing—at those that raised dust to soil thy robe, O Beautiful!

Thy judgment seat was in the flower-garden, in the birds' notes in springtime: in the shady river-banks, where the trees muttered in answer to the muttering of the waves.

O my Lover, they were pitiless in their passion.

They prowled in the dark to snatch thy ornaments to deck their own desires.

When they had struck thee and thou wert pained, it pierced me to the quick, and I cried to thee and said, "Take thy sword, O my Lover, and judge them!"

Ah, but thy justice was vigilant.

A mother's tears were shed on their insolence; the imperishable faith of a lover hid their spears of rebellion in its own wounds.

Thy judgment was in the mute pain of sleepless love; in the blush of the chaste; in the tears of the night of the desolate; in the pale morning light of forgiveness.

O Terrible, they in their reckless greed climbed thy gate at night, breaking into thy storehouse to rob thee.

But the weight of their plunder grew immense, too heavy to carry or to remove.

Thereupon I cried to thee and said, "Forgive them, O Terrible!"

Thy forgiveness burst in storms, throwing them down, scattering their thefts in the dust.

Thy forgiveness was in the thunderstone; in the shower of blood; in the angry red of the sunset.


## XXXVII

UPAGUPTA, the disciple of Buddha, lay asleep on the dust by the city wall of Mathura.

Lamps were all out, doors were all shut, and stars were all hidden by the murky sky of August.

Whose feet were those tinkling with anklets, touching his breast of a sudden?

He woke up startled, and the light from a woman's lamp struck his forgiving eyes.

It was the dancing-girl, starred with jewels, clouded with a pale-blue mantle, drunk with the wine of her youth.

She lowered her lamp and saw the young face, austerely beautiful.

"Forgive me, young ascetic," said the woman; "graciously come to my house. The dusty earth is not a fit bed for you."

The ascetic answered, "Woman, go on your way; when the time is ripe I will come to you."

Suddenly the black night showed its teeth in a flash of lightning.

The storm growled from the corner of the sky, and the woman trembled in fear.

·     ·     ·     ·

The branches of the wayside trees were aching with blossom.

Gay notes of the flute came floating in the warm spring air from afar.

The citizens had gone to the woods, to the festival of flowers.

From the mid-sky gazed the full moon on the shadows of the silent town.

The young ascetic was walking in the lonely street, while overhead the lovesick *koels* urged from the mango branches their sleepless plaint.

Upagupta passed through the city gates, and stood at the base of the rampart.

What woman lay in the shadow of the wall at his feet, struck with the black pestilence, her body spotted with sores, hurriedly driven away from the town?

The ascetic sat by her side, taking her head on his knees, and moistened her lips with water and smeared her body with balm.

"Who are you, merciful one?" asked the woman.

"The time, at last, has come to visit you, and I am here," replied the young ascetic.

## XXXVIII

THIS is no mere dallying of love between us, my lover.

Again and again have swooped down upon me the screaming nights of storm, blowing out my lamp: dark doubts have gathered, blotting out all stars from my sky.

Again and again the banks have burst, letting the flood sweep away my harvest, and wailing and despair have rent my sky from end to end.

This have I learnt, that there are blows of pain in your love, never the cold apathy of death.

### XXXIX

THE wall breaks asunder, light, like divine laughter, bursts in.
                Victory, O Light!
The heart of the night is pierced!
With your flashing sword cut in twain the tangle of doubt and feeble desires!
                Victory!
Come, Implacable!
Come, you who are terrible in your whiteness.
O Light, your drum sounds in the march of fire, and the red torch is held on high; death dies in a burst of splendour!

### XL

O FIRE, my brother, I sing victory to you.
You are the bright red image of fearful freedom.
You swing your arms in the sky, you sweep your impetuous fingers across the harp-string, your dance music is beautiful.

When my days are ended and the gates are opened you will burn to ashes this cordage of hands and feet.
My body will be one with you, my heart will be caught in the whirls of your frenzy, and the burning heat that was my life will flash up and mingle itself in your flame.

### XLI

THE Boatman is out crossing the wild sea at night.

The mast is aching because of its full sails filled with the violent wind.

Stung with the night's fang the sky falls upon the sea, poisoned with black fear.

The waves dash their heads against the dark unseen, and the Boatman is out crossing the wild sea.

The Boatman is out, I know not for what tryst, startling the night with the sudden white of his sails.

I know not at what shore, at last, he lands to reach the silent courtyard where the lamp is burning and to find her who sits in the dust and waits.

What is the quest that makes his boat care not for storm nor darkness?

Is it heavy with gems and pearls?

Ah, no, the Boatman brings with him no treasure. but only a white rose in his hand and a song on his lips.

It is for her who watches alone at night with her lamp burning.

She dwells in the wayside hut.

Her loose hair flies in the wind and hides her eyes.

The storm shrieks through her broken doors, the light flickers in her earthen lamp flinging shadows on the walls.

Through the howl of the winds she hears him call her name, she whose name is unknown.

It is long since the Boatman sailed.

It will be long before the day breaks and he knocks at the door.

The drums will not be beaten and none will know.

Only light shall fill the house, blessed shall be the dust, and the heart glad.

All doubts shall vanish in silence when the Boatman comes to the shore.

## XLII

I CLING to this living raft, my body, in the narrow
stream of my earthly years. I leave it when the crossing
is over.

And then?

I do not know if the light there and the darkness are
the same.

The Unknown is the perpetual freedom:
He is pitiless in his love.
He crushes the shell for the pearl, dumb in the prison
of the dark.

You muse and weep for the days that are done, poor
heart!
Be glad that days are to come!
The hour strikes, O pilgrim!
It is time for you to take the parting of the ways!
His face will be unveiled once again and you shall
meet.

### XLIII

OVER the relic of Lord Buddha King Bimbisār built a
shrine, a salutation in white marble.

There in the evening would come all the brides and
daughters of the King's house to offer flowers and light
lamps.

When the son became King in his time he washed his
father's creed away with blood, and lit sacrificial fires
with its sacred books.

The autumn day was dying.
The evening hour of worship was near.
Shrimati, the Queen's maid, devoted to Lord Buddha,
having bathed in holy water, and decked the golden

tray with lamps and fresh white blossoms, silently raised her dark eyes to the Queen's face.

The Queen shuddered in fear and said, "Do you not know, foolish girl, that death is the penalty for whoever brings worship to Buddha's shrine?

"Such is the King's will."

Shrimati bowed to the Queen, and turning away from her door came and stood before Amitā, the newly wed bride of the King's son.

A mirror of burnished gold on her lap, the newly wed bride was braiding her dark long tresses and painting the red spot of good luck at the parting of her hair.

Her hands trembled when she saw the young maid, and she cried, "What fearful peril would you bring me? Leave me this instant."

Princess Shuklā sat at the window reading her book of romance by the light of the setting sun.

She started when she saw at her door the maid with the sacred offerings.

Her book fell down from her lap, and she whispered in Shrimati's ears, "Rush not to death, daring woman!"

Shrimati walked from door to door.

She raised her head and cried, "O women of the King's house, hasten!

"The time for our Lord's worship is come!"

Some shut their doors in her face and some reviled her.

The last gleam of daylight faded from the bronze dome of the palace tower.

Deep shadows settled in street-corners: the bustle of the city was hushed: the gong at the temple of Shiva announced the time of the evening prayer.

199

In the dark of the autumn evening, deep as a limpid lake, stars throbbed with light, when the guards of the palace garden were startled to see through the trees a row of lamps burning at the shrine of Buddha.

They ran with their swords unsheathed, crying, "Who are you, foolish one, reckless of death?"

"I am Shrimati," replied a sweet voice, "the servant of Lord Buddha."

The next moment her heart's blood coloured the cold marble with its red.

And in the still hour of stars died the light of the last lamp of worship at the foot of the shrine.

### XLIV

THE day that stands between you and me makes her last bow of farewell.

The night draws her veil over her face, and hides the one lamp burning in my chamber.

Your dark servant comes noiselessly and spreads the bridal carpet for you to take your seat there alone with me in the wordless silence till night is done.

### XLV

MY night has passed on the bed of sorrow, and my eyes are tired. My heavy heart is not yet ready to meet morning with its crowded joys.

Draw a veil over this naked light, beckon aside from me this glaring flash and dance of life.

Let thy mantle of tender darkness cover me in its folds, and cover my pain awhile from the pressure of the world.

## XLVI

THE time is past when I could repay her for all that I received.

Her night has found its morning and thou hast taken her to thy arms: and to thee I bring my gratitude and my gifts that were for her.

For all hurts and offences to her I come to thee for forgiveness.

I offer to thy service those flowers of my love that remained in bud when she waited for them to open.

## XLVII

I FOUND a few old letters of mine carefully hidden in her box—a few small toys for her memory to play with.

With a timorous heart she tried to steal these trifles from time's turbulent stream, and said, "These are mine only!"

Ah, there is no one now to claim them, who can pay their price with loving care, yet here they are still.

Surely there is love in this world to save her from utter loss, even like this love of hers that saved these letters with such fond care.

## XLVIII

BRING beauty and order into my forlorn life, woman, as you brought them into my house when you lived.

Sweep away the dusty fragments of the hours, fill the empty jars, and mend all that has been neglected.

Then open the inner door of the shrine, light the candle, and let us meet there in silence before our God.

## XLIX

THE pain was great when the strings were being tuned, my Master!

Begin your music, and let me forget the pain; let me feel in beauty what you had in your mind through those pitiless days.

The waning night lingers at my doors, let her take her leave in songs.

Pour your heart into my life-strings, my Master, in tunes that descend from your stars.

L

IN the lightning-flash of a moment I have seen the immensity of your creation in my life—creation through many a death from world to world.

I weep at my unworthiness when I see my life in the hands of the unmeaning hours,—but when I see it in your hands I know it is too precious to be squandered among shadows.

LI

I KNOW that at the dim end of some day the sun will bid me its last farewell.

Shepherds will play their pipes beneath the banyan trees, and cattle graze on the slope by the river, while my days will pass into the dark.

This is my prayer, that I may know before I leave why the earth called me to her arms.

Why her night's silence spoke to me of stars, and her daylight kissed my thoughts into flower.

Before I go may I linger over my last refrain, complet-

ing its music, may the lamp be lit to see your face and
the wreath woven to crown you.

## LII

WHAT music is that in whose measure the world is
rocked?

We laugh when it beats upon the crest of life, we
shrink in terror when it returns into the dark.

But the play is the same that comes and goes with the
rhythm of the endless music.

You hide your treasure in the palm of your hand, and
we cry that we are robbed.

But open and shut your palm as you will, the gain
and the loss are the same.

At the game you play with your own self you lose
and win at once.

## LIII

I HAVE kissed this world with my eyes and my limbs;
I have wrapt it within my heart in numberless folds; I
have flooded its days and nights with thoughts till the
world and my life have grown one,—and I love my life
because I love the light of the sky so enwoven with me.

If to leave this world be as real as to love it—then
there must be a meaning in the meeting and the parting
of life.

If that love were deceived in death, then the canker
of this deceit would eat into all things, and the stars
would shrivel and grow black.

## LIV

THE Cloud said to me, "I vanish"; the Night said, "I plunge into the fiery dawn."

The Pain said, "I remain in deep silence as his footprint."

"I die into the fulness," said my life to me.

The Earth said, "My lights kiss your thoughts every moment."

"The days pass," Love said, "but I wait for you."

Death said, "I ply the boat of your life across the sea."

TULSIDAS, the poet, was wandering, deep in thought, by the Ganges, in that lonely spot where they burn their dead.

He found a woman sitting at the feet of the corpse of her dead husband, gaily dressed as for a wedding.

She rose as she saw him, bowed to him, and said, "Permit me, Master, with your blessing, to follow my husband to heaven."

"Why such hurry, my daughter?" asked Tulsidas. "Is not this earth also His who made heaven?"

"For heaven I do not long," said the woman. "I want my husband."

Tulsidas smiled and said to her, "Go back to your home, my child. Before the month is over you will find your husband."

The woman went back with glad hope. Tulsidas came to her every day and gave her high thoughts to think, till her heart was filled to the brim with divine love.

When the month was scarcely over, her neighbours

came to her, asking, "Woman, have you found your husband?"

The widow smiled and said, "I have."

Eagerly they asked, "Where is he?"

"In my heart is my lord, one with me," said the woman.

## LVI

You came for a moment to my side and touched me with the great mystery of the woman that there is in the heart of creation.

She who is ever returning to God his own outflowing of sweetness; she is the ever fresh beauty and youth in nature; she dances in the bubbling streams and sings in the morning light; she with heaving waves suckles the thirsty earth; in her the Eternal One breaks in two in a joy that no longer may contain itself, and overflows in the pain of love.

## LVII

Who is she who dwells in my heart, the woman forlorn for ever?

I wooed her and I failed to win her.

I decked her with wreaths and sang in her praise.

A smile shone in her face for a moment, then it faded.

"I have no joy in thee," she cried, the woman in sorrow.

I bought her jewelled anklets and fanned her with a fan gem-studded; I made her a bed on a bedstead of gold.

There flickered a gleam of gladness in her eyes, then it died.

"I have no joy in these," she cried, the woman in sorrow.

I seated her upon a car of triumph and drove her from end to end of the earth.

Conquered hearts bowed down at her feet, and shouts of applause rang in the sky.

Pride shone in her eyes for a moment, then it was dimmed in tears.

"I have no joy in conquest," she cried, the woman in sorrow.

I asked her, "Tell me, whom do you seek?"

She only said, "I wait for him of the unknown name."

Days pass by and she cries, "When will my beloved come whom I know not, and be known to me for ever?"

## LVIII

YOURS is the light that breaks forth from the dark, and the good that sprouts from the cleft heart of strife.

Yours is the house that opens upon the world, and the love that calls to the battlefield.

Yours is the gift that still is a gain when everything is a loss, and the life that flows through the caverns of death.

Yours is the heaven that lies in the common dust, and you are there for me, you are there for all.

## LIX

WHEN the weariness of the road is upon me, and the thirst of the sultry day; when the ghostly hours of the dusk throw their shadows across my life, then I cry not for your voice only, my friend, but for your touch.

There is an anguish in my heart for the burden of its riches not given to you.

Put out your hand through the night, let me hold it and fill it and keep it; let me feel its touch along the lengthening stretch of my loneliness.

## LX

THE odour cries in the bud, "Ah me, the day departs, the happy day of spring, and I am a prisoner in petals!"

Do not lose heart, timid thing!

Your bonds will burst, the bud will open into flower, and when you die in the fulness of life, even then the spring will live on.

The odour pants and flutters within the bud, crying, "Ah me, the hours pass by, yet I do not know where I go, or what it is I seek!"

Do not lose heart, timid thing!

The spring breeze has overheard your desire, the day will not end before you have fulfilled your being.

Dark is the future to her, and the odour cries in despair, "Ah me, through whose fault is my life so unmeaning?

"Who can tell me why I am at all?"

Do not lose heart, timid thing!

The perfect dawn is near when you will mingle your life with all life and know at last your purpose.

## LXI

SHE is still a child, my lord.

She runs about your palace and plays, and tries to make of you a plaything as well.

She heeds not when her hair tumbles down and her careless garment drags in the dust.

She falls asleep when you speak to her and answers not—and the flower you give her in the morning slips to the dust from her hands.

When the storm bursts and darkness is over the sky she is sleepless; her dolls lie scattered on the earth and she clings to you in terror.

She is afraid that she may fail in service to you.

But with a smile you watch her at her game.

You know her.

The child sitting in the dust is your destined bride; her play will be stilled and deepened into love.


## LXII

"WHAT is there but the sky, O Sun, that can hold thine image?"

"I dream of thee, but to serve thee I can never hope," the dewdrop wept and said; "I am too small to take thee unto me, great lord, and my life is all tears."

"I illumine the limitless sky, yet I can yield myself up to a tiny drop of dew," thus the Sun said; "I shall become but a sparkle of light and fill you, and your little life will be a laughing orb."


## LXIII

NOT for me is the love that knows no restraint, but like the foaming wine that having burst its vessel in a moment would run to waste.

Send me the love which is cool and pure like your rain that blesses the thirsty earth and fills the homely earthen jars.

Send me the love that would soak down into the centre of being, and from there would spread like the unseen sap through the branching tree of life, giving birth to fruits and flowers.

Send me the love that keeps the heart still with the fulness of peace.

## LXIV

THE sun had set on the western margin of the river among the tangle of the forest.

The hermit boys had brought the cattle home, and sat round the fire to listen to the master, Gautama, when a strange boy came, and greeted him with fruits and flowers, and, bowing low at his feet, spoke in a bird-like voice—"Lord, I have come to thee to be taken into the path of the supreme Truth.

"My name is Satyakāma."

"Blessings be on thy head," said the master.

"Of what clan art thou, my child? It is only fitting for a Brahmin to aspire to the highest wisdom."

"Master," answered the boy, "I know not of what clan I am. I shall go and ask my mother."

Thus saying, Satyakāma took leave, and wading across the shallow stream, came back to his mother's hut, which stood at the end of the sandy waste at the edge of the sleeping village.

The lamp burnt dimly in the room, and the mother stood at the door in the dark waiting for her son's return.

She clasped him to her bosom, kissed him on his hair, and asked him of his errand to the master.

"What is the name of my father, dear mother?" asked the boy.

"It is only fitting for a Brahmin to aspire to the highest wisdom, said Lord Gautama to me."

The woman lowered her eyes, and spoke in a whisper.

"In my youth I was poor and had many masters. Thou didst come to thy mother Jabālā's arms, my darling, who had no husband."

The early rays of the sun glistened on the tree-tops of the forest hermitage.

The students, with their tangled hair still wet with their morning bath, sat under the ancient tree, before the master.

There came Satyakāma.

He bowed low at the feet of the sage, and stood silent.

"Tell me," the great teacher asked him, "of what clan art thou?"

"My lord," he answered, "I know it not. My mother said when I asked her, 'I had served many masters in my youth, and thou didst come to thy mother Jabālā's arms, who had no husband.'"

There rose a murmur like the angry hum of bees disturbed in their hive; and the students muttered at the shameless insolence of that outcast.

Master Gautama rose from his seat, stretched out his arms, took the boy to his bosom, and said, "Best of all Brahmins art thou, my child. Thou hast the noblest heritage of truth."

## LXV

MAYBE there is one house in this city where the gate opens for ever this morning at the touch of the sunrise, where the errand of the light is fulfilled.

The flowers have opened in hedges and gardens, and maybe there is one heart that has found in them this morning the gift that has been on its voyage from endless time.

## LXVI

LISTEN, my heart, in his flute is the music of the smell of wild flowers, of the glistening leaves and gleaming water, of shadows resonant with bees' wings.

The flute steals his smile from my friend's lips and spreads it over my life.

·　　·　　·　　·　　·

## LXIX

YOU were in the centre of my heart, therefore when my heart wandered she never found you; you hid yourself from my loves and hopes till the last, for you were always in them.

You were the inmost joy in the play of my youth, and when I was too busy with the play the joy was passed by.

You sang to me in the ecstasies of my life and I forgot to sing to you.

## LXX

WHEN you hold your lamp in the sky it throws its light on my face and its shadow falls over you.

When I hold the lamp of love in my heart its light falls on you and I am left standing behind in the shadow.

. . . . .

## LXXII

THE joy ran from all the world to build my body.

The lights of the skies kissed and kissed her till she woke.

Flowers of hurrying summers sighed in her breath and voices of winds and water sang in her movements.

The passion of the tide of colours in clouds and in forests flowed into her life, and the music of all things caressed her limbs into shape.

She is my bride,—she has lighted her lamp in my house.

## LXXIII

THE spring with its leaves and flowers has come into my body.

The bees hum there the morning long, and the winds idly play with the shadows.

A sweet fountain springs up from the heart of my heart.

My eyes are washed with delight like the dew-bathed morning, and life is quivering in all my limbs like the sounding strings of the lute.

Are you wandering alone by the shore of my life, where the tide is in flood, O lover of my endless days?

Are my dreams flitting round you like the moths with their many-coloured wings?

And are those your songs that are echoing in the dark caves of my being?

Who but you can hear the hum of the crowded hours that sounds in my veins to-day, the glad steps that dance in my breast, the clamour of the restless life beating its wings in my body?

## LXXIV

MY bonds are cut, my debts are paid, my door has been opened, I go everywhere.

They crouch in their corner and weave their web of pale hours, they count their coins sitting in the dust and call me back.

But my sword is forged, my armour is put on, my horse is eager to run.
I shall win my kingdom.

## LXXV

IT was only the other day that I came to your earth, naked and nameless, with a wailing cry.
To-day my voice is glad, while you, my lord, stand aside to make room that I may fill my life.

Even when I bring you my songs for an offering I have the secret hope that men will come and love me for them.
You love to discover that I love this world where you have brought me.

## LXXVI

TIMIDLY I cowered in the shadow of safety, but now, when the surge of joy carries my heart upon its crest, my heart clings to the cruel rock of its trouble.

I sat alone in a corner of my house thinking it too narrow for any guest, but now when its door is flung open by an unbidden joy I find there is room for thee and for all the world.

I walked upon tiptoe, careful of my person, perfumed, and adorned—but now when a glad whirlwind has overthrown me in the dust I laugh and roll on the earth at thy feet like a child.

## LXXVII

THE world is yours at once and for ever.

And because you have no want, my king, you have no pleasure in your wealth.

It is as though it were naught.

Therefore through slow time you give me what is yours, and ceaselessly win your kingdom in me.

Day after day you buy your sunrise from my heart, and you find your love carven into the image of my life.

To the birds you gave songs, the birds gave you songs in return.

You gave me only voice, yet asked for more, and I sing.

You made your winds light and they are fleet in their service. You burdened my hands that I myself may lighten them, and at last gain unburdened freedom for your service.

You created your Earth, filling its shadows with fragments of light.

There you paused; you left me empty-handed in the dust to create your heaven.

To all things else you give; from me you ask.

The harvest of my life ripens in the sun and the shower till I reap more than you sowed, gladdening your heart, O Master of the golden granary.

## LXXIX

LET me not pray to be sheltered from dangers but to be fearless in facing them.

Let me not beg for the stilling of my pain but for the heart to conquer it.

Let me not look for allies in life's battlefield but to my own strength.

Let me not crave in anxious fear to be saved but hope for the patience to win my freedom.

Grant me that I may not be a coward, feeling your mercy in my success alone; but let me find the grasp of your hand in my failure.

## LXXX

YOU did not know yourself when you dwelt alone, and there was no crying of an errand when the wind ran from the hither to the farther shore.

I came and you woke, and the skies blossomed with lights.

You made me open in many flowers; rocked me in the

cradles of many forms; hid me in death and found me again in life.

I came and your heart heaved; pain came to you and joy.
You touched me and tingled into love.

But in my eyes there is a film of shame and in my breast a flicker of fear; my face is veiled and I weep when I cannot see you.

Yet I know the endless thirst in your heart for sight of me, the thirst that cries at my door in the repeated knockings of sunrise.

### LXXXI

You, in your timeless watch, listen to my approaching steps, while your gladness gathers in the morning twilight and breaks in the burst of light.
The nearer I draw to you the deeper grows the fervour in the dance of the sea.

Your world is a branching spray of light filling your hands, but your heaven is in my secret heart; it slowly opens its buds in shy love.

### LXXXII

I will utter your name, sitting alone among the shadows of my silent thoughts.

I will utter it without words, I will utter it without purpose.

For I am like a child that calls its mother an hundred times, glad that it can say "Mother."

## LXXXIII

### 1

I FEEL that all the stars shine in me.

The world breaks into my life like a flood.

The flowers blossom in my body.

All the youthfulness of land and water smokes like an incense in my heart; and the breath of all things plays on my thoughts as on a flute.

### 2

When the world sleeps I come to your door.

The stars are silent, and I am afraid to sing.

I wait and watch, till your shadow passes by the balcony of night and I return with a full heart.

Then in the morning I sing by the roadside;

The flowers in the hedge give me answer and the morning air listens,

The travellers suddenly stop and look in my face, thinking I have called them by their names.

### 3

Keep me at your door ever attending to your wishes, and let me go about in your Kingdom accepting your call.

Let me not sink and disappear in the depth of languor.

Let not my life be worn out to tatters by penury of waste.

Let not those doubts encompass me,—the dust of distractions.

Let me not pursue many paths to gather many things.

Let me not bend my heart to the yoke of the many.

Let me hold my head high in the courage and pride of being your servant.

## LXXXIV

THE OARSMEN

Do you hear the tumult of death afar,
The call midst the fire-floods and poisonous clouds?
—The Captain's call to the steersman to turn the ship
    to an unnamed shore,
For that time is over—the stagnant time in the
    port—
Where the same old merchandise is bought and sold in
    an endless round,
Where dead things drift in the exhaustion and empti-
    ness of truth.

They wake up in sudden fear and ask,
    "Comrades, what hour has struck?
    When shall the dawn begin?"
The clouds have blotted away the stars—
Who is there then can see the beckoning finger of the
    day?
They run out with oars in hand, the beds are emptied,
    the mother prays, the wife watches by the door;
There is a wail of parting that rises to the sky,
And there is the Captain's voice in the dark:
"Come, sailors, for the time in the harbour is over!"

All the black evils in the world have overflowed their
   banks,
Yet, oarsmen, take your places with the blessing of
   sorrow in your souls!'
Whom do you blame, brothers? Bow your heads down!
The sin has been yours and ours.
The heat growing in the heart of God for ages—
The cowardice of the weak, the arrogance of the strong,
   the greed of fat prosperity, the rancour of the
   wronged, pride of race, and insult to man—
Has burst God's peace, raging in storm.

Like a ripe pod, let the tempest break its heart into
   pieces, scattering thunders.
Stop your bluster of dispraise and of self-praise,
And with the calm of silent prayer on your foreheads
   sail to that unnamed shore.

We have known sins and evils every day and death we
   have known;
They pass over our world like clouds mocking us with
   their transient lightning laughter.
Suddenly they have stopped, become a prodigy,
And men must stand before them saying:
"We do not fear you, O Monster! for we have lived
   every day by conquering you,
And we die with the faith that Peace is true, and Good
   is true, and true is the eternal One!"

If the Deathless dwell not in the heart of death,
If glad wisdom bloom not bursting the sheath of
   sorrow,
If sin do not die of its own revealment,

If pride break not under its load of decorations,
Then whence comes the hope that drives these men
    from their homes like stars rushing to their death
    in the morning light?
Shall the value of the martyrs' blood and mothers' tears
    be utterly lost in the dust of the earth, not buying
    Heaven with their price?
And when Man bursts his mortal bounds, is not the
    Boundless revealed that moment?

## LXXXV

### THE SONG OF THE DEFEATED

MY Master has bid me, while I stand at the roadside, to sing the song of Defeat, for that is the bride whom He woos in secret.

She has put on the dark veil, hiding her face from the crowd, but the jewel glows on her breast in the dark.

She is forsaken of the day, and God's night is waiting for her with its lamps lighted and flowers wet with dew.

She is silent with her eyes downcast; she has left her home behind her, from her home has come that wailing in the wind.

But the stars are singing the love-song of the eternal to a face sweet with shame and suffering.

The door has been opened in the lonely chamber, the call has sounded, and the heart of the darkness throbs with awe because of the coming tryst.

## LXXXVI

### THANKSGIVING

THOSE who walk on the path of pride crushing the lowly life under their tread, covering the tender green of the earth with their footprints in blood;

Let them rejoice, and thank thee, Lord, for the day is theirs.

But I am thankful that my lot lies with the humble who suffer and bear the burden of power, and hide their faces and stifle their sobs in the dark.

For every throb of their pain has pulsed in the secret depth of thy night, and every insult has been gathered into thy great silence.

And the morrow is theirs.

O Sun, rise upon the bleeding hearts blossoming in flowers of the morning, and the torchlight revelry of pride shrunken to ashes.

# THE POST OFFICE

# THE CHARACTERS

MADHAV

AMAL, his adopted child

SUDHA, a little flower-girl

THE DOCTOR

DAIRYMAN

WATCHMAN

GAFFER

VILLAGE HEADMAN, a bully

KING'S HERALD

ROYAL PHYSICIAN

# THE POST OFFICE

## ACT I

### (*Madhav's House*)

*Madhav.* What a state I am in! Before he came, nothing mattered; I felt so free. But now that he has come, goodness knows from where, my heart is filled with his dear self, and my home will be no home to me when he leaves. Doctor, do you think he——

*Physician.* If there's life in his fate, then he will live long. But what the medical scriptures say, it seems——

*Madhav.* Great heavens, what?

*Physician.* The scriptures have it: "Bile or palsy, cold or gout spring all alike."

*Madhav.* Oh, get along, don't fling your scriptures at me; you only make me more anxious; tell me what I can do.

*Physician* (*taking snuff*). The patient needs the most scrupulous care.

*Madhav.* That's true; but tell me how.

*Physician.* I have already mentioned, on no account must he be let out of doors.

*Madhav.* Poor child, it is very hard to keep him indoors all day long.

*Physician.* What else can you do? The autumn sun and the damp are both very bad for the little fellow—for the scriptures have it:

> "In wheezing, swooning, or in nervous fret,
> In jaundice or leaden eyes——"

225

*Madhav.* Never mind the scriptures, please. Eh, then we must shut the poor thing up. Is there no other method?

*Physician.* None at all: for "In the wind and in the sun——"

*Madhav.* What will your "in this and in that" do for me now? Why don't you let them alone and come straight to the point? What's to be done, then? Your system is very, very hard for the poor boy; and he is so quiet too with all his pain and sickness. It tears my heart to see him wince, as he takes your medicine.

*Physician.* The more he winces, the surer is the effect. That's why the sage Chyabana observes: "In medicine as in good advice, the least palatable is the truest." Ah, well! I must be trotting now.                    [*Exit*

(*Gaffer enters*)

*Madhav.* Well, I'm jiggered, there's Gaffer now.

*Gaffer.* Why, why, I won't bite you.

*Madhav.* No, but you are a devil to send children off their heads.

*Gaffer.* But you aren't a child, and you've no child in the house; why worry, then?

*Madhav.* Oh, but I have brought a child into the house.

*Gaffer.* Indeed, how so?

*Madhav.* You remember how my wife was dying to adopt a child?

*Gaffer.* Yes, but that's an old story; you didn't like the idea.

*Madhav.* You know, brother, how hard all this getting money in has been.   That somebody else's child would sail in and waste all this money earned with so much trouble—Oh, I hated the idea. But this boy clings to my heart in such a queer sort of way——

226

*Gaffer*. So that's the trouble! and your money goes all for him and feels jolly lucky it does go at all.

*Madhav*. Formerly, earning was a sort of passion with me; I simply couldn't help working for money. Now, I make money, and as I know it is all for this dear boy, earning becomes a joy to me.

*Gaffer*. Ah, well, and where did you pick him up?

*Madhav*. He is the son of a man who was a brother to my wife by village ties. He has had no mother since infancy; and now the other day he lost his father as well.

*Gaffer*. Poor thing: and so he needs me all the more.

*Madhav*. The doctor says all the organs of his little body are at loggerheads with each other, and there isn't much hope for his life. There is only one way to save him and that is to keep him out of this autumn wind and sun. But you are such a terror! What with this game of yours at your age, too, to get children out of doors!

*Gaffer*. God bless my soul! So I'm already as bad as autumn wind and sun, eh! But, friend, I know something, too, of the game of keeping them indoors. When my day's work is over I am coming in to make friends with this child of yours.                [*Exit*

(*Amal enters*)

*Amal*. Uncle, I say, Uncle!

*Madhav*. Hullo! Is that you, Amal?

*Amal*. Mayn't I be out of the courtyard at all?

*Madhav*. No, my dear, no.

*Amal*. See there, where Auntie grinds lentils in the quern, the squirrel is sitting with his tail up and with his wee hands he's picking up the broken grains of lentils and crunching them. Can't I run up there?

*Madhav.* No, my darling, no.

*Amal.* Wish I were a squirrel!—it would be lovely. Uncle, why won't you let me go about?

*Madhav.* Doctor says it's bad for you to be out.

*Amal.* How can the doctor know?

*Madhav.* What a thing to say! The doctor can't know and he reads such huge books!

*Amal.* Does his book-learning tell him everything?

*Madhav.* Of course, don't you know!

*Amal* (*with a sigh*). Ah, I am so stupid! I don't read books.

*Madhav.* Now, think of it; very, very learned people are all like you; they are never out of doors.

*Amal.* Aren't they really?

*Madhav.* No, how can they? Early and late they toil and moil at their books, and they've eyes for nothing else. Now, my little man, you are going to be learned when you grow up; and then you will stay at home and read such big books, and people will notice you and say, "He's a wonder."

*Amal.* No, no, Uncle; I beg of you, by your dear feet —I don't want to be learned; I won't.

*Madhav.* Dear, dear; it would have been my saving if I could have been learned.

*Amal.* No, I would rather go about and see everything that there is.

*Madhav.* Listen to that! See! What will you see, what is there so much to see?

*Amal.* See that far-away hill from our window—I often long to go beyond those hills and right away.

*Madhav.* Oh, you silly! As if there's nothing more to be done but just get up to the top of that hill and away! Eh! You don't talk sense, my boy. Now listen, since that hill stands there upright as a barrier, it means you can't get beyond it. Else, what was the use in heaping up so many large stones to make such a big affair of it, eh!

*Amal.* Uncle, do you think it is meant to prevent us crossing over? It seems to me because the earth can't speak it raises its hands into the sky and beckons. And those who live far off and sit alone by their windows can see the signal. But I suppose the learned people——

*Madhav.* No, they don't have time for that sort of nonsense. They are not crazy like you.

*Amal.* Do you know, yesterday I met some one quite as crazy as I am.

*Madhav.* Gracious me, really, how so?

*Amal.* He had a bamboo staff on his shoulder with a small bundle at the top, and a brass pot in his left hand, and an old pair of shoes on; he was making for those hills straight across that meadow there. I called out to him and asked, "Where are you going?" He answered, "I don't know; anywhere!" I asked again, "Why are you going?" He said, "I'm going out to seek work." Say, Uncle, have you to seek work?

*Madhav.* Of course I have to. There's many about looking for jobs.

*Amal.* How lovely! I'll go about like them too, finding things to do.

*Madhav.* Suppose you seek and don't find. Then——

*Amal.* Wouldn't that be jolly? Then I should go farther! I watched that man slowly walking on with his pair of worn-out shoes. And when he got to where the water flows under the fig tree, he stopped and washed his feet in the stream. Then he took out from his bundle some gram-flour, moistened it with water and began to

229

eat. Then he tied up his bundle and shouldered it again; tucked up his cloth above his knees and crossed the stream. I've asked Auntie to let me go up to the stream, and eat my gram-flour just like him.

*Madhav.* And what did your Auntie say to that?

*Amal.* Auntie said, "Get well and then I'll take you over there." Please, Uncle, when shall I get well?

*Madhav.* It won't be long, dear.

*Amal.* Really, but then I shall go right away the moment I'm well again.

*Madhav.* And where will you go?

*Amal.* Oh, I will walk on, crossing so many streams, wading through water. Everybody will be asleep with their doors shut in the heat of the day and I will tramp on and on seeking work far, very far.

*Madhav.* I see! I think you had better be getting well first; then——

*Amal.* But then you won't want me to be learned, will you, Uncle?

*Madhav.* What would you rather be, then?

*Amal.* I can't think of anything just now; but I'll tell you later on.

*Madhav.* Very well. But mind you, you aren't to call out and talk to strangers again.

*Amal.* But I love to talk to strangers!

*Madhav.* Suppose they had kidnapped you?

*Amal.* That would have been splendid! But no one ever takes me away. They all want me to stay in here.

*Madhav.* I am off to my work—but, darling, you won't go out, will you?

*Amal.* No, I won't. But, Uncle, you'll let me be in this room by the roadside. [*Exit Madhav*

*Dairyman.* Curds, curds, good nice curds.

*Amal.* Curdseller, I say, Curdseller.

*Dairyman.* Why do you call me? Will you buy some curds?

*Amal.* How can I buy? I have no money.

*Dairyman.* What a boy! Why call out then? Ugh! What a waste of time!

*Amal.* I would go with you if I could.

*Dairyman.* With me?

*Amal.* Yes, I seem to feel homesick when I hear you call from far down the road.

*Dairyman (lowering his yoke-pole).* Whatever are you doing here, my child?

*Amal.* The doctor says I'm not to be out, so I sit here all day long.

*Dairyman.* My poor child, whatever has happened to you?

*Amal.* I can't tell. You see, I am not learned, so I don't know what's the matter with me. Say, Dairyman, where do you come from?

*Dairyman.* From our village.

*Amal.* Your village? Is it very far?

*Dairyman.* Our village lies on the river Shamli at the foot of the Panch-mura hills.

*Amal.* Panch-mura hills! Shamli river! I wonder. I may have seen your village. I can't think when, though!

*Dairyman.* Have you seen it? Been to the foot of those hills?

*Amal.* Never. But I seem to remember having seen it. Your village is under some very old big trees, just by the side of the red road—isn't that so?

*Dairyman.* That's right, child.

*Amal.* And on the slope of the hill cattle grazing.

231

*Dairyman.* How wonderful! Cattle grazing in our village! Indeed there are!

*Amal.* And your women with red sarees fill their pitchers from the river and carry them on their heads.

*Dairyman.* Good, that's right! Women from our dairy village do come and draw their water from the river; but then it isn't every one who has a red saree to put on. But, my dear child, surely you must have been there for a walk some time.

*Amal.* Really, Dairyman, never been there at all. But the first day doctor lets me go out, you are going to take me to your village.

*Dairyman.* I will, my child, with pleasure.

*Amal.* And you'll teach me to cry curds and shoulder the yoke like you and walk the long, long road?

*Dairyman.* Dear, dear, did you ever? Why should you sell curds? No, you will read big books and be learned.

*Amal.* No, I never want to be learned—I'll be like you and take my curds from the village by the red road near the old banyan tree, and I will hawk it from cottage to cottage. Oh, how do you cry—"Curds, curds, fine curds"? Teach me the tune, will you?

*Dairyman.* Dear, dear, teach you the tune; what a notion!

*Amal.* Please do. I love to hear it. I can't tell you how queer I feel when I hear you cry out from the bend of that road, through the line of those trees! Do you know I feel like that when I hear the shrill cry of kites from almost the end of the sky?

*Dairyman.* Dear child, will you have some curds? Yes, do.

*Amal.* But I have no money.

*Dairyman.* No, no, no, don't talk of money! You'll make me so happy if you take some curds from me.

*Amal.* Say, have I kept you too long?

*Dairyman.* Not a bit; it has been no loss to me at all; you have taught me how to be happy selling curds.

[*Exit*

*Amal* (*intoning*). Curds, curds, fine curds—from the dairy village—from the country of the Panch-mura hills by the Shamli bank. Curds, good curds; in the early morning the women make the cows stand in a row under the trees and milk them, and in the evening they turn the milk into curds. Curds, good curds. Hello, there's the watchman on his rounds. Watchman, I say, come and have a word with me.

*Watchman.* What's all this row about? Aren't you afraid of the likes of me?

*Amal.* No, why should I be?

*Watchman.* Suppose I march you off, then?

*Amal.* Where will you take me to? Is it very far, right beyond the hills?

*Watchman.* Suppose I march you straight to the King?

*Amal.* To the King! Do, will you? But the doctor won't let me go out. No one can ever take me away. I've got to stay here all day long.

*Watchman.* Doctor won't let you, poor fellow! So I see! Your face is pale and there are dark rings round your eyes. Your veins stick out from your poor thin hands.

*Amal.* Won't you sound the gong, Watchman?

*Watchman.* Time has not yet come.

*Amal.* How curious! Some say time has not yet come, and some say time has gone by! But surely your time will come the moment you strike the gong!

233

*Watchman.* That's not possible; I strike up the gong only when it is time.

*Amal.* Yes, I love to hear your gong. When it is mid-day and our meal is over, Uncle goes off to his work and Auntie falls asleep reading her *Ramayana*, and in the courtyard under the' shadow of the wall our doggie sleeps with his nose in his curled-up tail; then your gong strikes out, "Dong, dong, dong!" Tell me, why does your gong sound?

*Watchman.* My gong sounds to tell the people, Time waits for none, but goes on for ever.

*Amal.* Where, to what land?

*Watchman.* That none knows.

*Amal.* Then I suppose no one has ever been there! Oh, I do wish to fly with the time to that land of which no one knows anything.

*Watchman.* All of us have to get there one day, my child.

*Amal.* Have I too?

*Watchman.* Yes, you too!

*Amal.* But doctor won't let me out.

*Watchman.* One day the doctor himself may take you there by the hand.

*Amal.* He won't; you don't know him. He only keeps me in.

*Watchman.* One greater than he comes and lets us free.

*Amal.* When will this great doctor come for me? I can't stick in here any more.

*Watchman.* Shouldn't talk like that, my child.

*Amal.* No. I am here where they have left me—I never move a bit. But, when your gong goes off, dong, dong, dong, it goes to my heart. Say, Watchman?

*Watchman.* Yes, my dear.

*Amal.* Say, what's going on there in that big house on the other side, where there is a flag flying high up and the people are always going in and out?

*Watchman.* Oh, there? That's our new Post Office.

*Amal.* Post Office? Whose?

*Watchman.* Whose? Why, the King's, surely!

*Amal.* Do letters come from the King to his office here?

*Watchman.* Of course. One fine day there may be a letter for you in there.

*Amal.* A letter for me? But I am only a little boy.

*Watchman.* The King sends tiny notes to little boys.

*Amal.* Oh, how splendid! When shall I have my letter? How do you know he'll write to me?

*Watchman.* Otherwise why should he set his Post Office here right in front of your open window, with the golden flag flying?

*Amal.* But who will fetch me my King's letter when it comes?

*Watchman.* The King has many postmen. Don't you see them run about with round gilt badges on their chests?

*Amal.* Well, where do they go?

*Watchman.* Oh, from door to door, all through the country.

*Amal.* I'll be the King's postman when I grow up.

*Watchman.* Ha! ha! Postman, indeed! Rain or shine, rich or poor, from house to house delivering letters— that's very great work!

*Amal.* That's what I'd like best. What makes you smile so? Oh, yes, your work is great too. When it is silent everywhere in the heat of the noonday, your gong sounds, Dong, dong, dong,—and sometimes when I wake up at night all of a sudden and find our lamp blown out, I can hear through the darkness your gong slowly sounding, Dong, dong, dong!

*Watchman.* There's the village headman! I must be off. If he catches me gossiping there'll be a great to-do.

*Amal.* The headman? Whereabouts is he?

*Watchman.* Right down the road there; see that huge palm-leaf umbrella hopping along? That's him!

*Amal.* I suppose the King's made him our headman here?

*Watchman.* Made him? Oh, no! A fussy busybody! He knows so many ways of making himself unpleasant that everybody is afraid of him. It's just a game for the likes of him, making trouble for everybody. I must be off now! Mustn't keep work waiting, you know! I'll drop in again to-morrow morning and tell you all the news of the town. [*Exit*

*Amal.* It would be splendid to have a letter from the King every day. I'll read them at the window. But, oh! I can't read writing. Who'll read them out to me, I wonder! Auntie reads her *Ramayana*; she may know the King's writing. If no one will, then I must keep them carefully and read them when I'm grown up. But if the postman can't find me? Headman, Mr. Headman, may I have a word with you?

*Headman.* Who is yelling after me on the highway? Oh, it's you, is it, you wretched monkey?

*Amal.* You're the headman. Everybody minds you.

*Headman* (*looking pleased*). Yes, oh yes, they do! They must!

236

*Amal.* Do the King's postmen listen to you?

*Headman.* They've got to. By Jove, I'd like to see——

*Amal.* Will you tell the postman it's Amal who sits by the window here?

*Headman.* What's the good of that?

*Amal.* In case there's a letter for me.

*Headman.* A letter for you! Whoever's going to write to you?

*Amal.* If the King does.

*Headman.* Ha! ha! What an uncommon little fellow you are! Ha! ha! the King, indeed; aren't you his bosom friend, eh! You haven't met for a long while and the King is pining for you, I am sure. Wait till to-morrow and you'll have your letter.

*Amal.* Say, Headman, why do you speak to me in that tone of voice? Are you cross?

*Headman.* Upon my word! Cross, indeed! You write to the King! Madhav is a devilish swell nowadays. He's made a little pile; and so kings and padishahs are everyday talk with his people. Let me find him once and I'll make him dance. Oh, you,—you snipper-snapper! I'll get the King's letter sent to your house—indeed I will!

*Amal.* No, no, please don't trouble yourself about it.

*Headman.* And why not, pray! I'll tell the King about you and he won't be long. One of his footmen will come presently for news of you. Madhav's impudence staggers me. If the King hears of this, that'll take some of his nonsense out of him.                [*Exit*

*Amal.* Who are you walking there? How your anklets tinkle! Do stop a while, won't you?

(*A Girl enters*)

237

*Girl.* I haven't a moment to spare; it is already late!

*Amal.* I see, you don't wish to stop; I don't care to stay on here either.

*Girl.* You make me think of some late star of the morning! Whatever's the matter with you?

*Amal.* I don't know; the doctor won't let me out.

*Girl.* Ah me! Don't go, then! Should listen to the doctor. People will be cross with you if you're naughty. I know, always looking out and watching must make you feel tired. Let me close the window a bit for you.

*Amal.* No, don't, only this one's open! All the others are shut. But will you tell me who you are? Don't seem to know you.

*Girl.* I am Sudha.

*Amal.* What Sudha?

*Sudha.* Don't you know? Daughter of the flower-seller here.

*Amal.* What do *you* do?

*Sudha.* I gather flowers in my basket.

*Amal.* Oh, flower-gathering! That is why your feet seem so glad and your anklets jingle so merrily as you walk. Wish I could be out too. Then I would pick some flowers for you from the very topmost branches right out of sight.

*Sudha.* Would you really? Do you know as much about flowers as I?

*Amal.* Yes, I *do*, quite as much. I know all about Champa of the fairy tale and his six brothers. If only they let me, I'll go right into the dense forest where you can't find your way. And where the honey-sipping humming-bird rocks himself on the end of the thinnest branch, I will blossom into a *champa*. Would you be my sister Parul?

*Sudha*. You are silly! How can I be sister Parul when I am Sudha and my mother is Sasi, the flower-seller? I have to weave so many garlands a day. It would be jolly if I could lounge here like you!

*Amal*. What would you do then, all the day long?

*Sudha*. I could have great times with my doll Benay the bride, and Meni the pussy-cat, and—but I say, it is getting late and I mustn't stop, or I won't find a single flower.

*Amal*. Oh, wait a little longer; I do like it so!

*Sudha*. Ah, well—now don't you be naughty. Be good and sit still, and on my way back home with the flowers I'll come and talk with you.

*Amal*. And you'll let me have a flower, then?

*Sudha*. No, how can I? It has to be paid for.

*Amal*. I'll pay when I grow up—before I leave to look for work out on the other side of that stream there.

*Sudha*. Very well, then.

*Amal*. And you'll come back when you have your flowers?

*Sudha*. I will.

*Amal*. You will, really?

*Sudha*. Yes, I will.

*Amal*. You won't forget me? I am Amal, remember that.

*Sudha*. I won't forget you, you'll see.          [*Exit*
          (*A Troop of Boys enter*)

*Amal*. Say, brothers, where are you all off to? Stop here a little.

*A Boy*. We're off to play.

*Amal*. What will you play at, brothers?

239

*A Boy.* We'll play at being ploughmen.

*Another Boy* (*showing a stick*). This is our ploughshare.

*Another Boy.* We two are the pair of oxen.

*Amal.* And you're going to play the whole day?

*A Boy.* Yes, all day long.

*Amal.* And you will come home in the evening by the road along the river bank?

*A Boy.* Yes.

*Amal.* Do you pass our house on your way home?

*A Boy.* Come out and play with us; yes, do.

*Amal.* Doctor won't let me out.

*A Boy.* Doctor! Do you mean to say you mind what the doctor says? Let's be off; it is getting late.

*Amal.* Don't go. Play on the road near this window. I could watch you, then.

*A Boy.* What can we play at here?

*Amal.* With all these toys of mine that are lying about. Here you are; have them. I can't play alone. They are getting dirty and are of no use to me.

*Boys.* How jolly! What fine toys! Look, here's a ship. There's old mother Jatai. Isn't this a gorgeous sepoy? And you'll let us have them all? You don't really mind?

*Amal.* No, not a bit; have them by all means.

*A Boy.* You don't want them back?

*Amal.* Oh, no, I shan't want them.

*A Boy.* Say, won't you get a scolding for this?

*Amal.* No one will scold me. But will you play with them in front of our door for a while every morning? I'll get you new ones when these are old.

*A Boy.* Oh, yes, we will. I say, put these sepoys into a line. We'll play at war; where can we get a musket? Oh, look here, this bit of reed will do nicely. Say, but you're off to sleep already.

*Amal.* I'm afraid I'm sleepy. I don't know, I feel like it at times. I have been sitting a long while and I'm tired; my back aches.

*A Boy.* It's hardly midday now. How is it you're sleepy? Listen! The gong's sounding the first watch.

*Amal.* Yes, Dong, dong, dong; it tolls me to sleep.

*A Boy.* We had better go, then. We'll come in again to-morrow morning.

*Amal.* I want to ask you something before you go. You are always out—do you know of the King's postmen?

*Boys.* Yes, quite well.

*Amal.* Who are they? Tell me their names.

*A Boy.* One's Badal.

*Another Boy.* Another's Sarat.

*Another Boy.* There's so many of them.

*Amal.* Do you think they will know me if there's a letter for me?

*A Boy.* Surely, if your name's on the letter they will find you out.

*Amal.* When you call in to-morrow morning, will you bring one of them along so that he'll know me?

*A Boy.* Yes, if you like.

**CURTAIN**

# ACT II

### (*Amal in Bed*)

*Amal.* Can't I go near the window to-day, Uncle? Would the doctor mind that too?

*Madhav.* Yes, darling; you see you've made yourself worse squatting there day after day.

*Amal.* Oh, no, I don't know if it's made me more ill, but I always feel well when I'm there.

*Madhav.* No, you don't; you squat there and make friends with the whole lot of people round here, old and young, as if they are holding a fair right under my eaves—flesh and blood won't stand that strain. Just see —your face is quite pale.

*Amal.* Uncle, I fear my fakir 'll pass and not see me by the window.

*Madhav.* Your fakir; whoever's that?

*Amal.* He comes and chats to me of the many lands where he's been. I love to hear him.

*Madhav.* How's that? I don't know of any fakirs.

*Amal.* This is about the time he comes in. I beg of you, by your dear feet, ask him in for a moment to talk to me here.

### (*Gaffer enters in a Fakir's guise*)

*Amal.* There you are. Come here, Fakir, by my bed-side.

*Madhav.* Upon my word, but this is——

*Gaffer* (*winking hard*). I am the Fakir.

*Madhav.* It beats my reckoning what you're not.

*Amal.* Where have you been this time, Fakir?

*Gaffer.* To the Isle of Parrots. I am just back.

*Madhav.* The Parrots' Isle!

*Gaffer.* Is it so very astonishing? I am not like you. A

journey doesn't cost a thing. I tramp just where I like.

*Amal (clapping).* How jolly for you! Remember your promise to take me with you as your follower when I'm well.

*Gaffer.* Of course, and I'll teach you so many travellers' secrets that nothing in sea or forest or mountain can bar your way.

*Madhav.* What's all this rigmarole?

*Gaffer.* Amal, my dear, I bow to nothing in sea or mountain; but if the doctor joins in with this uncle of yours, then I with all my magic must own myself beaten.

*Amal.* No. Uncle won't tell the doctor. And I promise to lie quiet; but the day I am well, off I go with the Fakir, and nothing in sea or mountain or torrent shall stand in my way.

*Madhav.* Fie, dear child, don't keep on harping upon going! It makes me so sad to hear you talk so.

*Amal.* Tell me, Fakir, what the Parrots' Isle is like.

*Gaffer.* It's a land of wonders; it's a haunt of birds. No men are there; and they neither speak nor walk, they simply sing and they fly.

*Amal.* How glorious! And it's by some sea?

*Gaffer.* Of course. It's on the sea.

*Amal.* And green hills are there?

*Gaffer.* Indeed, they live among the green hills; and in the time of the sunset when there is a red glow on the hillside, all the birds with their green wings go flocking to their nests.

*Amal.* And there are waterfalls!

*Gaffer.* Dear me, of course; you don't have a hill

without its waterfalls. Oh, it's like molten diamonds; and, my dear, what dances they have! Don't they make the pebbles sing as they rush over them to the sea! No devil of a doctor can stop them for a moment. The birds looked upon me as nothing but a man, merely a trifling creature without wings—and they would have nothing to do with me. Were it not so I would build a small cabin for myself among their crowd of nests and pass my days counting the sea-waves.

*Amal.* How I wish I were a bird! Then——

*Gaffer.* But that would have been a bit of a job; I hear you've fixed up with the dairyman to be a hawker of curds when you grow up; I'm afraid such business won't flourish among birds; you might land yourself into serious loss.

*Madhav.* Really this is too much. Between you two I shall turn crazy. Now, I'm off.

*Amal.* Has the dairyman been, Uncle?

*Madhav.* And why shouldn't he? He won't bother his head running errands for your pet fakir, in and out among the nests in his Parrots' Isle. But he has left a jar of curds for you saying that he is busy with his niece's wedding in the village, and has to order a band at Kamlipara.

*Amal.* But he is going to marry me to his little niece.

*Gaffer.* Dear me, we are in a fix now.

*Amal.* He said she would be my lovely little bride with a pair of pearl drops in her ears and dressed in a lovely red saree; and in the morning she would milk with her own hands the black cow and feed me with warm milk with foam on it from a brand-new earthen cruse; and in the evenings she would carry the lamp round the cow-house, and then come and sit by me to tell me tales of Champa and his six brothers.

*Gaffer*. How charming! It would even tempt me, a hermit! But never mind, dear, about this wedding. Let it be. I tell you that when you marry there'll be no lack of nieces in his household.

*Madhav*. Shut up! This is more than I can stand.

[*Exit*

*Amal*. Fakir, now that Uncle's off, just tell me, has the King sent me a letter to the Post Office?

*Gaffer*. I gather that his letter has already started; it is on the way here.

*Amal*. On the way? Where is it? Is it on that road winding through the trees which you can follow to the end of the forest when the sky is quite clear after rain?

*Gaffer*. That is where it is. You know all about it already.

*Amal*. I do, everything.

*Gaffer*. So I see, but how?

*Amal*. I can't say; but it's quite clear to me. I fancy I've seen it often in days long gone by. How long ago I can't tell. Do you know when? I can see it all: there, the King's postman coming down the hillside alone, a lantern in his left hand and on his back a bag of letters; climbing down for ever so long, for days and nights, and where at the foot of the mountain the waterfall becomes a stream he takes to the footpath on the bank and walks on through the rye; then comes the sugar-cane field and he disappears into the narrow lane cutting through the tall stems of sugar-canes; then he reaches the open meadow where the cricket chirps and where there is not a single man to be seen, only the snipe wagging their tails and poking at the mud with their bills. I can feel him coming nearer and nearer and my heart becomes glad.

*Gaffer.* My eyes are not young; but you make me see all the same.

*Amal.* Say, Fakir, do you know the King who has this Post Office?

*Gaffer.* I do; I go to him for my alms every day.

*Amal.* Good! When I get well I must have my alms too from him, mayn't I?

*Gaffer.* You won't need to ask, my dear; he'll give it to you of his own accord.

*Amal.* No, I will go to his gate and cry, "Victory to thee, O King!" and dancing to the tabor's sound, ask for alms. Won't it be nice?

*Gaffer.* It will be splendid, and if you're with me I shall have my full share. But what will you ask?

*Amal.* I shall say, "Make me your postman, that I may go about, lantern in hand, delivering your letters from door to door. Don't let me stay at home all day!"

*Gaffer.* What is there to be sad for, my child, even were you to stay at home?

*Amal.* It isn't sad. When they shut me in here first I felt the day was so long. Since the King's Post Office was put there I like more and more being indoors, and as I think I shall get a letter one day, I feel quite happy and then I don't mind being quiet and alone. I wonder if I shall make out what'll be in the King's letter?

*Gaffer.* Even if you didn't wouldn't it be enough if it just bore your name?

*(Madhav enters)*

*Madhav.* Have you any idea of the trouble you've got me into, between you two?

246

*Gaffer.* What's the matter?

*Madhav.* I hear you've let it get rumoured about that the King has planted his office here to send messages to both of you.

*Gaffer.* Well, what about it?

*Madhav.* Our headman Panchanan has had it told to the King anonymously.

*Gaffer.* Aren't we aware that everything reaches the King's ears?

*Madhav.* Then why don't you look out? Why take the King's name in vain? You'll bring me to ruin if you do.

*Amal.* Say, Fakir, will the King be cross?

*Gaffer.* Cross, nonsense! And with a child like you and a fakir such as I am? Let's see if the King be angry, and then won't I give him a piece of my mind!

*Amal.* Say, Fakir, I've been feeling a sort of darkness coming over my eyes since the morning. Everything seems like a dream. I long to be quiet. I don't feel like talking at all. Won't the King's letter come? Suppose this room melts away all on a sudden, suppose——

*Gaffer (fanning Amal).* The letter's sure to come to-day, my boy.

(*Doctor enters*)

*Doctor.* And how do you feel to-day?

*Amal.* Feel awfully well to-day, Doctor. All pain seems to have left me.

*Doctor (aside to Madhav).* Don't quite like the look of that smile. Bad sign that, his feeling well! Chakradhan has observed——

*Madhav.* For goodness' sake, Doctor, leave Chakradhan alone. Tell me what's going to happen?

*Doctor.* Can't hold him in much longer, I fear! I warned you before—this looks like a fresh exposure.

247

*Madhav.* No, I've used the utmost care, never let him out of doors; and the windows have been shut almost all the time.

*Doctor.* There's a peculiar quality in the air to-day. As I came in I found a fearful draught through your front door. That's most hurtful. Better lock it at once. Would it matter if this kept your visitors off for two or three days? If some one happens to call unexpectedly— there's the back door. You had better shut this window as well, it's letting in the sunset rays only to keep the patient awake.

*Madhav.* Amal has shut his eyes. I expect he is sleeping. His face tells me—— Oh, Doctor, I bring in a child who is a stranger and love him as my own, and now I suppose I must lose him!

*Doctor.* What's that? There's your headman sailing in! —What a bother! I must be going, brother. You had better stir about and see to the doors being properly fastened. I will send on a strong dose directly I get home. Try it on him—it may save him at last, if he can be saved at all.　　　　　[*Exeunt Madhav and Doctor*

(*The Headman enters*)

*Headman.* Hello, urchin!——

*Gaffer* (*rising hastily*). 'Sh, be quiet.

*Amal.* No, Fakir, did you think I was asleep? I wasn't. I can hear everything; yes, and voices far away. I feel that mother and father are sitting by my pillow and speaking to me.

(*Madhav enters*)

*Headman.* I say, Madhav, I hear you hobnob with bigwigs nowadays.

*Madhav.* Spare me your jokes, Headman; we are but common people.

*Headman.* But your child here is expecting a letter from the King.

*Madhav.* Don't you take any notice of him, a mere foolish boy!

*Headman.* Indeed, why not! It'll beat the King hard to find a better family! Don't you see why the King plants his new Post Office right before your window? Why, there's a letter for you from the King, urchin.

*Amal (starting up).* Indeed, really!

*Headman.* How can it be false? You're the King's chum. Here's your letter (*showing a blank slip of paper*). Ha, ha, ha! This is the letter.

*Amal.* Please don't mock me. Say, Fakir, is it so?

*Gaffer.* Yes, my dear. I as Fakir tell you it *is* his letter.

*Amal.* How is it I can't see? It all looks so blank to me. What is there in the letter, Mr. Headman?

*Headman.* The King says, "I am calling on you shortly; you had better have puffed rice for me.—Palace fare is quite tasteless to me now." Ha! ha! ha!

*Madhav (with folded palms).* I beseech you, Headman, don't you joke about these things——

*Gaffer.* Joking indeed! He would not dare.

*Madhav.* Are you out of your mind too, Gaffer?

*Gaffer.* Out of my mind; well then, I am; I can read plainly that the King writes he will come himself to see Amal, with the State Physician.

*Amal.* Fakir, Fakir, 'sh, his trumpet! Can't you hear?

*Headman.* Ha! ha! ha! I fear he won't until he's a bit more off his head.

*Amal.* Mr. Headman, I thought you were cross with me and didn't love me. I never could have believed you would fetch me the King's letter. Let me wipe the dust off your feet.

*Headman.* This little child does have an instinct of reverence. Though a little silly, he has a good heart.

*Amal.* It's hard on the fourth watch now, I suppose. Hark, the gong, "Dong, dong, ding—Dong, dong, ding." Is the evening star up? How is it I can't see——

*Gaffer.* Oh, the windows are all shut; I'll open them.

          *(A knocking outside)*

*Madhav.* What's that?—Who is it?—What a bother!

*Voice (from outside).* Open the door.

*Madhav.* Headman—I hope they're not robbers.

*Headman.* Who's there?—It is Panchanan, the headman, who calls.—Aren't you afraid to make that noise? Fancy! The noise has ceased! Panchanan's voice carries far.—Yes, show me the biggest robbers!——

*Madhav (peering out of the window).* No wonder the noise has ceased. They've smashed the outer door.

          *(The King's Herald enters)*

*Herald.* Our Sovereign King comes to-night!

*Headman.* My God!

*Amal.* At what hour of the night, Herald?

*Herald.* On the second watch.

*Amal.* When my friend the watchman will strike his gong from the city gates, "Ding dong ding, ding dong ding"—then?

*Herald.* Yes, then. The King sends his greatest physician to attend on his young friend.

          *(State Physician enters)*

*State Physician.* What's this? How close it is here! Open wide all the doors and windows. *(Feeling Amal's body.)* How do you feel, my child?

*Amal.* I feel very well, Doctor, very well. All pain is

gone. How fresh and open! I can see all the stars now twinkling from the other side of the dark.

*Physician.* Will you feel well enough to leave your bed when the King comes in the middle watches of the night?

*Amal.* Of course, I'm dying to be about for ever so long. I'll ask the King to find me the polar star.—I must have seen it often, but I don't know exactly which it is.

*Physician.* He will tell you everything. (*To Madhav.*) Arrange flowers through the room for the King's visit. (*Indicating the Headman.*) We can't have that person in here.

*Amal.* No, let him be, Doctor. He is a friend. It was he who brought me the King's letter.

*Physician.* Very well, my child. He may remain if he is a friend of yours.

*Madhav* (*whispering into Amal's ear*). My child, the King loves you. He is coming himself. Beg for a gift from him. You know our humble circumstances.

*Amal.* Don't you worry, Uncle.—I've made up my mind about it.

*Madhav.* What is it, my child?

*Amal.* I shall ask him to make me one of his postmen that I may wander far and wide, delivering his message from door to door.

*Madhav* (*slapping his forehead*). Alas, is that all?

*Amal.* What'll be our offerings to the King, Uncle, when he comes?

*Herald.* He has commanded puffed rice.

*Amal.* Puffed rice. Say, Headman, you're right. You said so. You knew all we didn't.

*Headman.* If you would send word to my house I could manage for the King's advent really nice——

*Physician.* No need at all. Now be quiet, all of you. Sleep is coming over him. I'll sit by his pillow; he's dropping asleep. Blow out the oil-lamp. Only let the star-light stream in. Hush, he sleeps.

*Madhav (addressing Gaffer).* What are you standing there for like a statue, folding your palms?—I am nervous.—Say, are there good omens? Why are they darkening the room? How will star-light help?

*Gaffer.* Silence, unbeliever!

(*Sudha enters*)

*Sudha.* Amal!

*Physician.* He's asleep.

*Sudha.* I have some flowers for him. Mayn't I give them into his own hand?

*Physician.* Yes, you may.

*Sudha.* When will he be awake?

*Physician.* Directly the King comes and calls him.

*Sudha.* Will you whisper a word for me in his ear?

*Physician.* What shall I say?

*Sudha.* Tell him Sudha has not forgotten him.

**CURTAIN**

# LOVER'S GIFT

# LOVER'S GIFT

. . . . .

## II

COME to my garden walk, my love. Pass by the fervid flowers that press themselves on your sight. Pass them by, stopping at some chance joy, which like a sudden wonder of sunset illumines, yet eludes.

For love's gift is shy, it never tells its name, it flits across the shade, spreading a shiver of joy along the dust. Overtake it or miss it for ever. But a gift that can be grasped is merely a frail flower, or a lamp with a flame that will flicker.

. . . . .

## IV

SHE is near to my heart as the meadow-flower to the earth; she is sweet to me as sleep is to tired limbs. My love for her is my life flowing in its fullness, like a river in autumn flood, running with serene abandonment. My songs are one with my love, like the murmur of a stream, that sings with all its waves and currents.

## V

I WOULD ask for still more, if I had the sky with all its stars, and the world with its endless riches; but I would

be content with the smallest corner of this earth if only
she were mine.

   •  •  •  "  •

## VIII

THERE is room for you. You are alone with your few
sheaves of rice. My boat is crowded, it is heavily laden,
but how can I turn you away? your young body is slim
and swaying; there is a twinkling smile in the edge
of your eyes, and your robe is coloured like the rain-
cloud.

 The travellers will land for different roads and homes.
You will sit for a while on the prow of my boat, and at
the journey's end none will keep you back.

 Where do you go, and to what home, to garner your
sheaves? I will not question you, but when I fold my
sails and moor my boat I shall sit and wonder in the
evening,—Where do you go, and to what home, to
garner your sheaves?

   •  •  •  •  •

## XIII

LAST night in the garden I offered you my youth's
foaming wine. You lifted the cup to your lips, you shut
your eyes and smiled while I raised your veil, unbound
your tresses, drawing down upon my breast your face
sweet with its silence, last night when the moon's dream
overflowed the world of slumber.

 To-day in the dew-cooled calm of the dawn you are
walking to God's temple, bathed and robed in white,
with a basketful of flowers in your hand. I stand aside in

the shade under the tree, with my head bent, in the calm of the dawn by the lonely road to the temple.

· · · · ·

## XVI

SHE dwelt here by the pool with its landing-stairs in ruins. Many an evening she had watched the moon made dizzy by the shaking of bamboo leaves, and on many a rainy day the smell of the wet earth had come to her over the young shoots of rice.

Her pet name is known here among those date-palm groves and in the courtyards where girls sit and talk while stitching their winter quilts. The water in this pool keeps in its depth the memory of her swimming limbs, and her wet feet had left their marks, day after day, on the footpath leading to the village.

The women who come to-day with their vessels to the water have all seen her smile over simple jests, and the old peasant, taking his bullocks to their bath, used to stop at her door every day to greet her.

Many a sailing-boat passes by this village; many a traveller takes rest beneath that banyan tree; the ferry-boat crosses to yonder ford carrying crowds to the market; but they never notice this spot by the village road, near the pool with its ruined landing-stairs,— where dwelt she whom I love.

· · · · ·

## XVIII

YOUR days will be full of cares, if you must give me your heart. My house by the cross-roads has its doors open and my mind is absent,—for I sing.

I shall never be made to answer for it, if you must give me your heart. If I pledge my word to you in tunes now, and am too much in earnest to keep it when music is silent, you must forgive me; for the law laid down in May is best broken in December.

Do not always keep remembering it, if you must give me your heart. When your eyes sing with love, and your voice ripples with laughter, my answers to your questions will be wild, and not miserly accurate in facts,—they are to be believed for ever and then forgotten for good.

## XIX

IT is written in the book that Man, when fifty, must leave the noisy world, to go to the forest seclusion. But the poet proclaims that the forest hermitage is only for the young. For it is the birthplace of flowers and the haunt of birds and bees; and hidden nooks are waiting there for the thrill of lovers' whispers. There the moonlight, that is all one kiss for the *mālati* flowers, has its deep message, but those who understand it are far below fifty.

And alas, youth is inexperienced and wilful, therefore it is but meet that the old should take charge of the household, and the young take to the seclusion of forest shades and the severe discipline of courting.

·   ·   ·   ·   ·

## XXII

I SHALL gladly suffer the pride of culture to die out in my house, if only in some happy future I am born a herd-boy in the Brinda forest.

258

The herd-boy who grazes his cattle sitting under the banyan tree, and idly weaves *gunja* flowers into garlands, who loves to splash and plunge in the Jamuna's cool deep stream.

He calls his companions to wake up when morning dawns, and all the houses in the lane hum with the sound of the churn, clouds of dust are raised by the cattle, the maidens come out in the courtyard to milk the kine.

As the shadows deepen under the *tomal* trees, and the dusk gathers on the river-banks; when the milkmaids, while crossing the turbulent water, tremble with fear; and loud peacocks, with tails outspread, dance in the forest, he watches the summer clouds.

When the April night is sweet as a fresh-blown flower, he disappears in the forest with a peacock's plume in his hair; the swing ropes are twined with flowers on the branches; the south wind throbs with music, and the merry shepherd boys crowd on the banks of the blue river.

No, I will never be the leader, brothers, of this new age of new Bengal; I shall not trouble to light the lamp of culture for the benighted. If only I could be born, under the shady *asoka* groves, in some village of Brinda, where milk is churned by the maidens!

. . . . . . . . . .

## XXVIII

I DREAMT that she sat by my head, tenderly ruffling my hair with her fingers, playing the melody of her touch. I looked at her face and struggled with my tears, till the agony of unspoken words burst my sleep like a bubble.

I sat up and saw the glow of the Milky Way above my window, like a world of silence on fire, and I wondered if at this moment she had a dream that rhymed with mine.

·        ·        ·        ·        ·

### XXXIX

THERE is a looker-on who sits behind my eyes. It seems he has seen things in ages and worlds beyond memory's shore, and those forgotten sights glisten on the grass and shiver on the leaves. He has seen under new veils the face of the one beloved, in twilight hours of many a nameless star. Therefore his sky seems to ache with the pain of countless meetings and partings, and a longing pervades this spring breeze,—the longing that is full of the whisper of ages without beginning.

### XL

A MESSAGE came from my youth of vanished days, saying, "I wait for you among the quiverings of unborn May, where smiles ripen for tears and hours ache with songs unsung."

It says, "Come to me across the worn-out track of age, through the gates of death. For dreams fade, hopes fail, the gathered fruits of the year decay, but I am the eternal truth, and you shall meet me again and again in your voyage of life from shore to shore."

·        ·        ·        ·        ·

ARE you a mere picture, and not as true as those stars, true as this dust? They throb with the pulse of things, but you are immensely aloof in your stillness, painted form.

The day was when you walked with me, your breath warm, your limbs singing of life. My world found its speech in your voice, and touched my heart with your face. You suddenly stopped in your walk, in the shadow-side of the Forever, and I went on alone.

Life, like a child, laughs, shaking its rattle of death as it runs; it beckons me on, I follow the unseen; but you stand there, where you stopped behind that dust and those stars; and you are a mere picture.

No, it cannot be. Had the life-flood utterly stopped in you, it would stop the river in its flow, and the foot-fall of dawn in her cadence of colours. Had the glimmering dusk of your hair vanished in the hopeless dark, the woodland shade of summer would die with its dreams.

Can it be true that I forgot you? We haste on without heed, forgetting the flowers on the roadside hedge. Yet they breathe unaware into our forgetfulness, filling it with music. You have moved from my world, to take seat at the root of my life, and therefore is this forgetting—remembrance lost in its own depth.

You are no longer before my songs, but one with them. You came to me with the first ray of dawn. I lost you with the last gold of evening. Ever since I am always finding you through the dark. No, you are no mere picture.

DYING, you have left behind you the great sadness of
the Eternal in my life. You have painted my thought's
horizon with the sunset colours of your departure,
leaving a track of tears across the earth to love's heaven.
Clasped in your dear arms, life and death united in me
in a marriage bond.

I think I can see you watching there in the balcony
with your lamp lighted, where the end and the beginning of all things meet. My world went hence through
the doors that you opened—you holding the cup of
death to my lips, filling it with life from your own.

· · · · ·

## XLVII

THE road is my wedded companion. She speaks to me
under my feet all day, she sings to my dreams all night.

My meeting with her had no beginning, it begins
endlessly at each daybreak, renewing its summer in
fresh flowers and songs, and her every new kiss is the
first kiss to me.

The road and I are lovers. I change my dress for her
night after night, leaving the tattered cumber of the
old in the wayside inns when the day dawns.

## XLVIII

I TRAVELLED the old road every day, I took my fruits to
the market, my cattle to the meadows, I ferried my boat
across the stream and all the ways were well known to
me.

One morning my basket was heavy with wares. Men

were busy in the fields, the pastures crowded with cattle; the breast of earth heaved with the mirth of ripening rice.

Suddenly there was a tremor in the air, and the sky seemed to kiss me on my forehead. My mind started up like the morning out of mist.

I forgot to follow the track. I stepped a few paces from the path, and my familiar world appeared strange to me, like a flower I had only known in bud.

My everyday wisdom was ashamed. I went astray in the fairyland of things. It was the best luck of my life that I lost my path that morning, and found my eternal childhood.

## XLIX

WHERE is heaven? you ask me, my child,—the sages tell us it is beyond the limits of birth and death, unswayed by the rhythm of day and night; it is not of this earth.

But your poet knows that its eternal hunger is for time and space, and it strives evermore to be born in the fruitful dust. Heaven is fulfilled in your sweet body, my child, in your palpitating heart.

The sea is beating its drums in joy, the flowers are a-tiptoe to kiss you. For heaven is born in you, in the arms of the mother-dust.

. . . . .

## LII

TIRED of waiting, you burst your bonds, impatient flowers, before the winter had gone. Glimpses of the unseen comer reached your wayside watch, and you

263

rushed out running and panting, impulsive jasmines, troops of riotous roses.

You were the first to march to the breach of death, your clamour of colour and perfume troubled the air. You laughed and pressed and pushed each other, bared your breast and dropped in heaps.

The Summer will come in its time, sailing in the flood-tide of the south wind. But you never counted slow moments to be sure of him. You recklessly spent your all in the road, in the terrible joy of faith.

You heard his footsteps from afar, and flung your mantle of death for him to tread upon. Your bonds break even before the rescuer is seen, you make him your own ere he can come and claim you.

· · · · ·

## LIV

IN the beginning of time, there rose from the churning of God's dream two women. One is the dancer at the court of paradise, the desired of men, she who laughs and plucks the minds of the wise from their cold meditations and of fools from their emptiness; and scatters them like seeds with careless hands in the extravagant winds of March, in the flowering frenzy of May.

The other is the crowned queen of heaven, the mother, throned on the fullness of golden autumn; she who in the harvest-time brings straying hearts to the smile sweet as tears, the beauty deep as the sea of silence,—brings them to the temple of the Unknown, at the holy confluence of Life and Death.

· · · · ·

## LVI

THE evening was lonely for me, and I was reading a book till my heart became dry, and it seemed to me that beauty was a thing fashioned by the traders in words. Tired I shut the book and snuffed the candle. In a moment the room was flooded with moonlight.

Spirit of Beauty, how could you, whose radiance overbrims the sky, stand hidden behind a candle's tiny flame? How could a few vain words from a book rise like a mist, and veil her whose voice has hushed the heart of earth into ineffable calm?

.    .    .    .    .

## LVIII

THINGS throng and laugh loud in the sky; the sands and dust dance and whirl like children. Man's mind is aroused by their shouts; his thoughts long to be the playmates of things.

Our dreams, drifting in the stream of the vague, stretch their arms to clutch the earth,—their efforts stiffen into bricks and stones, and thus the city of man is built.

Voices come swarming from the past,—seeking answers from the living moments. Beats of their wings fill the air with tremulous shadows, and sleepless thoughts in our minds leave their nests to take flight across the desert of dimness, in the passionate thirst for forms. They are lampless pilgrims, seeking the shore of light, to find themselves in things. They will be lured into poets' rhymes, they will be housed in the towers of the town not yet planned, they have their call to arms from the battlefields of the future, they are bidden to join hands in the strifes of peace yet to come.

·     ·     ·     ·     ·

## LX

TAKE back your coins, King's Councillor. I am of those women you sent to the forest shrine to decoy the young ascetic who had never seen a woman. I failed in your bidding.

Dimly day was breaking when the hermit boy came to bathe in the stream, his tawny locks crowded on his shoulders, like a cluster of morning clouds, and his limbs shining like a streak of sunbeam. We laughed and sang as we rowed in our boat; we jumped into the river in a mad frolic, and danced around him, when the sun rose staring at us from the water's edge in a flush of divine anger.

Like a child-god, the boy opened his eyes and watched our movements, the wonder deepening till his eyes shone like morning stars. He lifted his clasped hands and chanted a hymn of praise in his bird-like young voice, thrilling every leaf of the forest. Never such words were sung to a mortal woman before; they were like the silent hymn to the dawn which rises from the hushed hills.  The women hid their mouths with their hands, their bodies swaying with laughter, and a spasm of doubt ran across his face. Quickly came I to his side, sorely pained, and, bowing to his feet, I said, "Lord, accept my service."

I led him to the grassy bank, wiped his body with the end of my silken mantle, and, kneeling on the ground, I dried his feet with my trailing hair. When I raised my face and looked into his eyes, I thought I felt the world's first kiss to the first woman,—Blessed am I, blessed is God, who made me a woman. I heard him say to me, "What God unknown are you? Your touch is the touch of the Immortal, your eyes have the mystery of the midnight."

Ah, no, not that smile, King's Councillor,—the dust of worldly wisdom has covered your sight, old man. But this boy's innocence pierced the mist and saw the shining truth, the woman divine. . . .

The women clapped their hands, and laughed their obscene laugh, and with veils dragging on the dust and hair hanging loose they began to pelt him with flowers.

Alas, my spotless sun, could not my shame weave fiery mist to cover you in its folds? I fell at his feet and cried, "Forgive me." I fled like a stricken deer through shade and sun, and cried as I fled, "Forgive me." The women's foul laughter pressed me like a crackling fire, but the words ever rang in my ears, "What God unknown are you?"

# CROSSING

# CROSSING

. . . . . .

## IV

ACCEPT me, my lord, accept me for this while.

Let those orphaned days that passed without thee be
forgotten.

Only spread this little moment wide across thy lap,
holding it under thy light.

I have wandered in pursuit of voices that drew me yet
led me nowhere.

Now let me sit in peace and listen to thy words in the
soul of my silence.

Do not turn away thy face from my heart's dark secrets,
but burn them till they are alight with thy fire.

## V

THE scouts of a distant storm have pitched their cloud-
tents in the sky; the light has paled; the air is damp
with tears in the voiceless shadows of the forest.

The peace of sadness is in my heart like the brooding
silence upon the master's lute before the music
begins.

My world is still with the expectation of the great pain
of thy coming into my life.

. . . . .

## VIII

THE lantern which I carry in my hand makes enemy of
the darkness of the farther road.

And this wayside becomes a terror to me, where even
the flowering tree frowns like a spectre of scowling
menace; and the sound of my own steps comes back
to me in the echo of muffled suspicion.

Therefore I pray for thy own morning light, when the
far and the near will kiss each other and death
and life will be one in love.

## IX

WHEN thou savest me the steps are lighter in the march
of thy worlds.

When stains are washed away from my heart it
brightens the light of thy sun.

That the bud has not blossomed in beauty in my life
spreads sadness in the heart of creation.

When the shroud of darkness will be lifted from my
soul it will bring music to thy smile.

## X

THOU hast given me thy love, filling the world with
thy gifts.

They are showered upon me when I do not know them,
for my heart is asleep and dark is the night.

Yet though lost in the cavern of my dreams I have been
thrilled with fitful gladness;

And I know that in return for the treasure of thy great
worlds thou wilt receive from me one little flower
of love in the morning when my heart awakes.

.   .   .   .   .

## XVII

Pick up this life of mine from the dust.

Keep it under your eyes, in the palm of your right
hand.

Hold it up in the light, hide it under the shadow of
death; keep it in the casket of the night with your
stars, and then in the morning let it find itself
among flowers that blossom in worship.

## XVIII

I know that this life, missing its ripeness in love, is not
altogether lost.

I know that the flowers that fade in the dawn, the
streams that strayed in the desert, are not altogether lost.

I know that whatever lags behind in this life laden with
slowness is not altogether lost.

I know that my dreams that are still unfulfilled, and
my melodies still unstruck, are clinging to some
lute-strings of thine, and they are not altogether
lost.

·     ·     ·     ·     ·

## XX

The day is dim with rain.

Angry lightnings glance through the tattered cloud-
veils

And the forest is like a caged lion shaking its mane in
despair.

On such a day amidst the winds beating their wings,
let me find my peace in thy presence,

For the sorrowing sky has shadowed my solitude, to
deepen the meaning of thy touch about my heart.

·   ·   ·   ·   ·

### XXIII

I CAME nearest to you, though I did not know it,—
when I came to hurt you.
I owned you at last as my master when I fought against
you to be defeated.
I merely made my debt to you burdensome when I
robbed you in secret.
I struggled in my pride against your current only to feel
all your force in my breast.
Rebelliously I put out the light in my house, and your
sky surprised me with its stars.

·   ·   ·   ·   ·

### XXV

I HID myself to evade you.
Now that I am caught at last, strike me, see if I flinch.
Finish the game for good.
If you win in the end, strip me of all that I have.
I have had my laughter and songs in wayside booths and
stately halls,—now that you have come into my life,
make me weep, see if you can break my heart.

### XXVI

WHEN I awake in thy love my night of ease will be
ended.
Thy sunrise will touch my heart with its touchstone of

fire, and my voyage will begin in its orbit of triumphant suffering.

I shall dare to take up death's challenge and carry thy voice in the heart of mockery and menace.

I shall bare my breast against the wrongs hurled at thy children, and take the risk of standing by thy side where none but thee remains.

.    .    .    .

## XXIX

I HAVE met thee where the night touches the edge of the day; where the light startles the darkness into dawn, and the waves carry the kiss of the one shore to the other.

From the heart of the fathomless blue comes one golden call, and across the dusk of tears I try to gaze at thy face and know not for certain if thou art seen.

## XXX

IF love be denied me then why does the morning break its heart in songs, and why are these whispers that the south wind scatters among the new-born leaves?

If love be denied me then why does the midnight bear in yearning silence the pain of the stars?

And why does this foolish heart recklessly launch its hope on the sea whose end it does not know?

## XXXIX

No guest had come to my house for long, my doors
were locked, my windows barred; I thought my
night would be lonely.

When I opened my eyes I found the darkness had
vanished.

I rose up and ran and saw the bolts of my gates all
broken, and through the open door your wind and
light waved their banner.

When I was a prisoner in my own house, and the doors
were shut, my heart ever planned to escape and to
wander.

Now at my broken gate I sit still and wait for your
coming.

You keep me bound by my freedom.

.    .    .    .    .

## XLII

FREE me as free are the birds of the wilds, the wanderers
of unseen paths.

Free me as free are the deluge of rain, and the storm
that shakes its locks and rushes on to its unknown
end.

Free me as free is the forest fire, as is the thunder that
laughs aloud and hurls defiance to darkness.

.    .    .    .    .

## XLVII

I LIVED on the shady side of the road and watched my
neighbours' gardens across the way revelling in the
sunshine.

I felt I was poor, and from door to door went with my
   hunger.

The more they gave me from their careless abundance
   the more I became aware of my beggar's bowl.

Till one morning I awoke from my sleep at the sudden
   opening of my door, and you came and asked for
   alms.

In despair I broke the lid of my chest open and was
   startled into finding my own wealth.

## XLVIII

THOU hast taken him to thine arms and crowned him
   with death, him who ever waited outside like a
   beggar at life's feast.

Thou hast put thy right hand on his failures and kissed
   him with peace that stills life's turbulent thirst.

Thou hast made him one with all kings and with the
   ancient world of wisdom.

·   ·   ·   ·   ·

## LIII

I HAVE come to thee to take thy touch before I begin
   my day.

Let thy eyes rest upon my eyes for awhile.

Let me take to my work the assurance of thy comradeship, my friend.

Fill my mind with thy music to last through the desert
   of noise!

Let thy Love's sunshine kiss the peaks of my thoughts
   and linger in my life's valley where the harvest
   ripens.

## LIV

STAND before my eyes, and let thy glance touch my
    songs into a flame.
Stand among thy stars and let me find kindled in their
    lights my own fire of worship.
The earth is waiting at the world's wayside;
Stand upon the green mantle she has flung upon thy
    path; and let me feel in her grass and meadow
    flowers the spread of my own salutation.
Stand in my lonely evening where my heart watches
    alone; fill her cup of solitude, and let me feel in
    me the infinity of thy love.

## LV

LET thy love play upon my voice and rest on my silence.
Let it pass through my heart into all my movements.
Let thy love like stars shine in the darkness of my sleep
    and dawn in my awakening.
Let it burn in the flame of my desires
And flow in all currents of my own love.
Let me carry thy love in my life as a harp does its music,
    and give it back to thee at last with my life.

## LVI

YOU hide yourself in your own glory, my King.
The sand-grain and the dew-drop are more proudly
    apparent than yourself.
The world unabashed calls all things its own that are
    yours—yet it is never brought to shame.
You make room for us while standing aside in silence;
    therefore love lights her own lamp to seek you and
    comes to your worship unbidden.

## LVII

WHEN from the house of feast I came back home, the
    spell of the midnight quieted the dance in my
    blood.
My heart became silent at once like a deserted theatre
    with its lamps out.
My mind crossed the dark and stood among the stars,
    and I saw that we were playing unafraid in the
    silent courtyard of our King's palace.

    •     •     •     •     •

## LX

WITH his morning songs he knocks at our door bringing
    his greetings of sunrise.
With him we take our cattle to the fields and play our
    flute in the shade.
We lose him to find him again and again in the market
    crowd.
In the busy hour of the day we come upon him of a
    sudden, sitting on the wayside grass.
We march when he beats his drum,
We dance when he sings.
We stake our joys and sorrows to play his game to the
    end.
He stands at the helm of our boat,
With him we rock on the perilous waves.
For him we light our lamp and wait when our day is
    done.

    •     •     •     •     •

## LXII

WHEN bells sounded in your temple in the morning,
  men and women hastened down the woodland path
  with their offerings of fresh flowers.
But I lay on the grass in the shade and let them pass by.
I think it was well that I was idle, for then my flowers
  were in bud.
At the end of the day they have bloomed, and I go to
  my evening worship.

. . . . .

## LXVIII

THERE are numerous strings in your lute, let me add
  my own among them.
Then when you smite your chords my heart will break
  its silence and my life will be one with your song.
Amidst your numberless stars let me place my own
  little lamp.
In the dance of your festival of lights my heart will
  throb and my life will be one with your smile.

## LXIX

LET my song be simple as the waking in the morning,
  as the dripping of dew from the leaves,
Simple as the colours in clouds and showers of rain in
  the midnight.
But my lute-strings are newly strung and they dart
  their notes like spears sharp in their newness.
Thus they miss the spirit of the wind and hurt the light
  of the sky; and these strains of my songs fight hard
  to push back thy own music.

## LXX

I HAVE seen thee play thy music in life's dancing-hall;
in the sudden leaf-burst of spring thy laughter has
come to greet me; and lying among field flowers I
have heard in the grass thy whisper.

The child has brought to my house the message of thy
hope, and the woman the music of thy love.

Now I am waiting on the seashore to feel thee in death,
to find life's refrain back again in the star-songs of
the night.

## LXXI

I REMEMBER my childhood when the sunrise, like my
play-fellow, would burst in to my bedside with its
daily surprise of morning; when the faith in the
marvellous bloomed like fresh flowers in my heart
every day, looking into the face of the world in
simple gladness; when insects, birds and beasts, the
common weeds, grass and the clouds had their
fullest value of wonder; when the patter of rain at
night brought dreams from the fairyland, and
mother's voice in the evening gave meaning to the
stars.

And then I think of death, and the rise of the curtain
and the new morning and my life awakened in its
fresh surprise of love.

## LXXII

WHEN my heart did not kiss thee in love, O world,
thy light missed its full splendour and thy sky
watched through the long night with its lighted
lamp.

My heart came with her songs to thy side, whispers
  were exchanged, and she put her wreath on thy neck.
I know she has given thee something which will be
  treasured with thy stars.

### LXXIII

THOU hast given me thy seat at thy window from the
  early hour.
I have spoken to thy silent servants of the road running
  on thy errands, and have sung with thy choir of the
  sky.
I have seen the sea in calm bearing its immeasurable
  silence, and in storm struggling to break open its
  own mystery of depth.
I have watched the earth in its prodigal feast of youth,
  and in its slow hours of brooding shadows.
Those who went to sow seeds have heard my greetings,
  and those who brought their harvest home or their
  empty baskets have passed by my songs.
Thus at last my day has ended and now in the evening
  I sing my last song to say that I have loved thy
  world.

### LXXIV

IT has fallen upon me, the service of thy singer.
In my songs I have voiced thy spring flowers, and
  given rhythm to thy rustling leaves.
I have sung into the hush of thy night and peace of thy
  morning.
The thrill of the first summer rains has passed into my
  tunes, and the waving of the autumn harvest.
Let not my song cease at last, my Master, when thou

breakest my heart to come into my house, but let it burst into thy welcome.

. . . . . .

## LXXVII

"TRAVELLER, where do you go?"

"I go to bathe in the sea in the redd'ning dawn, along the tree-bordered path."

"Traveller, where is that sea?"

"There where this river ends its course, where the dawn opens into morning, where the day droops to the dusk."

"Traveller, how many are they who come with you?"

"I know not how to count them.

They are travelling all night with their lamps lit, they are singing all day through land and water."

"Traveller, how far is the sea?"

"How far is it, we all ask.

The rolling roar of its water swells to the sky when we hush our talk.

It ever seems near yet far."

"Traveller, the sun is waxing strong."

"Yes, our journey is long and grievous.

Sing who are weary in spirit, sing who are timid of heart."

"Traveller, what if the night overtakes you?"

"We shall lie down to sleep till the new morning dawns with its songs, and the call of the sea floats in the air."

## LXXVIII

COMRADE of the road,
Here are my traveller's greetings to thee.
O Lord of my broken heart, of leave-taking and loss,
    of the grey silence of the dayfall,
My greetings of the ruined house to thee!
O Light of the new-born morning,
Sun of the everlasting day,
My greetings of the undying hope to thee!
My guide,
I am a wayfarer of an endless road,
My greetings of a wanderer to thee!

# STRAY BIRDS

# STRAY BIRDS

## I

STRAY birds of summer come to my window to sing and
fly away.
  And yellow leaves of autumn, which have no songs,
flutter and fall there with a sigh.

## II

O TROUPE of little vagrants of the world, leave your
footprints in my words.

## III

THE world puts off its mask of vastness to its lover.
  It becomes small as one song, as one kiss of the
eternal.

## IV

IT is the tears of the earth that keep her smiles in
bloom.

## V

THE mighty desert is burning for the love of a blade of
grass who shakes her head and laughs and flies away.

## VI

IF you shed tears when you miss the sun, you also miss
the stars.

## VII

THE sands in your way beg for your song and your movement, dancing water. Will you carry the burden of their lameness?

## VIII

HER wistful face haunts my dreams like the rain at night.

## IX

ONCE we dreamt that we were strangers.
  We wake up to find that we were dear to each other.

## X

SORROW is hushed into peace in my heart like the evening among the silent trees.

## XI

SOME unseen fingers, like an idle breeze, are playing upon my heart the music of the ripples.

## XII

"WHAT language is thine, O sea?"
  "The language of eternal question."
"What language is thy answer, O sky?"
  "The language of eternal silence."

## XIII

LISTEN, my heart, to the whispers of the world with which it makes love to you.

## XIV

THE mystery of creation is like the darkness of night—
it is great. Delusions of knowledge are like the fog of
the morning.

XV

DO not seat your love upon a precipice because it is
high.

XVI

I SIT at my window this morning where the world like
a passer-by stops for a moment, nods to me and goes.

XVII

THESE little thoughts are the rustle of leaves; they have
their whisper of joy in my mind.

XVIII

WHAT you are you do not see, what you see is your
shadow.

XIX

MY wishes are fools, they shout across thy songs, my
Master.
      Let me but listen.

XX

I CANNOT choose the best.
      The best chooses me.

XXI

THEY throw their shadows before them who carry their
lantern on their back.

### XXII

THAT I exist is a perpetual surprise which is life.

### XXIII

"WE, the rustling leaves, have a voice that answers the storms, but who are you, so silent?"
"I am a mere flower."

### XXIV

REST belongs to the work as the eyelids to the eyes.

### XXV

MAN is a born child, his power is the power of growth.

### XXVI

GOD expects answers for the flowers he sends us, not for the sun and the earth.

### XXVII

THE light that plays, like a naked child, among the green leaves happily knows not that man can lie.

### XXVIII

O BEAUTY, find thyself in love, not in the flattery of thy mirror.

### XXIX

MY heart beats her waves at the shore of the world and writes upon it her signature in tears with the words, "I love thee."

## XXX

"Moon, for what do you wait?"
  "To salute the sun for whom I must make way."

XXXI

The trees come up to my window like the yearning
voice of the dumb earth.

XXXII

His own mornings are new surprises to God.

XXXIII

Life finds its wealth by the claims of the world, and its
worth by the claims of love.

XXXIV

The dry river-bed finds no thanks for its past.

XXXV

The bird wishes it were a cloud.
  The cloud wishes it were a bird.

XXXVI

The waterfall sings, "I find my song, when I find my
freedom."

XXXVII

I cannot tell why this heart languishes in silence.
  It is for small needs it never asks, or knows or
remembers.

WOMAN, when you move about in your household service your limbs sing like a hill stream among its pebbles.

THE sun goes to cross the Western sea, leaving its last salutation to the East.

Do not blame your food because you have no appetite.

THE trees, like the longings of the earth, stand a-tiptoe to peep at the heaven.

YOU smiled and talked to me of nothing and I felt that for this I had been waiting long.

THE fish in the water is silent, the animal on the earth is noisy, the bird in the air is singing.

But Man has in him the silence of the sea, the noise of the earth and the music of the air.

THE world rushes on over the strings of the lingering heart making the music of sadness.

HE has made his weapons his gods.

When his weapons win he is defeated himself.

GOD finds himself by creating.

SHADOW, with her veil drawn, follows Light in secret meekness, with her silent steps of love.

THE stars are not afraid to appear like fireflies.

I THANK thee that I am none of the wheels of power but I am one with the living creatures that are crushed by it.

THE mind, sharp but not broad, sticks at every point but does not move.

YOUR idol is shattered in the dust to prove that God's dust is greater than your idol.

MAN does not reveal himself in his history, he struggles up through it.

WHILE the glass lamp rebukes the earthen for calling it cousin, the moon rises, and the glass lamp, with a bland smile, calls her,—"My dear, dear sister."

## LIV

LIKE the meeting of the seagulls and the waves we meet and come near. The seagulls fly off, the waves roll away and we depart.

## LV

MY day is done, and I am like a boat drawn on the beach, listening to the dance-music of the tide in the evening.

## LVI

LIFE is given to us, we earn it by giving it.

## LVII

WE come nearest to the great when we are great in humility.

## LVIII

THE sparrow is sorry for the peacock at the burden of its tail.

## LIX

NEVER be afraid of the moments—thus sings the voice of the everlasting.

## LX

THE hurricane seeks the shortest road by the no-road, and suddenly ends its search in the Nowhere.

## LXI

TAKE my wine in my own cup, friend.
It loses its wreath of foam when poured into that of others.

## LXII

THE Perfect decks itself in beauty for the love of the Imperfect.

## LXIII

GOD says to man, "I heal you, therefore I hurt, love you, therefore punish."

## LXIV

THANK the flame for its light, but do not forget the lampholder standing in the shade with constancy of patience.

## LXV

TINY grass, your steps are small, but you possess the earth under your tread.

## LXVI

THE infant flower opens its bud and cries, "Dear World, please do not fade."

## LXVII

GOD grows weary of great kingdoms, but never of little flowers.

## LXVIII

WRONG cannot afford defeat but Right can.

## LXIX

"I GIVE my whole water in joy," sings the waterfall, "though little of it is enough for the thirsty."

### LXX

WHERE is the fountain that throws up these flowers in a ceaseless outbreak of ecstasy?

### LXXI

THE woodcutter's axe begged for its handle from the tree.
  The tree gave it.

### LXXII

IN my solitude of heart I feel the sigh of this widowed evening veiled with mist and rain.

### LXXIII

CHASTITY is a wealth that comes from abundance of love.

### LXXIV

THE mist, like love, plays upon the heart of the hills and brings out surprises of beauty.

### LXXV

WE read the world wrong and say that it deceives us.

### LXXVI

THE poet wind is out over the sea and the forest to seek his own voice.

### LXXVII

EVERY child comes with the message that God is not yet discouraged of man.

### LXXVIII

THE grass seeks her crowd in the earth.
  The tree seeks his solitude of the sky.

MAN barricades against himself.

YOUR voice, my friend, wanders in my heart, like the muffled sound of the sea among these listening pines.

WHAT is this unseen flame of darkness whose sparks are the stars?

LET life be beautiful like summer flowers and death like autumn leaves.

HE who wants to do good knocks at the gate; he who loves finds the gate open.

IN death the many becomes one; in life the one becomes many.

Religion will be one when God is dead.

THE artist is the lover of Nature, therefore he is her slave and her master.

"How far are you from me, O Fruit?"
"I am hidden in your heart, O Flower."

### LXXXVII

THIS longing is for the one who is felt in the dark, but not seen in the day.

### LXXXVIII

"YOU are the big drop of dew under the lotus leaf, I am the smaller one on its upper side," said the dewdrop to the lake.

### LXXXIX

THE scabbard is content to be dull when it protects the keenness of the sword.

### XC

IN darkness the One appears as uniform; in the light the One appears as manifold.

### XCI

THE great earth makes herself hospitable with the help of the grass.

### XCII

THE birth and death of the leaves are the rapid whirls of the eddy whose wider circles move slowly among stars.

### XCIII

POWER said to the world, "You are mine."
   The world kept it prisoner on her throne.
   Love said to the world, "I am thine."
   The world gave it the freedom of her house.

### XCIV

THE mist is like the earth's desire.
   It hides the sun for whom she cries.

## XCV

Be still, my heart, these great trees are prayers.

## XCVI

The noise of the moment scoffs at the music of the Eternal.

## XCVII

I think of other ages that floated upon the stream of life and love and death and are forgotten, and I feel the freedom of passing away.

## XCVIII

The sadness of my soul is her bride's veil.
It waits to be lifted in the night.

## XCIX

Death's stamp gives value to the coin of life; making it possible to buy with life what is truly precious.

## C

The cloud stood humbly in a corner of the sky.
The morning crowned it with splendour.

## CI

The dust receives insult and in return offers her flowers.

## CII

Do not linger to gather flowers to keep them, but walk on, for flowers will keep themselves blooming all your way.

### CIII

Roots are the branches down in the earth.
  Branches are roots in the air.

### CIV

The music of the far-away summer flutters around the autumn seeking its former nest.

### CV

Do not insult your friend by lending him merits from your own pocket.

### CVI

The touch of the nameless days clings to my heart like mosses round the old tree.

### CVII

The echo mocks her origin to prove she is the original.

### CVIII

God is ashamed when the prosperous boasts of his special favour.

### CIX

I cast my own shadow upon my path, because I have a lamp that has not been lighted.

### CX

Man goes into the noisy crowd to drown his own clamour of silence.

THAT which ends in exhaustion is death, but the perfect ending is in the endless.

THE sun has his simple robe of light. The clouds are decked with gorgeousness.

THE hills are like shouts of children who raise their arms, trying to catch stars.

THE road is lonely in its crowd, for it is not loved.

THE power that boasts of its mischiefs is laughed at by the yellow leaves that fall, and clouds that pass by.

THE earth hums to me to-day in the sun, like a woman at her spinning, some ballad of the ancient time in a forgotten tongue.

THE grass-blade is worthy of the great world where it grows.

DREAM is a wife who must talk,
    Sleep is a husband who silently suffers.

THE night kisses the fading day whispering to his ear, "I am death, your mother. I am to give you fresh birth."

I FEEL thy beauty, dark night, like that of the loved woman when she has put out the lamp.

I CARRY in my world that flourishes the worlds that have failed.

DEAR friend, I feel the silence of your great thoughts of many a deepening eventide on this beach when I listen to these waves.

THE bird thinks it is an act of kindness to give the fish a lift in the air.

"IN the moon thou sendest thy love letters to me," said the night to the sun.

"I leave my answers in tears upon the grass."

THE Great is a born child; when he dies he gives his great childhood to the world.

NOT hammer-strokes, but dance of the water sings the pebbles into perfection.

BEES sip honey from flowers and hum their thanks
when they leave.

The gaudy butterfly is sure that the flowers owe
thanks to him.

CXXVIII

TO be outspoken is easy when you do not wait to speak
the complete truth.

CXXIX

ASKS the Possible of the Impossible, "Where is your
dwelling-place?"

"In the dreams of the impotent," comes the answer.

CXXX

IF you shut your door to all errors truth will be shut out

CXXXI

I HEAR some rustle of things behind my sadness of
heart,—I cannot see them.

CXXXII

LEISURE in its activity is work.

The stillness of the sea stirs in waves.

CXXXIII

THE leaf becomes flower when it loves.

The flower becomes fruit when it worships.

THE roots below the earth claim no rewards for making the branches fruitful.

THIS rainy evening the wind is restless.

I look at the swaying branches and ponder over the greatness of all things.

STORM of midnight, like a giant child awakened in the untimely dark, has begun to play and shout.

THOU raisest thy waves vainly to follow thy lover, O sea, thou lonely bride of the storm.

"I AM ashamed of my emptiness," said the Word to the Work.

"I know how poor I am when I see you," said the Work to the Word.

TIME is the wealth of change, but the clock in its parody makes it mere change and no wealth.

TRUTH in her dress finds facts too tight.

In fiction she moves with ease.

## CXLI

WHEN I travelled to here and to there, I was tired of thee, O Road, but now when thou leadest me to everywhere I am wedded to thee in love.

## CXLII

LET me think that there is one among those stars that guides my life through the dark unknown.

## CXLIII

WOMAN, with the grace of your fingers you touched my things and order came out like music.

## CXLIV

ONE sad voice has its nest among the ruins of the years. It sings to me in the night,—"I loved you."

## CXLV

THE flaming fire warns me off by its own glow. Save me from the dying embers hidden under ashes.

## CXLVI

I HAVE my stars in the sky,
But oh for my little lamp unlit in my house.

## CXLVII

THE dust of the dead words clings to thee. Wash thy soul with silence.

305

### CXLVIII

Gaps are left in life through which comes the sad music of death.

### CXLIX

The world has opened its heart of light in the morning.
Come out, my heart, with thy love to meet it.

### CL

My thoughts shimmer with these shimmering leaves and my heart sings with the touch of this sunlight; my life is glad to be floating with all things into the blue of space, into the dark of time.

### CLI

God's great power is in the gentle breeze, not in the storm.

### CLII

This is a dream in which things are all loose and they oppress. I shall find them gathered in thee when I awake and shall be free.

### CLIII

"Who is there to take up my duties?" asked the setting sun.
"I shall do what I can, my Master," said the earthen lamp.

### CLIV

By plucking her petals you do not gather the beauty of the flower.

## CLV

SILENCE will carry your voice like the nest that holds the sleeping birds.

## CLVI

THE Great walks with the Small without fear.
  The Middling keeps aloof.

## CLVII

THE night opens the flowers in secret and allows the day to get thanks.

## CLVIII

POWER takes as ingratitude the writhings of its victims.

## CLIX

WHEN we rejoice in our fullness, then we can part with our fruits with joy.

## CLX

THE raindrops kissed the earth and whispered,—"We are thy homesick children, mother, come back to thee from the heaven."

## CLXI

THE cobweb pretends to catch dewdrops and catches flies.

## CLXII

LOVE! when you come with the burning lamp of pain in your hand, I can see your face and know you as bliss.

"THE learned say that your lights will one day be no more," said the firefly to the stars.
  The stars made no answer.

CLXIV

IN the dusk of the evening the bird of some early dawn comes to the nest of my silence.

CLXV

THOUGHTS pass in my mind like flocks of ducks in the sky.
  I hear the voice of their wings.

CLXVI

THE canal loves to think that rivers exist solely to supply it with water.

CLXVII

THE world has kissed my soul with its pain, asking for its return in songs.

CLXVIII

THAT which oppresses me, is it my soul trying to come out in the open, or the soul of the world knocking at my heart for its entrance?

CLXIX

THOUGHT feeds itself with its own words and grows.

I HAVE dipped the vessel of my heart into this silent hour; it has filled with love.

EITHER you have work or you have not.

When you have to say, "Let us do something," then begins mischief.

THE sunflower blushed to own the nameless flower as her kin.

The sun rose and smiled on it, saying, "Are you well, my darling?"

"WHO drives me forward like fate?"

"The Myself striding on my back."

THE clouds fill the water-cups of the river, hiding themselves in the distant hills.

I SPILL water from my water-jar as I walk on my way.

Very little remains for my home.

THE water in a vessel is sparkling; the water in the sea is dark.

The small truth has words that are clear; the great truth has great silence.

## CLXXVII

YOUR smile was the flowers of your own fields, your talk was the rustle of your own mountain pines, but your heart was the woman that we all know.

## CLXXVIII

IT is the little things that I leave behind for my loved ones,—great things are for everyone.

## CLXXIX

WOMAN, thou hast encircled the world's heart with the depth of thy tears as the sea has the earth.

## CLXXX

THE sunshine greets me with a smile.
    The rain, his sad sister, talks to my heart.

## CLXXXI

MY flower of the day dropped its petals forgotten.
    In the evening it ripens into a golden fruit of memory.

## CLXXXII

I AM like the road in the night listening to the footfalls of its memories in silence.

## CLXXXIII

THE evening sky to me is like a window, and a lighted lamp, and a waiting behind it.

### CLXXXIV

HE who is too busy doing good finds no time to be good.

### CLXXXV

I AM the autumn cloud, empty of rain, see my fullness in the field of ripened rice.

### CLXXXVI

THEY hated and killed and men praised them.
  But God in shame hastens to hide its memory under the green grass.

### CLXXXVII

TOES are the fingers that have forsaken their past.

### CLXXXVIII

DARKNESS travels towards light, but blindness towards death.

### CLXXXIX

THE pet dog suspects the universe for scheming to take its place.

### CXC

SIT still, my heart, do not raise your dust.
  Let the world find its way to you.

### CXCI

THE bow whispers to the arrow before it speeds forth—
"Your freedom is mine."

311

WOMAN, in your laughter you have the music of the
fountain of life.

A MIND all logic is like a knife all blade.
　　It makes the hand bleed that uses it.

GOD loves man's lamp-lights better than his own great
stars.

THIS world is the world of wild storms kept tame with
the music of beauty.

"MY heart is like the golden casket of thy kiss," said
the sunset cloud to the sun.

BY touching you may kill, by keeping away you may
possess.

THE cricket's chirp and the patter of rain come to me
through the dark, like the rustle of dreams from my
past youth.

"I HAVE lost my dewdrop," cries the flower to the
morning sky that has lost all its stars.

THE burning log bursts in flame and cries,—"This is my flower, my death."

THE wasp thinks that the honey-hive of the neighbouring bees is too small.

His neighbours ask him to build one still smaller.

"I CANNOT keep your waves," says the bank to the river.

"Let me keep your footprints in my heart."

THE day, with the noise of this little earth, drowns the silence of all worlds.

THE song feels the infinite in the air, the picture in the earth, the poem in the air and the earth;

For its words have meaning that walks and music that soars.

WHEN the sun goes down to the West, the East of his morning stands before him in silence.

LET me not put myself wrongly to my world and set it against me.

PRAISE shames me, for I secretly beg for it.

LET my doing nothing when I have nothing to do become untroubled in its depth of peace like the evening in the seashore when the water is silent.

MAIDEN, your simplicity, like the blueness of the lake, reveals your depth of truth.

THE best does not come alone.
It comes with the company of the all.

GOD's right hand is gentle, but terrible is his left hand.

MY evening came among the alien trees and spoke in a language which my morning stars did not know.

NIGHT's darkness is a bag that bursts with the gold of the dawn.

OUR desire lends the colours of the rainbow to the mere mists and vapours of life.

GOD waits to win back his own flowers as gifts from man's hands.

MY sad thoughts tease me asking me their own names.

THE service of the fruit is precious, the service of the flower is sweet, but let my service be the service of the leaves in its shade of humble devotion.

MY heart has spread its sails to the idle winds for the shadowy island of Anywhere.

MEN are cruel, but Man is kind.

MAKE me thy cup and let my fulness be for thee and for thine.

THE storm is like the cry of some god in pain whose love the earth refuses.

THE world does not leak because death is not a crack.

## CCXXIII

LIFE has become richer by the love that has been lost.

## CCXXIV

MY friend, your great heart shone with the sunrise of the East like the snowy summit of a lonely hill in the dawn.

## CCXXV

THE fountain of death makes the still water of life play.

## CCXXVI

THOSE who have everything but thee, my God, laugh at those who have nothing but thyself.

## CCXXVII

THE movement of life has its rest in its own music.

## CCXXVIII

KICKS only raise dust and not crops from the earth.

## CCXXIX

OUR names are the light that glows on the sea waves at night and then dies without leaving its signature.

## CCXXX

LET him only see the thorns who has eyes to see the rose.

## CCXXXI

SET the bird's wings with gold and it will never again soar in the sky.

THE same lotus of our clime blooms here in the alien water with the same sweetness, under another name.

IN heart's perspective the distance looms large.

THE moon has her light all over the sky, her dark spots to herself.

DO not say, "It is morning," and dismiss it with a name of yesterday. See it for the first time as a new-born child that has no name.

SMOKE boasts to the sky, and Ashes to the earth, that they are brothers to the fire.

THE raindrop whispered to the jasmine, "Keep me in your heart for ever."

The jasmine sighed, "Alas," and dropped to the ground.

TIMID thoughts, do not be afraid of me.

I am a poet.

THE dim silence of my mind seems filled with crickets' chirp—the grey twilight of sound.

ROCKETS, your insult to the stars follows yourself back to the earth.

THOU hast led me through my crowded travels of the day to my evening's loneliness.

I wait for its meaning through the stillness of the night.

THIS life is the crossing of a sea, where we meet in the same narrow ship.

In death we reach the shore and go to our different worlds.

THE stream of truth flows through its channels of mistakes.

MY heart is homesick to-day for the one sweet hour across the sea of time.

THE bird-song is the echo of the morning light back from the earth.

"ARE you too proud to kiss me?" the morning light asks the buttercup.

"How may I sing to thee and worship, O Sun?" asked the little flower.

"By the simple silence of thy purity," answered the sun.

MAN is worse than an animal when he is an animal.

CCXLIX

DARK clouds become heaven's flowers when kissed by light.

CCL

LET not the sword-blade mock its handle for being blunt.

CCLI

THE night's silence, like a deep lamp, is burning with the light of its Milky Way.

CCLII

AROUND the sunny island of life swells day and night death's limitless song of the sea.

CCLIII

Is not this mountain like a flower, with its petals of hills, drinking the sunlight?

CCLIV

THE real with its meaning read wrong and emphasis misplaced is the unreal.

CCLV

FIND your beauty, my heart, from the world's movement, like the boat that has the grace of the wind and the water.

### CCLVI

THE eyes are not proud of their sight but of their eyeglasses.

### CCLVII

I LIVE in this little world of mine and am afraid to make it the least less. Lift me into thy world and let me have the freedom gladly to lose my all.

### CCLVIII

THE false can never grow into truth by growing in power.

### CCLIX

MY heart, with its lapping waves of song, longs to caress this green world of the sunny day.

### CCLX

WAYSIDE grass, love the star, then your dreams will come out in flowers.

### CCLXI

LET your music, like a sword, pierce the noise of the market to its heart.

### CCLXII

THE trembling leaves of this tree touch my heart like the fingers of an infant child.

### CCLXIII

THE little flower lies in the dust.
  It sought the path of the butterfly.

### CCLXIV

I AM in the world of the roads.

The night comes. Open thy gate, thou world of the home.

### CCLXV

I HAVE sung the songs of thy day.

In the evening let me carry thy lamp through the stormy path.

### CCLXVI

I DO not ask thee into the house.

Come into my infinite loneliness, my Lover.

### CCLXVII

DEATH belongs to life as birth does.

The walk is in the raising of the foot as in the laying of it down.

### CCLXVIII

I HAVE learnt the simple meaning of thy whispers in flowers and sunshine—teach me to know thy words in pain and death.

### CCLXIX

THE night's flower was late when the morning kissed her, she shivered and sighed and dropped to the ground.

### CCLXX

THROUGH the sadness of all things I hear the crooning of the Eternal Mother.

### CCLXXI

I came to your shore as a stranger, I lived in your house
as a guest, I leave your door as a friend, my earth.

### CCLXXII

Let my thoughts come to you, when I am gone, like
the afterglow of sunset at the margin of starry silence.

### CCLXXIII

Light in my heart the evening star of rest and then let
the night whisper to me of love.

### CCLXXIV

I am a child in the dark.
   I stretch my hands through the coverlet of night for
thee, Mother.

### CCLXXV

The day of work is done. Hide my face in your arms,
Mother.
   Let me dream.

### CCLXXVI

The lamp of meeting burns long; it goes out in a
moment at the parting.

### CCLXXVII

One word keep for me in thy silence, O World, when
I am dead, "I have loved."

## CCLXXVIII

WE live in this world when we love it.

## CCLXXIX

LET the dead have the immortality of fame, but the living the immortality of love.

## CCLXXX

I HAVE seen thee as the half-awakened child sees his mother in the dusk of the dawn and then smiles and sleeps again.

## CCLXXXI

I SHALL die again and again to know that life is inexhaustible.

## CCLXXXII

WHILE I was passing with the crowd in the road I saw thy smile from the balcony and I sang and forgot all noise.

## CCLXXXIII

LOVE is life in its fulness like the cup with its wine.

## CCLXXXIV

THEY light their own lamps and sing their own words in their temples.

But the birds sing thy name in thine own morning light,—for thy name is joy.

## CCLXXXV

LEAD me in the centre of thy silence to fill my heart with songs.

LET them live who choose in their own hissing world of fireworks.

My heart longs for thy stars, my God.

LOVE'S pain sang round my life like the unplumbed sea, and love's joy sang like birds in its flowering groves.

PUT out the lamp when thou wishest.

I shall know thy darkness and shall love it.

WHEN I stand before thee at the day's end thou shalt see my scars and know that I had my wounds and also my healing.

SOME day I shall sing to thee in the sunrise of some other world, "I have seen thee before in the light of the earth, in the love of man."

CLOUDS come floating into my life from other days no longer to shed rain or usher storm but to give colour to my sunset sky.

TRUTH raises against itself the storm that scatters its seeds broadcast.

### CCXCIII

THE storm of the last night has crowned this morning with golden peace.

### CCXCIV

TRUTH seems to come with its final word; and the final word gives birth to its next.

### CCXCV

BLESSED is he whose fame does not outshine his truth.

### CCXCVI

SWEETNESS of thy name fills my heart when I forget mine—like thy morning sun when the mist is melted.

### CCXCVII

THE silent night has the beauty of the mother and the clamorous day of the child.

### CCXCVIII

THE world loved man when he smiled. The world became afraid of him when he laughed.

### CCXCIX

GOD waits for man to regain his childhood in wisdom.

### CCC

LET me feel this world as thy love taking form, then my love will help it.

## CCCI

THY sunshine smiles upon the winter days of my heart, never doubting of its spring flowers.

## CCCII

GOD kisses the finite in his love and man the infinite.

## CCCIII

THOU crossest desert lands of barren years to reach the moment of fulfilment.

## CCCIV

GOD's silence ripens man's thoughts into speech.

## CCCV

THOU wilt find, Eternal Traveller, marks of thy footsteps across my songs.

## CCCVI

LET me not shame thee, Father, who displayest thy glory in thy children.

## CCCVII

CHEERLESS is the day, the light under frowning clouds is like a punished child with traces of tears on its pale cheeks, and the cry of the wind is like the cry of a wounded world. But I know I am travelling to meet my Friend.

## CCCVIII

TO-NIGHT there is a stir among the palm leaves, a swell in the sea, Full Moon, like the heart-throb of the world. From what unknown sky hast thou carried in thy silence the aching secret of love?

## CCCIX

I DREAM of a star, an island of light, where I shall be born and in the depth of its quickening leisure my life will ripen its works like the rice-field in the autumn sun.

## CCCX

THE smell of the wet earth in the rain rises like a great chant of praise from the voiceless multitude of the insignificant.

## CCCXI

THAT love can ever lose is a fact that we cannot accept as truth.

## CCCXII

WE shall know some day that death can never rob us of that which our soul has gained, for her gains are one with herself.

## CCCXIII

GOD comes to me in the dusk of my evening with the flowers from my past kept fresh in his basket.

## CCCXIV

WHEN all the strings of my life will be tuned, my Master, then at every touch of thine will come out the music of love.

## CCCXV

LET me live truly, my Lord, so that death to me become true.

MAN's history is waiting in patience for the triumph of the insulted man.

I FEEL thy gaze upon my heart this moment like the sunny silence of the morning upon the lonely field whose harvest is over.

I LONG for the Island of Songs across this heaving Sea of Shouts.

THE prelude of the night is commenced in the music of the sunset, in its solemn hymn to the ineffable dark.

I HAVE scaled the peak and found no shelter in fame's bleak and barren height. Lead me, my Guide, before the light fades, into the valley of quiet where life's harvest mellows into golden wisdom.

THINGS look phantastic in this dimness of the dusk— the spires whose bases are lost in the dark and tree-tops like blots of ink. I shall wait for the morning and wake up to see thy city in the light.

I HAVE suffered and despaired and known death and I am glad that I am in this great world.

### CCCXXIII

THERE are tracts in my life that are bare and silent. They are the open spaces where my busy days had their light and air.

### CCCXXIV

RELEASE me from my unfulfilled past clinging to me from behind making death difficult.

### CCCXXV

LET this be my last word, that I trust in thy love.

# THE CYCLE OF SPRING

# THE CYCLE OF SPRING

## INTRODUCTION

### Characters of the Prelude

KING, VIZIER, GENERAL (BIJOY VARMA)
CHINESE AMBASSADOR, PUNDIT (SRUTI-BHUSHAN)
POET (KABI-SHEKHAR), GUARDS, COURTIERS, HERALD

*The stage is on two levels: the higher, at the back, for the Song-
preludes alone, concealed by a purple curtain; the lower
only being discovered when the drop goes up. Diagonally
across the extreme left of the lower stage is arranged the
King's Court, with various platforms for the various
dignitaries ascending to the canopied throne. The body of
the stage is left free for the "Play" when that develops.*

### (Enter some Courtiers)

[*The names of the speakers are not given in the margin, as they
can easily be guessed.*]

Hush! Hush!

What is the matter?

The King is in great distress.

How dreadful!

Who is that over there, playing on his flute?

Why? What's the matter?

The King is greatly disturbed.

333

How dreadful!

What are those wild children doing, making so much noise?

They are the Mandal family.

Then tell the Mandal family to keep their children quiet.

Where can that Vizier have gone to?

Here I am! What's the matter?

Haven't you heard the news?

No, what?

The King is greatly troubled in his mind.

Well, I've got some very important news about the frontier war.

War we may have, but not the news.

Then the Chinese Ambassador is waiting to see His Majesty.

Let him wait. Anyhow he can't see the King.

Can't see the King?—Ah, here is the King at last. Look at him coming this way, with a mirror in his hand. "Long live the King. Long live the King."

If it please Your Majesty, it is time to go to the Court.

Time to go? Yes, time to go, but not to the Court.

What does Your Majesty mean?

Haven't you heard? The bell has just been rung to dismiss the Court.

When? What bell? We haven't heard any bell.

How could you hear? They have rung it in my ears alone.

Oh, Sire! No one can have had the impertinence to do that.

Vizier! They are ringing it now.

Pardon me, Sire, if I am very stupid; but I cannot understand.

Look at this, Vizier, look at this.

Your Majesty's hair——

Can't you see there's a bell-ringer there?

Oh, Your Majesty! Are you playing a joke?

The joke is not mine, but His, who has got the whole world by the ear, and is having His jest. Last night, when the Queen was putting a garland of jasmines round my neck, she cried out with alarm, "King, what is this? Here are two grey hairs behind your ear."

Oh, please, Sire, don't worry so much about a little thing like that. Why! The royal physician——

Vizier! The founder of our dynasty had his royal physician too. But what could he do? Death has left his card of invitation behind my ear. The Queen wanted, then and there, to pluck out the grey hairs. But I said, "Queen, what's the use? You may remove Death's

335

invitation, but can you remove Death, the Inviter?" So, for the present——

Yes, Sire, for the present, let us attend to business.

Business, Vizier! I have no time for business. Send for the Pundit. Send for Sruti-bhushan.

But, Sire, the General——

The General?—No, no, not the General. Send for the Pundit.

But the news from the frontier——

Vizier, the news has come to me from the last great frontier of all, the frontier of Death. Send for the Pundit.

But if Your Majesty will give me one moment, the Ambassador from the great Emperor of China——

Vizier, a greater Emperor has sent his embassy to me. Call Sruti-bhushan.

Very well, Sire. But your father-in-law——

It is not my father-in-law whom I want now. Send for the Pundit.

But if it please you to hear me this once. The Poet, Kabi-shekhar, is waiting with his new book called *The Garden of Poesy*.

Let your Poet disport himself, jumping about on the topmost branches of his Garden of Poesy, but send for the Pundit.

Very well, Sire. I will send for him at once.

Tell him to bring his book of devotions with him, called *The Ocean of Renunciation*.

Yes, Sire.

But, Vizier! Who are those outside making all that noise? Go out and stop them at once. I must have peace.

If it please Your Majesty, there is a famine in Nagapatam and the headmen of the villages are praying to be allowed to see your face.

My time is short, Vizier! I must have peace.

They say their time is shorter. They are at death's door. They, too, want peace,—peace from the burning of hunger.

Vizier! The burning of hunger is quenched at last on the funeral pyre.

Then these wretched people——

Wretched!—Listen to the advice of a wretched King to his wretched subjects. It is futile to be impatient, and try to break through the net of the inexorable Fisherman. Sooner or later, Death the Fisherman will have his haul.

Well then?

Let me have the Pundit, and his *Ocean of Renunciation*.

And in this scarcity——

Vizier! The real scarcity is of time, and not of food. We are all suffering from starvation of time. None of us has enough of it, neither the King nor his people.

Then——

Then know that our petitions for more time will all go to the last fire of doom. So why strain our voice in prayer?—Ah, here is Sruti-bhushan at last. My reverence to you.

Pundit, do tell the King that the Goddess of Fortune deserts him who gives way to melancholy.

Sruti-bhushan, what is my Vizier whispering to you?

He tells me, King, to instruct you in the ways of fortune.

What instruction can you give?

There is a verse in my book of devotions which runs as follows:

> Fortune, as fickle as lotus-flower,
> Closes her favours when comes the hour.
> Oh, foolish man, how can you trust her,
> Who comes of a sudden, and goes in a fluster?

Ah, Pundit! One breath of your teaching blows out the false flame of ambition. Our teacher has said:

> "Teeth fall out, hair grows grey,
>   Yet man clings to hope that plays him false."

Well, King, now that you have introduced the subject of hope, let me give you another verse from the *Ocean of Renunciation*. It runs as follows:

> That fetters are binding, all are aware;
> But fetters of hope are strange, I declare.
> Hope's captive is tossed in the whirlpool's wake,
> And only grows still when the fetters break.

338

Ah, Pundit! Your words are priceless. Vizier, give him a hundred gold sequins at once. What's that noise outside?

It is the famine-stricken people.

Tell them to hold their peace.

Let Sruti-bhushan, with his book of devotions, go and try to bring them peace; and, in the meanwhile, Your Majesty might discuss war matters——

No, no. Let the war matters come later. I can't let Sruti-bhushan go yet.

King, you said something to me, a moment ago, about a gift of gold. Now mere gold, by itself, does not confer any permanent benefit. It is said in my book of devotions, called *The Ocean of Renunciation*:

> *He who gives gold, gives only pain;*
> *When the gold is spent grief comes again.*
> *When a lakh, or crore, of gold is spent,*
> *Grief only remains in the empty tent.*

Ah, Pundit! How exquisite! So you don't want any gold, my Master?

No, King, I don't want gold, but something more permanent, which would make your merit permanent also. I should be quite content, if you gave me the living of Kanchanpur. For it is said in the *Renuncia-tion*——

No, Pundit, I quite understand. You needn't quote scripture to support your claim. I understand quite well—Vizier!

339

Yes, Your Majesty.

See that the rich province of Kanchanpur is settled on the Pundit.—What's the matter now outside there? What are they crying for?

If it please Your Majesty, it is the people.

Why do they cry so repeatedly?

Their cry is repeated, I admit, but the reason remains most monotonously the same. They are starving.

But, King, I must tell you before I forget it. It is the one desire of my wife to make her whole body jingle, from head to foot, in praise of your munificence; but, alas, the sound is too feeble for want of proper ornaments.

I understand you, Pundit. Vizier! Order ornaments from the Court Jeweller for Sruti-bhushan's wife immediately.

And, King, while he is about it, would you tell the Vizier that we are both of us distracted in our devotions by house-repairs. Let him ask the royal masons to put up a thoroughly well-built house, where we can practise our devotions in peace.

Very well, Pundit.—Vizier!

Yes, Your Majesty.

Give the order at once.

Sire, your treasury is empty. Funds are wanting.

Pooh! That's an old story. I hear that every year. It

340

is your business to increase the funds, and mine to increase the wants. What do you say, Sruti-bhushan?

King, I cannot blame the Vizier. He is looking after your treasures in this world. We are looking after your treasures in the next. So where he sees want, we see wealth. Now, if you would only let me dive deep once more into the *Ocean of Renunciation* you will find it written as follows:

> *That King's coffers are well stored,*
> *Where wealth alone on worth is poured.*

Pundit, your company is most valuable.

Your Majesty, Sruti-bhushan knows its value to a farthing. Come, Sruti-bhushan, make haste. Let us collect all the wealth you need for your Treasury of Devotion. For wealth has the ugly habit of diminishing fast. If we are not quick about it, little will remain to enable us to observe our renunciation with all splendour. ·

Yes, Vizier, let us go at once. (*To the King.*) When he is making such a fuss about a tiny matter like this, it is best to pacify him first and then return to you afterwards.

Pundit, I am afraid that, some day, you will leave my royal protection altogether and retire to the forest.

King, so long as I find contentment in a King's palace, it is as good as a hermitage for my peace of mind. I must now leave you, King. Vizier, let us go.

[*The Vizier and Pundit go out*

Oh, dear me! Whatever shall I do? Here's the Poet coming. I am afraid he'll make me break all my good resolutions.—Oh, my grey hairs, cover my ears, so that the Poet's allurements may not enter.

Why, King, what's the matter? I hear you want to send away your Poet.

What have I to do with poets, when poetry brings me this parting message?

What parting message?

Look at this behind my ear. Don't you see it?

See what? Grey hairs? Why, King, don't you worry about that.

Poet, Nature is trying to rub out the green of youth, and to paint everything white.

No, no, King. You haven't understood the artist. On that white ground, Nature will paint new colours.

I don't see any sign of colours yet.

They are all within. In the heart of the white dwell all the colours of the rainbow.

Oh, Poet, do be quiet. You disturb me when you talk like that.

King, if this youth fades, let it fade. Another Queen of Youth is coming. And she is putting a garland of pure white jasmines round your head, in order to be your bride. The wedding festival is being made ready, behind the scene.

Oh, dear, Poet! You will undo everything. Do go away. Ho there, Guard! Go at once and call Sruti-bhushan.

What will you do with him, King, when he comes?

I will compose my mind, and practise my renunciation.

Ah, King, when I heard that news, I came at once. For I can be your companion in this practice of renunciation.

You?

Yes, I, King. We Poets exist for this very purpose. We set men free from their desires.

I don't understand you. You talk in riddles.

What? You can't understand me? And yet you have been reading my poems all this while!—There is renunciation in our words, renunciation in the metre, renunciation in our music. That is why fortune always forsakes us; and we in turn always forsake fortune. We go about, all day long, initiating the youths in the sacred cult of fortune-forsaking.

What does it say to us?

It says:
"Ah, brothers, don't cling to your goods and chattels,
And sit ever in the corner of your room.
Come out, come out into the open world.
Come out into the highways of life.
Come out, ye youthful Renouncers."

But, Poet, do you really mean to say that the highway of the open world is the pathway of renunciation?

Why not, King? In the open world all is change, all is life, all is movement. And he who ever moves and journeys with this life-movement, dancing and playing on his flute as he goes, he is the true Renouncer. He is the true disciple of the minstrel Poet.

But how then can I get peace? I must have peace.

Oh, King, we haven't the least desire for peace. We are the Renouncers.

But ought we not to get that treasure, which is said to be never-changing?

No, we don't covet any never-changing treasures. We are the Renouncers.

What do you mean? Oh, dear, Poet, you will undo everything if you talk like that. You are destroying my peace of mind. Call Sruti-bhushan. Let some one call the Pundit.

What I mean, King, is this. We are the true Renouncers, because change is our very secret. We lose, in order to find. We have no faith in the never-changing.

What do you mean?

Haven't you noticed the detachment of the rushing river, as it runs splashing from its mountain cave? It gives itself away so swiftly, and only thus it finds itself. What is never-changing, for the river, is the desert sand, where it loses its course.

Ah, but listen, Poet—listen to those cries there outside. That is your world. How do you deal with that?

King, they are your starving people.

My people, Poet? Why do you call them that? They

344

are the world's people, not mine. Have I created their miseries? What can your youthful Poet Renouncers do to relieve sufferings like theirs? Tell me that.

King, it is we alone who can truly bear those sufferings, because we are like the river that flows on in gladness, thus lightening our burden, and the burden of the world. But the hard, metalled road is fixed and never-changing. And so it makes the burden more burdensome. The heavy loads groan and creak along it, and cut deep gashes in its breast. We Poets call to every one to carry all their joys and sorrows lightly, in a rhythmic measure. Our call is the Renouncers' call.

Ah, Poet, now I don't care a straw for Sruti-bhushan. Let the Pundit go hang. But, do you know what my trouble is now? Though I can't, for the life of me, understand your words, the music haunts me. Now, it's just the other way round with the Pundit. His words are clear enough, and they obey the rules of syntax quite correctly. But the tune!—No, it's no use telling you any further.

King, our words don't speak, they sing.

Well, Poet, what do you want to do now?

King, I'm going to have a race through those cries which are rising outside your gate.

What do you mean? Famine relief is for men of business. Poets oughtn't to have anything to do with things like that.

King, business men always make their business so out of tune. That is why we Poets hasten to tune it.

345

Now come, my dear Poet, do speak in plainer language.

King, they work because they must. We work, because we are in love with life. That is why they condemn us as unpractical, and we condemn them as lifeless.

But who is right, Poet? Who wins? You, or they?

We, King, we. We always win.

But, Poet, your proof——

King, the greatest things in the world disdain proof. But if you could for a time wipe out all the poets and all their poetry from the world, then you would soon discover, by their very absence, where the men of action got their energy from, and who really supplied the life-sap to their harvest-field. It is not those who have plunged deep down into the Pundit's *Ocean of Renunciation*, nor those who are always clinging to their possessions; it is not those who have become adepts in turning out quantities of work, nor those who are ever telling the dry beads of duty,—it is not these who win at last. But it is those who love, because they live. These truly win, for they truly surrender. They accept pain with all their strength and with all their strength they remove pain. It is they who create, because they know the secret of true joy, which is the secret of detachment.

Well then, Poet, if that be so, what do you ask me to do now?

I ask you, King, to rise up and move. That cry outside
346

yonder is the cry of life to life. And if the life within you is not stirred, in response to that call without, then there is cause for anxiety indeed,—not because duty has been neglected, but because you are dying.

But, Poet, surely we must die, sooner or later?

No, King, that's a lie. When we feel for certain that we are alive, then we know for certain that we shall go on living. Those who have never put life to the test, in all possible ways, these keep on crying out:

> Life is fleeting, Life is waning,
> Life is like a dew-drop on a lotus leaf.

But isn't life inconstant?

Only because its movement is unceasing. The moment you stop this movement, that moment you begin to play the drama of Death.

Poet, are you speaking the truth? Shall we really go on living?

Yes, we shall really go on living.

Then, Poet, if we are going to go on living, we must make our life worth its eternity. Is not that so?

Yes, indeed.

Ho, Guard!

Yes, Your Royal Highness.

Call the Vizier at once.

Yes, Your Royal Highness.

(*Vizier enters*)

What is Your Majesty's pleasure?

347

Vizier! Why on earth have you kept me waiting so long?

I was very busy, Your Majesty.

Busy? What were you busy about?

I was dismissing the General.

Why should you dismiss the General? We have got to discuss war matters with him.

And arrangements had to be made for the state departure of the Chinese Ambassador.

What do you mean by his state departure?

If it please Your Majesty, you did not grant him an interview. So he——

Vizier! You surprise me. Is this the way you manage state affairs? What has happened to you? Have you lost your senses?

Then, again, Sire, I was trying to find a way to pull down the Poet's house. At first, no one would undertake it. Then, at last, all the Pundits of the Royal School of Grammar and Logic came up with their proper tools and set to work.

Vizier! Are you mad this morning? Pull down the Poet's house? Why, you might as well kill all the birds in the garden and make them up into a pie.

If it please Your Majesty, you need not be annoyed. We shan't have to pull down the house after all; for the moment Sruti-bhushan heard it was to be demolished, he decided to take possession of it himself.

What, Vizier! That's worse still. Why! The Goddess of Music would break her harp in pieces against my head if she even heard of such a thing. No, that can't be.

Then, Your Majesty, there was another thing to be got through. We had to deliver over the province of Kanchanpur to the Pundit.

No, Vizier! What a mess you are making! That must go to our Poet.

To me, King? No. My poetry never accepts reward.

Well, well! Let the Pundit have it.

And, last of all, Sire, I have issued orders to the soldiers to disperse the crowd of famine-stricken people.

Vizier, you are doing nothing but blunder. The best way to disperse the famished people is with food, not force.

(*Guard enters*)

May it please Your Royal Highness.

What's the matter, Guard?

May it please Your Royal Highness, here is Sruti-bhushan, the Pundit, coming back with his *Book of Devotions*.

Oh, stop him, Vizier, stop him. He will undo everything. Don't let him come upon me unawares like this. In a moment of weakness I may suddenly find myself out of my depth in the *Ocean of Renunciation*. Poet! Don't give me time for that. Do something. Do anything. Have you got anything ready to hand? Any play toward? Any poem? Any masque? Any——

Yes, King. I have got the very thing. But whether it is a drama, or a poem, or a play, or a masque, I cannot say.

Shall I be able to understand the sense of what you have written?

No, King, what a poet writes is not meant to have any sense.

What then?

To have the tune itself.

What do you mean? Is there no philosophy in it?

No, none at all, thank goodness.

What does it say, then?

King, it says "I exist." Don't you know the meaning of the first cry of the new-born child? The child, when it is born, hears at once the cries of the earth and water and sky, which surround him,—and they all cry to him, "We exist," and his tiny little heart responds, and cries out in its turn, "I exist." My poetry is like the cry of that new-born child. It is a response to the cry of the Universe.

Is it nothing more than that, Poet?

No, nothing more. There is life in my song, which cries, "In joy and in sorrow, in work and in rest, in life and in death, in victory and in defeat, in this world and in the next, all hail to the 'I exist.'"

Well, Poet, I can assure you, if your play hasn't got any philosophy in it, it won't pass muster in these days.

That's true, King. The newer people, of this modern age, are more eager to amass than to realize. They are, in their generation, wiser than the children of light.

Whom shall we ask, then, for an audience? Shall we ask the young students of our royal school?

No, King, they cut up poetry with their logic. They are like the young-horned deer trying their new horns on the flower-beds.

Whom should I ask, then?

Ask those whose hair is turning grey.

What do you mean, Poet?

The youth of these middle-aged people is a youth of detachment. They have just crossed the waters of pleasure, and are in sight of the land of pure gladness. They don't want to eat fruit, but to produce it.

I, at least, have now reached that age of discretion, and ought to be able to appreciate your songs. Shall I ask the General?

Yes, ask him.

And the Chinese Ambassador?

Yes, ask him too.

I hear my father-in-law has come.

Well, ask him too, but I have my doubts about his youthful sons.

But don't forget his daughter.

Don't worry about her. She won't let herself be forgotten.

And Sruti-bhushan? Shall I ask him?

No, King, no. Decidedly, no. I have no grudge against him. Why should I inflict this on him?

Very well, Poet. Off with you. Make your stage preparations.

No, King. We are going to act this play without any special preparations. Truth looks tawdry when she is overdressed.

But, Poet, there must be some canvas for a background.

No. Our only background is the mind. On that we shall summon up a picture with the magic wand of music.

Are there any songs in the play?

Yes, King. The door of each act will be opened by the key of song.

What is the subject of the songs?

The Disrobing of Winter.

But, Poet, we haven't read about that in any Mythology.

In the world-myth this song comes round in its turn. In the play of the seasons, each year, the mask of the Old Man, Winter, is pulled off, and the form of Spring

352

is revealed in all its beauty. Thus we see that the old is ever new.

Well, Poet, so much for the songs: but what about the remainder?

Oh, that is all about life.

Life? What is life?

This is how it runs: A band of young companions have run off in pursuit of one Old Man. They have taken a vow to catch him. They enter into a cave; they take hold of him, and then——

Then, what? What did they see?

Ah! That will be told in its own good time.

But I haven't understood one thing. Your drama and your songs,—have they different subjects, or the same?

The same, King. The play of Spring in nature is the counterpart of the play of Youth in our lives. It is simply from the lyrical drama of the World Poet that I have stolen this plot.

Who, then, are the chief characters?

One is called the Leader.

Who is he, Poet?

He is the guiding impulse in our life. Another is Chandra.

Who is he?

He who makes life dear to us.

And who else?

Then there is Dada, to whom duty is the essence of life, not joy.

Is there any one else?

Yes, the blind Minstrel.

Blind?

Because he does not see with his eyes, therefore he sees with his whole body and mind and soul.

Who else is there, in your play, among the chief actors?

You are there, King.

I?

Yes, you, King. For if you stayed out of it, instead of coming into it, then the King would begin to abuse the Poet and send for Sruti-bhushan again. And then there would be no hope of salvation for him. For the World Poet himself would be defeated. And the South Wind of Spring would have to retire, without receiving its homage.

## ACT I

*The Heralds of Spring are abroad. There are songs in the rust-ling bamboo leaves, in birds' nests, and in blossoming branches.*

### SONG-PRELUDE

*The purple secondary curtain* [1] *goes up, disclosing the elevated*

[1] Neither the secondary curtain nor the drop is again used during the play. The action is continuous, either on the front stage or on the rear stage, the latter being darkened when not actually in use.

*rear stage with a skyey background of dark blue, on which appear the horn of the crescent moon and the silver points of stars. Trees in the foreground, with two rope swings entwined with garlands of flowers. Flowers everywhere in profusion. On the extreme left the mouth of a dark cavern dimly seen. Boys representing the "Bamboo" disclosed, swinging.*

## SONG OF THE BAMBOO

O South Wind, the Wanderer, come and rock me,
    Rouse me into the rapture of new leaves.
I am the wayside bamboo tree, waiting for your breath
    To tingle life into my branches.

O South Wind, the Wanderer, my dwelling is in the end of
    the lane.
    I know your wayfaring, and the language of your footsteps.
        Your least touch thrills me out of my slumber,
        Your whisper gleans my secrets.

*(Enter a troop of girls, dancing, representing birds)*

## SONG OF THE BIRD

The sky pours its light into our hearts,
    We fill the sky with songs in answer.
We pelt the air with our notes
    When the air stirs our wings with its madness.
        O Flame of the Forest,
All your flower-torches are ablaze;
You have kissed our songs red with the passion of your youth.
In the spring breeze the mango-blossoms launch their messages
    to the unknown
And the new leaves dream aloud all day.

O Sirish, you have cast your perfume-net round our hearts,
　　Drawing them out in songs.

(Disclosed among the branches of trees, suddenly lighted up,
　　boys representing champak blossoms)


## SONG OF THE BLOSSOMING CHAMPAK

My shadow dances in your waves,
　　everflowing river,
I, the blossoming champak, stand unmoved on the bank,
　　with my flower-vigils.
My movement dwells in the stillness of my depth,
　　In the delicious birth of new leaves,
　　　In flood of flowers,
　　　In unseen urge of new life towards the light.
Its stirring thrills the sky, and the silence of the dawn is moved.


## Morning

[The rear stage is now darkened. On the main stage, bright,
　　enter a band of youths whose number may be anything
　　between three and thirty. They sing.]

　The fire of April leaps from forest to forest,
　　Flashing up in leaves and flowers
　　　from all nooks and corners.
　The sky is thriftless with colours,
　　The air delirious with songs.
　The wind-tost branches of the woodland
　　　Spread their unrest in our blood.
　The air is filled with bewilderment of mirth;
　　And the breeze rushes from flower to flower, asking their
　　names.

April pulls hard, brother, April pulls very hard.

How do you know that?

If he didn't, he would never have pulled Dada outside his den.

Well, I declare! Here is Dada, our cargo-boat of moral-maxims, towed against the current of his own pen and ink.

*Chandra.* But you mustn't give April all the credit for that. For I, Chandra, have hidden the yellow leaves of his manuscript book among the young buds of the *pial* forest, and Dada is out looking for it.

The manuscript book banished! What a good riddance!

We ought to strip off Dada's grey philosopher's cloak also.

*Chandra.* Yes, the very dust of the earth is tingling with youth, and yet there's not a single touch of Spring in the whole of Dada's body.

*Dada.* Oh, do stop this fooling. What a nuisance you are making of yourselves! We aren't children any longer.

*Chandra.* Dada, the age of this earth is scarcely less than yours; and yet it is not ashamed to look fresh.

Dada, you are always struggling with those quatrains of yours, full of advice that is as old as death, while the earth and the water are ever striving to be new.

357

Dada, how in the world can you go on writing verses like that, sitting in your den?

*Dada.* Well, you see, I don't cultivate poetry as an amateur gardener cultivates flowers. *My* poems have substance and weight in them.

Yes, they are like the turnips, which cling to the ground.

*Dada.* Well, then, listen to me——

How awful! Here's Dada going to run amuck with his quatrains.

Oh dear, oh dear! The quatrains are let loose. There's no holding them in.

To all passers-by I give notice that Dada's quatrains have gone mad, and are running amuck.

*Chandra.* Dada! Don't take any notice of their fun. Go on with your reading. If no one else can survive it, I think I can. I am not a coward like these fellows.

Come on, then, Dada. We won't be cowards. We will keep our ground, and not yield an inch, but only listen.

We will receive the spear-thrusts of the quatrains on our breast, not on our back.

But for pity's sake, Dada, give us only one—not more.

*Dada.* Very well. Now listen:

> *If bamboos were made only into flutes,*
> *They would droop and die with very shame,*

*They hold their heads high in the sky,*
*Because they are variously useful.*

Please, gentlemen, don't laugh. Have patience while
I explain. The meaning is——

The meaning?

What? Must the infantry charge of meaning follow
the cannonading of your quatrains, to complete the
rout?

*Dada.* Just one word to make you understand. It
means, that if the bamboos were no better than those
noisy instruments——

No, Dada, we must not understand.

I defy you to make us understand.

Dada, if you use force to make us understand we shall
use force to force ourselves not to understand.

*Dada.* The gist of the quatrain is this, that if we do
no good to the world, then——

Then the world will be very greatly relieved.

*Dada.* There is another verse that makes it clearer:

*There are numerous stars in the midnight sky,*
*Which hang in the air for no purpose;*
*If they would only come down to earth,*
*For the street lighting they might be useful.*

I see we must make clearer our meaning. Catch him.
Let's raise him up, shoulder high, and take him back
to his den.

*Dada.* Why are you so excited to-day? Have you any particular business to do?

Yes, we have very urgent business,—very urgent indeed.

*Dada.* What is your business about?

We are out to seek a play for **our** Spring festival.

*Dada.* Play! Day and night, play!

(*They sing*)
> We are free, my friends, from the fear of work,
>   For we know that work is play,—
>     the play of life.
> It is Play, to fight and toss,
>     between life and death;
> It is Play that flashes in the laughter of light in the
>     infinite heart;
>   It roars in the wind,
>     and surges in the sea.

Oh, here comes our Leader. Brothers—our Leader, our Leader!

*Leader.* Hallo! What a noise you make!

Was it that which made you come out of doors?

*Leader.* Yes.

Well, we did it for that very purpose.

*Leader.* You don't want me to remain indoors?

Why remain indoors? This outer world has been made with a lavish expenditure of sun and moon and stars.

Let us enjoy it, and then we can save God's face for indulging in such extravagance.

*Leader.* What were you discussing?

This:

(*They sing*)

*Play blooms in flower
    and ripens in fruit
In the sunshine of eternal youth.
Play bursts up in the blood-red fire,
    and licks into ashes the decaying and the dead.*

Our Dada's objection was about this play.

*Dada.* Shall I tell you the reason why?

Yes, Dada, you may tell us, but we shan't promise to listen.

*Dada.* Here it is:

*Time is the capital of work,
And Play is its defalcation.
Play rifles the house, and then wastes its spoil,
Therefore the wise call it worse than useless.*

*Chandra.* But surely, Dada, you are talking nonsense. Time itself is Play. Its only object is Pas-time.

*Dada.* Then what is Work?

*Chandra.* Work is the dust raised by the passing of Time.

*Dada.* Leader, you must give us your answers.

*Leader.* No. I never give answers. I lead on from one question to another. That is my leadership.

361

*Dada.* Everything else has its limits, but your child-ishness is absolutely unbounded.

Do you know the reason? It is because we are really nothing but children. And everything else has its limitations except the child.

*Dada.* Won't you ever attain Age?

No, we shall never attain Age.

We shall die old, but never attain Age.

*Chandra.* When we meet Age, we shall shave his head, and put him on a donkey, and send him across the river.

Oh, you can save yourself the trouble of shaving his head, for Age is bald.

*(They sing)*

Our hair shall never turn grey,
  Never.
There is no blank in this world for us,
  no break in our road,
It may be an illusion that we follow,
But it shall never play us false,
  Never.

*(The Leader sings)*

Our hair shall never turn grey,
  Never.

We will never doubt the world and shut our eyes to ponder.
  *Never.*
We will not grope in the maze of our mind.
We flow with the flood of things, from the mountain to the sea,
We will never be lost in the desert sand,
  *Never.*

We can tell, by his looks, that Dada will some day go to that Old Man, to receive his lessons.

*Leader.* Which Old Man?

The Old Man of the line of Adam.

He dwells in a cave, and never thinks of dying.

*Leader.* Where did you learn about him?

Oh, every one talks about him. And it is in the books also.

*Leader.* What does he look like?

Some say he is white, like the skull of a dead man. And some say he is dark, like the socket of a skeleton's eye.

But haven't you heard any news of him, Leader?

*Leader.* I don't believe in him at all.

Well, that goes entirely against current opinion. That Old Man is more existent than anything else. He lives within the ribs of creation.

According to our Pundit, it is we who have no existence. You can't be certain whether we are, or are not.

*Chandra.* We? Oh, we are too brand-new altogether. We haven't yet got our credentials to prove that we exist.

*Leader.* Have you really gone and opened communication with the Pundits?

Why? What harm is there in that, Leader?

*Leader.* You will become pale, like the white mist in

autumn. Even the least colour of blood will disappear from your mind. I have a suggestion.

What, Leader? What?

*Leader.* You were looking out for a play?

Yes, yes, we got quite frantic about it.

We thought it over so vigorously that people had to run to the King's court to lodge a complaint.

*Leader.* Well, I can suggest a play which will be new.

What?—What?—Tell us.

*Leader.* Go and capture the Old Man.

That is new, no doubt, but we very much doubt if it's a play.

*Leader.* I am sure you won't be able to do it.

Not do it? We shall.

*Leader.* No, never.

Well, then, suppose we do capture him, what will you give us?

*Leader.* I shall accept you as my preceptor.

Preceptor! You want to make us grey, and cold, and old, before our time. .

*Leader.* Then what do you want me to do?

If we capture him, then we shall take away your leadership.

*Leader.* That will be a great relief to me. You have

made all my bones out of joint already. Very well, then it's all settled?

Yes, settled. We shall bring him to you by the next full moon of Spring.

But what are we going to do with him?

*Leader.* You shall let him join in your Spring Festival.

Oh no, that will be outrageous. Then the mango flowers will run to seed at once.

And all the cuckoos will become owls.

And the bees will go about reciting Sanskrit verses, making the air hum with m's and n's.

*Leader.* And your skull will be so top-heavy with prudence that it will be difficult for you to keep on your feet.

How awful!

*Leader.* And you will have rheumatics in all your joints.

How awful!

*Leader.* And you will become your own elder brothers, pulling your own ears to set yourselves right.

How awful!

*Leader.* And——

No more "ands." We are ready to surrender.

We will abandon our game of capturing the Old Man.

We will put it off till the cold weather. In this Springtime your company will be enough for us.

*Leader.* Ah, I see! You have already got the chill of the Old Man in your bones.

Why? What are the symptoms?

*Leader.* You have no enthusiasm. You back out at the very start. Why don't you make a trial?

Very well. Agreed. Come on.

Let us go after the Old Man. We will pluck him out, like a grey hair, wherever we find him.

*Leader.* But the Old Man is an adept in the business of plucking out. His best weapon is the hoe.

You needn't try to frighten us like that. When we are out for adventure, we must leave behind all fears, all quatrains, all Pundits, and all Scriptures.

(*They sing*)

*We are out on our way*
  *And we fear not the Robber, the Old Man.*
*Our path is straight, it is broad,*
  *Our burden is light, for our pocket is bare,*
*Who can rob us of our folly?*
  *For us there is no rest, nor ease, nor praise, nor success,*
*We dance in the measure of fortune's rise and fall,*
  *We play our game, or win or lose,*
    *And we fear not the Robber.*

# ACT II

## SONG-PRELUDE

*[Spring's Heralds try to rob Winter of his outfit of age.]*

*Rear stage lighted up, disclosing Old Winter teased by the boys and girls representing Spring's Heralds.*

### SONG OF THE HERALDS OF SPRING

*We seek our playmates,*
*Waking them up from all corners*
*before it is morning.*
*We call them in bird-songs,*
*Beckon them in nodding branches.*
*We spread our spell for them*
*in the splendour of clouds.*
*We laugh at solemn Death*
*Till he joins in our laughter.*
*We tear open Time's purse,*
*Taking back his plunder from him.*
*You shall lose your heart to us, O Winter.*
*It will gleam in the trembling leaves*
*And break into flowers.*

### SONG OF WINTER

*Leave me, let me go.*
*I sail for the bleak North, for the peace of the frozen shore.*
*Your laughter is untimely, my friends.*
*You turn my farewell tunes into the welcome song of the*
*Newcomer,*
*And all things draw me back again into the dancing ring of*
*their hearts.*

### Song of the Heralds of Spring

*Life's spies are we, lurking in ambush everywhere.*
*We wait to rob you of your last savings of withered hours*
    *to scatter them in the wayward winds.*
*We shall bind you in flower-chains*
    *where Spring keeps his captives,*
*For we know you carry your jewels of youth*
    *hidden in your grey rags.*

### (Noon)

[*The rear stage is darkened. The band of Youths enters on the*
    *main stage. No actual change in the scenery is necessary—*
    *this being left to the imagination of the audience.*]

Ferryman! Ferryman! Open your door.

*Ferryman.* What do you want?

We want the Old Man.

*Ferryman.* Which old man?

Not which old man? We want *the* Old Man.

*Ferryman.* Who is he?

The true and original Old Man.

*Ferryman.* Oh! I understand. What do you want him
for?

For our Spring Festival.

*Ferryman.* For your Spring Festival? Are you become
mad?

Not a sudden becoming. We have been like this from
the beginning.

And we shall go on like this to the end.

(*They sing*)
*The Piper pipes in the centre, hidden from sight,*
*And we become frantic, we dance.*
*The March wind, seized with frenzy,*
*Runs and reels, and sways with noisy branches.*
*The sun and stars are drawn in the whirl of rapture.*

Now, Ferryman, give us news of the Old Man.

You ply your boat from one landing-stage to another.
Surely you know where——

*Ferryman.* My business is limited only to the path.
But whose path it is, and what it means, I have no
occasion to enquire. For my goal is the landing-stage,
not the house.

Very well. Let us go, let us try all the ways.

(*They sing*)
*The Piper pipes in the centre, hidden from sight.*
  *Ah, the turbulent tune, to whose time the oceans dance,*
    *And dance our heaving hearts.*
*Fling away all burdens and cares, brother,*
  *Do not be doubtful of your path,*
*For the path wakes up of itself*
  *Under the dancing steps of freedom.*

*Ferryman.* There comes the Watchman. Ask him. I
know about the way; but he knows about the wayfarers.

*Watchman.* Who are you?

We are just what you see. That's our only descrip-
tion.

369

*Watchman.* But what do you want?

We want the Old Man.

*Watchman.* Which old man?

That eternal Old Man.

*Watchman.* How absurd! While you are seeking him, he is after you.

Why?

*Watchman.* He is fond of warming his cold blood with the wine of hot youth.

We'll give him a warm enough reception. All we want is to see him. Have you seen him?

*Watchman.* My watch is at night. I see my people, but don't know their features. But, look here, every one knows that he is the great kidnapper; and you want to kidnap him! It's midsummer madness.

The secret is out. It doesn't take long to discover that we are mad.

*Watchman.* I am the Watchman. The people I see passing along the road are all very much alike. Therefore, when I see anything queer, it always strikes me.

Just listen to him. All the respectable people of our neighbourhood say just the same thing—that we are queer.

Yes, we're queer. There's no mistake about that.

*Watchman.* But all this is utter childishness.

Do you hear that? It's exactly what our Dada says.

370

We have been going on with our childishness through unremembered ages.

And now we have become confirmed children.

And we have a leader, who is a perfect veteran in childhood. He rushes along so recklessly that he drops off his age at every step he runs.

*Watchman.* And who are you?

We are butterflies, freed from the cocoon of Age.

*Watchman (aside).* Mad. Raving mad.

*Ferryman.* Then what will you all do now?

*Chandra.* We shall go——

*Watchman.* Where?

*Chandra.* That we haven't decided.

*Watchman.* You have decided to go, but not where to go?

*Chandra.* Yes, that will be settled as we go along.

*Watchman.* What does that mean?

*Chandra.* It means this song.

(*They sing*)

*We move and move without rest,*
*We move while the wanderers' stars shine in the sky and fade.*
*We play the tune of the road*
*While our limbs scatter away the laughter of movement,*
*And our many-coloured mantle of youth flutters about in the air.*

*Watchman.* Is it your custom to answer questions by songs?

*Chandra.* Yes, otherwise the answer becomes too unintelligible.

*Watchman.* Then you think your songs intelligible?

*Chandra.* Yes, quite, because they contain music.

(*They sing*)

*We move and move without rest.*
  *World, the Rover, loves his comrades of the road.*
*His call comes across the sky,*
  *The seasons lead the way, strewing the path with flowers.*

*Watchman.* No ordinary being ever breaks out singing, like this, in the middle of talking.

*Chandra.* Again we are found out. We are no ordinary beings.

*Watchman.* Have you got no work to do?

*Chandra.* No, we are on a holiday.

*Watchman.* Why?

*Chandra.* Lest our time should all be wasted.

*Watchman.* I don't quite understand you.

*Chandra.* Then we shall be obliged to sing again.

*Watchman.* No, no. There's no need to do that. I don't hope to understand you any better, even if you do sing.

*Chandra.* Everybody has given up the hope of understanding us.

*Watchman.* But how can things get on with you, if you behave like this?

*Chandra.* Oh, there's no need for things to get on with us, so long as we ourselves get on.

*Watchman.* Mad! Quite mad! Raving mad!

*Chandra.* Why, here comes our Dada.

Dada, what made you lag behind?

*Chandra.* Don't you know? We are free as the wind, because we have no substance in us. But Dada is like the rain-cloud of August. He must stop, every now and then, to unburden himself.

*Dada.* Who are you?

*Ferryman.* I am the Ferryman.

*Dada.* And who are you?

*Watchman.* I am the Watchman.

*Dada.* I am delighted to see you. I want to read you something that I have written. It contains nothing frivolous, but only the most important lessons.

*Ferryman.* Very good. Let us have it then.

*Watchman.* Our master used to tell us that there are plenty of men to say good things, but very few to listen. That requires strength of mind. Now, go on, Sir, go on.

*Dada.* I saw, in the street, one of the King's officers dragging along a merchant. The King had made up a false charge, in order to get his money. This gave me an inspiration. You must know that I never write a single line which is not inspired by some actual fact. You can

**373**

put my verses to the test in the open streets and markets——

*Ferryman.* Please, Sir, do let us hear what you have written.

*Dada.*　　*The sugar-cane filling itself with juice*
*Is chewed and sucked dry by all beggars.*
*O foolish men, take your lesson from this;*
*Those trees are saved, which are fruitful.*

You will understand that the sugar-cane gets into trouble, simply because it tries to keep its juice. But nobody is so foolish as to kill the tree that freely gives fruit.

*Watchman.* What splendid writing, Ferryman!

*Ferryman.* Yes, Watchman, it contains great lessons for us.

*Watchman.* It gives me food for thought. If only I had here our neighbour, the Scribe! I should like to take this down. Do send round to tell the people of the place to assemble.

*Chandra.* But, Ferryman, you promised to come out with us. Yet, if once Dada begins to quote his quatrains, there will be——

*Ferryman.* Go along with you. None of your madness here. We are fortunate now in having met our master. Let us improve the occasion with good words. We are all of us getting old. Who knows when we shall die?

All the more reason why you should cultivate our company.

*Chandra.* You can always find another Dada. But when

374

once we are dead, God will never repeat the blunder of another absurdity like us again.

(*Enter Oilman*)

*Oilman.* Ho! Watchman.

*Watchman.* Who is there? Is that the Oilman?

*Oilman.* The child I was bringing up was kidnapped last night.

*Watchman.* By whom?

*Oilman.* By the Old Man.

*Youths* (*together*). Old Man? You don't mean it. Old Man?

*Oilman.* Yes, Sirs, the Old Man; what makes you so glad?

Oh, that's a bad habit of ours. We become glad for no reason whatever.

*Watchman* (*aside*). Mad! Raving mad!

Have you seen the Old Man?

*Oilman.* I think I saw him in the distance last night.

*First Youth.* What did he look like?

*Oilman.* Black. More black than our brother here, the Watchman. Black as night, with two eyes on his breast shining like two glow-worms.

That won't suit us. That would be awkward for our Spring Festival.

*Chandra.* We shall have to change our date from the

375

full moon to the dark moon. For the dark moon has no end of eyes on her breast.

*Watchman.* But I warn you, my friends, you are not doing wisely.

No, we are not.

We are found out again. We never do anything wisely. It is contrary to our habit.

*Watchman.* Do you take this to be a joke? I warn you, my friends, it is dangerous.

Dangerous? That's the best joke of all.

(*They sing*)

> *We are neither too good nor wise,*
>     *That is all the merit we have.*
> *Our calumny spreads from land to land,*
>     *And danger dogs our steps.*
> *We take great care to forget what is taught us.*
> *We say things different from the book,*
>     *Bringing upon us trouble,*
>       *And rebuke from the learned.*

*Watchman.* Ah, Sir, you spoke about some Leader. Where is he? He could have kept you in order, if he were with you.

He never stays with us, lest he should have to keep us in order.

He simply launches us on our way, and then slips off.

*Watchman.* That's a poor idea of leadership.

*Chandra.* He is never concerned about his leadership. That is why we recognize him as our Leader.

376

*Watchman.* Then he has got a very easy task.

*Chandra.* It is no easy task to lead men. But it is easy enough to drive them.

(They sing)

*We are not too good nor wise,*
*That is all the merit we have.*
*In a luckless moment we were born,*
*When the star of wisdom was the dimmest.*
*We can hope for no profit from our adventures,*
*We move on, because we must.*

Dada, come on. Let us go.

*Watchman.* No, no, Sir. Don't you get yourself into mischief in their company.

*Ferryman.* You read your verses, Sir, to us. Our neighbours will be here soon. They will be greatly profited.

*Dada.* No. I'm not going to move a step from here.

Then let us move. The men in the street can't bear us.

That's because we rattle them too much.

You hear the hum of human bees, they smell the honey of Dada's quatrains.

*Youths* (*together*). They come! They come!

(Enter Village folk)

*Villager.* Is it true that there is going to be a reading? Who are you? Are *you* going to read?

No. We commit all kinds of atrocities, but not that. This one merit will bring us salvation.

*Villager.* What do they say? They seem to be talking in riddles.

*Chandra.* We only say things which we perfectly understand ourselves, and they are riddles to you. Dada repeats to you things which you understand perfectly, and these sound to you the very essence of wisdom.

(*Boy enters*)

*Boy.* I couldn't catch him.

Whom?

*Boy.* The Old Man, whom you are seeking.

Have you seen him?

*Boy.* Yes, I thought I saw him going by in a car.

Where? In what direction?

*Boy.* I couldn't make out exactly. The dust raised by his wheels is still whirling in the air.

Then let us go.

He has filled the sky with dead leaves.

[*They go out*

*Watchman.* They are mad! Quite mad! Raving mad!

# ACT III

## SONG-PRELUDE

[*Winter is being unmasked—his hidden youth about to be disclosed.*]

*The rear stage lighted up, disclosing Winter and the Heralds of Spring.*

### SONG OF THE HERALDS OF SPRING

*How grave he looks,*
*how laughably old,*
*How solemnly quiet among death preparations!*
*Come, friends, help him to find himself*
*before he reaches home.*
*Change his pilgrim's robe*
*into the dress of the singing youth,*
*Snatch away his bag of dead things*
*And confound his calculations.*

*(Another group sings)*

*The time comes when the world shall know*
*that you're not banished in your own shadows;*
*Your heart shall burst in torrents*
*Out of the clasp of the ice;*
*And your North wind turn its face*
*Against the haunts of the flitting phantoms.*
*There sounds the magician's drum,*
*And the sun waits with laughter in his glance,*
*To see your grey turn into green.*

*(Evening)*

[*The rear stage is darkened; the light on the main stage dimmed to the greyness of dark.*]

*Band of Youths.* They all cry, "There, there," and when we look for it, we find nothing but dust and dry leaves.

I thought I had a glimpse of the flag on his car through the cloud.

It is difficult to follow his track. Now it seems East: now it seems West.

And so we are tired, chasing shadows all day long. And the day has been lost.

I tell you the truth. Fear comes more and more into my mind, as the day passes.

We have made a mistake. The morning light whispered in our ears, "Bravo, march on." And now, the evening light is mocking us for that.

I am afraid we have been deceived. I am beginning to feel greater respect for Dada's quatrains than before. We shall all be soon sitting down on the ground composing quatrains.

And then the whole neighbourhood will come, swarming round us. And they will get such immense benefit from our wisdom that they will never leave us.

And we shall settle down like a great big boulder, cold and immovable.

And they will cling to us, as we sit there, like a thick fog.

What would our Leader think of us, I wonder, if he could hear us now?

I am sure it is our Leader who has led us astray. He
380

makes us toil for nothing, while he himself remains idle.

Let us go back and fight with him. We will tell him that we won't move a step further, but sit with our legs tucked under us. These legs are wretched vagabonds. They are always trudging the road.

We will keep our hands fast behind our backs.

There is no mischief in the back; all the trouble is in the front.

Of all our limbs, the back is the most truthful. It says to us, "Lie down."

When we are young, that braggart breast is a great swell; but, in the end, we can only rely on our back.

The little stream that flows past our village comes to my mind. That morning we thought that it said to us, "Forward! Forward!" But what it really said was, "False! False!" The world is all false.

Our Pundit used to tell us that.

We shall go straight to the Pundit, when we get back.

We shall never stir one step outside the limit of the Pundit's Scriptures.

What a mistake we made! We thought that moving itself was something heroic.

But really not to move, that is heroic, because it is defying the whole moving world.

Brave rebels that we are, we shall *not* move. We shall have the audacity to sit still, and never move an inch.

"Life and youth are fleeting," the Scripture says. Let life and youth go to the dogs, we shall not move.

"Our minds and wealth are fleeting," adds the Scripture. "Give them up and sit still," say we.

Let us go back to the point from which we started.

But that would be to move.

What then?

There sit down, where we have come to.

And let us imagine that there we had been before we ever came there.

Yes, yes, that will keep our minds still. If we know that we have come from somewhere else, then the mind longs for that somewhere else.

That land of somewhere else is a very dangerous place.

There the ground moves, and also the roads. But as for us——

*(They sing)*

*We cling to our seats and never stir,*
*We allow our flowers to fade in peace,*
*    and avoid the trouble of bearing fruit.*
*Let the starlights blazon their eternal folly,*
*    We quench our flames.*
*Let the forest rustle and the ocean roar,*
*    We sit mute.*
*Let the call of the flood-tide come from the sea,*
*    We remain still.*

Do you hear that laughter?

Yes, yes, it is laughter.

What a relief! We have never heard that sound for an age.

We had been choking for want of the breath of laughter.

This laughter comes to us like the April rain.

Whose is it?

Cannot you guess? It is our Chandra.

What a marvellous gift of laughter he has! It is like a waterfall. It dashes all the black stones out of the path.

It is like sunlight. It cuts the mist to pieces with its sword.

Now all danger of quatrain fever is over. Let us get up.

From this moment there will be nothing but work for us. As the Scripture says, "Everything in this world is fleeting, and he only lives who does his duty and achieves fame."

Why are you quoting that? Are you still suffering from the quatrain fever?

What do you mean by fame? Does the river take any heed of its foam? Fame is that foam on life's stream.

(*Enter Chandra with a blind Minstrel*)

Well, Chandra, what makes you so glad?

*Chandra.* I have got the track of the Old Man.

From whom?

*Chandra.* From this old Minstrel.

He seems to be blind.

*Chandra.* Yes, that is why he has not got to seek the road.

What do you say? Shall you be able to lead us right?

*Minstrel.* Yes.

But how?

*Minstrel.* Because I can hear the footsteps.

We also have ears, but——

*Minstrel.* I hear with my whole being.

*Chandra.* They all started up with fear when I asked about the Old Man. Only this Minstrel seemed to have no fear. I suppose because he cannot see, he is not afraid.

*Minstrel.* Do you know why I have no fear? When the sun of my life set, and I became blind, the dark night revealed all its lights, and, from that day forward, I have been no more afraid of the dark.

Then let us go. The evening star is up.

*Minstrel.* Let me sing, and walk on as I sing, and you follow me. I cannot find my way, if I do not sing.

What do you mean?

*Minstrel.* My songs precede, I follow.

(*He sings*)

*Gently, my friend, gently walk to your silent chamber.*
*I know not the way, I have not the light,*
*Dark is my life and my world.*

384

I have only the sound of your steps
   to guide me in this wilderness.

Gently, my friend, gently walk along the dark shore.
   Let the hint of the way come in whisper,
Through the night, in the April breeze.
   I have only the scent of your garland
      to guide me in this wilderness.


## ACT IV

### SONG-PRELUDE

[*There enter a troupe of young things, and they introduce
themselves in a song as follows:*]

#### THE SONG OF RETURNING YOUTH

Again and again we say "Good-bye,"
   To come back again and again.
Oh, who are you?
I am the flower vakul.
And who are you?
I am the flower parul.
And who are these?
We are mango blossoms landed on the shore of light.
   We laugh and take leave when the time beckons us.
We rush into the arms of the ever-returning.
   But who are you?
   I am the flower shimul.
   And who are you?
   I am the kamini bunch.
And who are these?
We are the jostling crowd of new leaves.

385

*[Winter is revealed as Spring and answers to the questions put by the chorus of young things.]*

### THE SONG OF BURDENS DROPPED

*Do you own defeat at the hand of youth?*
    *Yes.*
*Have you met at last the ageless Old, who ever grows new?*
    *Yes.*
*Have you come out of the walls that crumble and bury those*
      *whom they shelter?*
    *Yes.*

              *(Another group sings)*

*Do you own defeat at the hands of life?*
    *Yes.*
*Have you passed through death to stand at last face to face with*
      *the Deathless?*
    *Yes.*
*Have you dealt the blow to the demon dust, that swallows your*
      *city Immortal?*
    *Yes.*

        *(Spring's flowers surround him and sing)*

### THE SONG OF FRESH BEAUTY

*We waited by the wayside counting moments*
    *till you appeared in the April morning.*
*You come as a soldier-boy winning life at death's gate,—*
      *Oh, the wonder of it!*
*We listen amazed at the music of your young voice.*
    *Your mantle is blown in the wind*
      *like the fragrance of the Spring.*
*The white spray of malati flowers in your hair*
      *shines like star-clusters.*

*A fire burns through the veil of your smile,—*
*Oh, the wonder of it!*
*And who knows where your arrows are hidden*
*which smite death?*

(*Night*)

[*The rear stage is darkened, and the light on the main stage
dimmed to the heavy purple blackness of mourning.*]

(*Enter the Band of Youths*)

Chandra has gone away again, leaving us behind.

It is difficult to keep him still.

We get our rest by sitting down, but he gets his by
walking on.

He has gone across the river with the blind Minstrel,
in whose depth of blindness Chandra is seeking the
invisible light.

That is why our Leader calls him the Diver.

Our life becomes utterly empty when Chandra is
away.

Do you feel as though something was in the air?

The sky seems to be looking into our face, like a
friend bidding farewell.

This little stream of water is trickling through the
*casuarina* grove. It seems like the tears of midnight.

We have never gazed upon the earth before with such
intentness.

When we run forward at full speed, our eyes keep

gazing in front of us, and we see nothing on either side of us.

If things did not move on and vanish, we should see no beauty anywhere.

If youth had only the heat of movement, it would get parched and withered. But there is ever the hidden tear, which keeps it fresh.

The cry of the world is not only "I have," but also "I give." In the first dawning light of creation, "I have" was wedded to "I give." If this bond of union were to snap, then everything would go to ruin.

I don't know where that blind Minstrel has landed us at last.

It seems as though these stars in the sky above us are the gazing of countless eyes we met in all forgotten ages. It seems as if, through the flowers, there came the whisper of those we have forgotten, saying Remember us.

Our hearts will break if we do not sing.

*(They sing)*

*Did you leave behind you your love, my heart,*
*    and miss peace through all your days?*
*And is the path you followed lost and forgotten,*
*    making your return hopeless?*
*I go roaming listening to brooks' babble,*
*    to the rustle of leaves.*
*And it seems to me that I shall find the way,*
*    that reaches the land of lost love*
*        beyond the evening stars.*

388

What a strange tune is this, that comes out of the music of Spring!

It seems like the tune of yellow leaves.

Spring has stored up its tears in secret for us all this while.

It was afraid we should not understand it, because we were so youthful.

It wanted to beguile us with smiles.

But we shall sleep our hearts to-night in the sadness of the other shore.

Ah, the dear earth! The beautiful earth! She wants all that we have—the touch of our hands, the song of our hearts.

She wants to draw out from us all that is within, hidden even from ourselves.

This is her sorrow, that she finds out some things only to know that she has not found all. She loses before she attains.

Ah, the dear earth! We shall never deceive you.

(*They sing*)

*I shall crown you with my garland,*
  *before I take leave.*
*You ever spoke to me in all my joys and sorrows.*
  *And now, at the end of the day, my own heart will break in*
    *speech.*
*Words came to me, but not the tune,*
  *and the song that I never sang to you*
*remains hidden behind my tears.*

Brother, did you notice that some one seemed to have passed by?

The only thing you feel is this passing by.

I felt the touch of the mantle of some wayfarer.

We came out to capture somebody, but now we feel the longing to be captured ourselves.

Ah, here comes the Minstrel. Where have you brought us? The breath of the wayfaring world touches us here,—the breath of the starry sky.

We came seeking a new form of play. But now we have forgotten what play it was.

We wanted to catch the Old Man.

And everybody said that he was terrifying, a bodiless head, a gaping mouth, a dragon eager to swallow the moon of the youth of the world. But now we are no longer afraid. The flowers go, the leaves go, the waves in the river go, and we shall also follow them. Ah, blind Minstrel, strike your lute and sing to us. Who knows what is the hour of the night?

*(The Minstrel sings)*

*Let me give my all to him, before I am asked,*
  *whom the world offers its all.*
*When I came to him for my gifts, I was not afraid;*
  *And I will not fear, when I come to him,*
    *to give up what I have.*
*The morning accepts his gold with songs,*
  *the evening pays him back the debt of gold and is glad.*
*The joy of the blooming flower comes to fruit*
  *with shedding of its leaves.*

*Hasten, my heart, and spend yourself in love,*
*before the day is done.*

Minstrel, why is Chandra still absent?

*Minstrel.* Don't you know that he has gone?

Gone?—Where?

*Minstrel.* He said, "I shall go and conquer him."

Whom?

*Minstrel.* The One who is feared by all. He said,
"Why else am I young?"

Ah, that was fine.—Dada goes to read his quatrains
to the village people, and Chandra has disappeared,—
for what purpose nobody knows.

*Minstrel.* He said, "Men have always been fighting for
a cause. It is the shock of that which ruffles the breeze
of this Spring."

The shock?

*Minstrel.* Yes, the message that man's fight is not yet
over.

Is this the message of Spring?

*Minstrel.* Yes. Those who have been made immortal
by death have sent their message in these fresh leaves
of Spring. It said, "We never doubted the way. We
never counted the cost: we rushed out: we blossomed.
If we had sat down to debate, then where would be the
Spring?"

Has that made Chandra mad?

*Minstrel.* He said——

*The Spring flowers have woven my wreath of victory,*
  *The South wind breathes its breath of fire in my blood.*
*The voice of the house-corner wails in vain from behind.*
  *Death stands before me, offering its crown.*
*The tempest of youth sweeps the sky-harp with its fingers;*
  *My heart dances in its wild rhythm.*
*Gathering and storing are not for me,*
  *I spend and scatter.*
*And prudence and comfort bid me adieu in despair.*

But where has he gone to?

*Minstrel.* He said, "I cannot keep waiting by the way-side any longer. I must go and meet him, and conquer him."

But which way did he take?

*Minstrel.* He has entered the cave.

How is that? It is so fearfully dark. Did he, without making any enquiries——

*Minstrel.* Yes, he went in to make enquiries himself.

When will he come back?

I don't believe he will ever come back.

But if Chandra leaves us, then life is not worth living.

What shall we say to our Leader?

The Leader also will leave us.

Didn't he leave any message for us before he disappeared?

*Minstrel.* He said, "Wait for me. I shall return."

Return? How are we to know it?

*Minstrel.* He said, "I will conquer, and then come back again."

Then we shall wait for him all night.

But, Minstrel, where have we got to wait for him?

*Minstrel.* Before that cave, from whence the stream of water comes flowing out.

Which way did he go to get there?

The darkness there is like a dark sword.

*Minstrel.* He followed the sound of the night-bird's wings.

Why did you not go with him?

*Minstrel.* He left me behind to give you hope.

When did he go?

*Minstrel.* In the first hour of the watch.

Now the third hour has passed, I think. The air is chilly.

I dreamt that three women, with their hair hanging loose——

Oh, leave off your dream-women. I am sick of your dreams.

Everything appears darkly ominous. I didn't notice before the hooting of the owl. But now——

Do you hear that dog whining on the far bank of the river?

It seems as though a witch were riding upon him and lashing him.

Surely, if it had been possible, Chandra would have come back by now.

How I wish this night were over!

Do you hear the woman's cry?

Oh, the women, the women. They are ever crying and weeping. But they cannot turn those back who must go forward.

It is getting unbearable to sit still like this. Men imagine all sorts of things when they sit still. Let us go also. As soon as we are started on our way fear will leave us.

But who will show us the way?

There is the blind Minstrel.

What do you say, Minstrel? Can you show us the way?

*Minstrel.* Yes.

But we can hardly believe you. How can you find out the path by simply singing?

If Chandra never comes back, you shall.

We never knew that we loved Chandra so intensely. We made light of him all these days.

When we are in the playing mood, we become so intent on the play that we neglect the playmate.

But, if he once comes back, we shall never neglect him any more.

I am afraid that we have often given him pain.

Yet his love rose above all that. We never knew how beautiful he was, when we could see him every day.

(*They sing*)
*When there was light in my world*
*You stood outside my eyes.*
*Now that there is none,*
*You come into my heart.*
*When there were dolls for me, I played;*
*You smiled and watched from the door.*
*Now that the dolls have crumbled to dust,*
*You come and sit by me.*
*And I have only my heart for my music,*
*When my lute-strings have broken.*

That Minstrel sits so still and silent. I don't like it.

He looks ominous,—like the lowering autumn cloud.

Let us dismiss him.

No, no. It gives us heart, when he sits there.

Don't you see that there is no sign of fear in his face?

It seems as if some messages were striking his forehead. His body appears to espy some one in the distance. There seem to be eyes on the tips of his fingers.

Simply by watching him we can see that some one is coming through the dark.

Look. He is standing up. He is turning towards the East, and making his obeisance.

Yet there is nothing to be seen, not even a streak of light.

Why not ask him what it is that he sees?

No, don't disturb him.

Do you know, it seems to me that the morning has dawned in him.

As if the ferry-boat of light had reached the shore of his forehead.

His mind is still, like the morning sky.

The storm of birds' songs will burst out presently.

He is striking his lute. His heart is singing.

Hush. He is singing.

(*The Minstrel sings*)

*Victory to thee, victory for ever,*
  *O brave heart.*
*Victory to life, to joy, to love,*
  *To eternal light.*
*The night shall wane, the darkness shall vanish,*
  *Have faith, brave heart.*
*Wake up from sleep, from languor of despair,*
  *Receive the light of new dawn with a song.*

(*A ray of light hovers before the cavern*)

Ah! There he is. Chandra! Chandra!

Hush. Don't make any noise. I cannot see him distinctly.

Ah! It cannot be any other than Chandra.

Oh, what joy!

Chandra! Come!

Chandra! How could you leave us for so long?

Have you been able to capture the Old Man?

*Chandra.* Yes, I have.

But we don't see him.

*Chandra.* He is coming.

But what did you see in the cave? Tell us.

*Chandra.* No, I cannot tell you.

Why?

*Chandra.* If my mind were a voice, then I could tell you.

But could you see him whom you captured? Was he the Old Man of the World?

The Old Man who would like to drink up the sea of youth in his insatiable thirst.

Was it the One who is like the dark night, whose eyes are fixed on his breast, whose feet are turned the wrong way round, who walks backwards?

Was it the One who wears the garland of skulls, and lives in the burning-ground of the dead?

*Chandra.* I do not know, I cannot say. But he is coming. You shall see him.

*Minstrel.* Yes, I see him.

[*The light strengthens and gradually throughout the scene grows to a culminating brilliance at the close.*]

Where?

*Minstrel.* Here.

He is coming out of the cave.—Some one is coming out of the cave.

How wonderful!

*Chandra.* Why, it is you?

Our Leader!

Our Leader!

Our Leader!

Where is the Old Man?

*Leader.* He is nowhere.

Nowhere?

*Leader.* Yes, nowhere.

Then what is he?

*Leader.* He is a dream.

Then you are the real?

*Leader.* Yes.

And we are the real?

*Leader.* Yes.

Those who saw you from behind imagined you in all kinds of shapes.

We didn't recognize you through the dust.

You seemed old.

And then you came out of the cave,—and now you look like a boy.

It seems just as if we had seen you for the first time.

*Chandra.* You are first every time. You are first over and over again.

*Leader.* Chandra! You must own your defeat. You couldn't catch the Old Man.

*Chandra.* Let our festival begin. The sun is up.

Minstrel, if you keep so still, you will swoon away. Sing something.

(*The Minstrel sings*)

I lose thee, to find thee back again and again,
  My beloved.
Thou leavest me, that I may receive thee all the more,
  when thou returnest.
Thou canst vanish behind the moment's screen
  Only because thou art mine for evermore,
    My beloved.
When I go in search of thee, my heart trembles,
  spreading ripples across my love.
Thou smilest through thy disguise of utter absence,
  and my tears sweeten thy smile.

Do you hear the hum?

Yes.

They are not bees, but the people of the place.

Then Dada must be near at hand with his quatrains.

*Dada.* Is this the Leader?

Yes, Dada.

*Dada.* Oh, I am so glad you have come. I must read my collection of quatrains.

No. No. Not the whole collection, but only one.

*Dada.* Very well. One will do.

399

*The sun is at the gate of the East, his drum of victory sound-
ing in the sky.*
*The Night says I am blessed, my death is bliss.*
*He receives his alms of gold, filling his wallet,—and departs.*

That is to say——

No. We don't want your that is to say.

*Dada.* It means——

Whatever it means, we are determined not to know
it.

*Dada.* What makes you so desperate?

It is our festival day.

*Dada.* Ah, is that so? Then let me go to all the
neighbours——

No, you mustn't go there.

*Dada.* But is there any need for me here?

Yes.

Then my quatrains——

*Chandra.* We shall colour your quatrains with such a
thick brush that no one will know whether they have
any meaning at all.

And then you will be without any means.

The neighbourhood will desert you.

The Watchman will take you to be a fool.

And the Pundit will take you to be a blockhead.

And your own people will consider you to be useless.

And the outside people will consider you queer.

*Chandra.* But we shall crown you, Dada, with a crown of new leaves.

We shall put a garland of jasmine round your neck.

And there will be no one else except ourselves who will know your true worth.

### THE SONG OF THE FESTIVAL OF SPRING

*[In which all the persons of the drama, not excepting Sruti-bhushan, unite on the main stage in the dance of Spring.]*

> *Come and rejoice,*
> *for April is awake.*
> *Fling yourselves into the flood of being,*
> *bursting the bondage of the past.*
>
> *April is awake.*
> *Life's shoreless sea*
> *is heaving in the sun before you.*
> *All the losses are lost,*
> *and death is drowned in its waves.*
> *Plunge into the deep without fear,*
> *with the gladness of April in your heart.*

# THE FUGITIVE
## AND OTHER POEMS

# THE FUGITIVE, AND OTHER POEMS

## I

### I

DARKLY you sweep on, Eternal Fugitive, round whose bodiless rush stagnant space frets into eddying bubbles of light.

Is your heart lost to the Lover calling you across his immeasurable loneliness?

Is the aching urgency of your haste the sole reason why your tangled tresses break into stormy riot and pearls of fire roll along your path as from a broken necklace?

Your fleeting steps kiss the dust of this world into sweetness, sweeping aside all waste; the storm centred with your dancing limbs shakes the sacred shower of death over life and freshens her growth.

Should you in sudden weariness stop for a moment, the world would rumble into a heap, an encumbrance, barring its own progress, and even the least speck of dust would pierce the sky throughout its infinity with an unbearable pressure.

My thoughts are quickened by this rhythm of unseen feet round which the anklets of light are shaken.

They echo in the pulse of my heart, and through my blood surges the psalm of the ancient sea.

I hear the thundering flood tumbling my life from world to world and form to form, scattering my being in an endless spray of gifts, in sorrowings and songs.

The tide runs high, the wind blows, the boat dances like thine own desire, my heart!

Leave the hoard on the shore and sail over the unfathomed dark towards limitless light.

·   ·   ·   ·   ·

It was growing dark when I asked her, "What strange land have I come to?"

She only lowered her eyes, and the water gurgled in the throat of her jar, as she walked away.

The trees hang vaguely over the bank, and the land appears as though it already belonged to the past.

The water is dumb, the bamboos are darkly still, a wristlet tinkles against the water-jar from down the lane.

Row no more, but fasten the boat to this tree,—for I love the look of this land.

The evening star goes down behind the temple dome, and the pallor of the marble landing haunts the dark water.

Belated wayfarers sighed; for light from hidden windows is splintered into the darkness by intervening wayside trees and bushes. Still that wristlet tinkles against the water-jar, and retreating steps rustle from down the lane littered with leaves.

The night deepens, the palace towers loom spectre-like, and the town hums wearily.

Row no more, but fasten the boat to a tree.

Let me seek rest in this strange land, dimly lying under the stars, where darkness tingles with the tinkle of a wristlet knocking against a water-jar.

## IV

O THAT I were stored with a secret, like unshed rain in summer clouds—a secret, folded up in silence, that I could wander away with.

O that I had some one to whisper to, where slow waters lap under trees that doze in the sun.

The hush this evening seems to expect a footfall, and you ask me for the cause of my tears.

I cannot give a reason why I weep, for that is a secret still withheld from me.

. . . . .

## VII

I AM like the night to you, little flower.

I can only give you peace and a wakeful silence hidden in the dark.

When in the morning you open your eyes, I shall leave you to a world a-hum with bees, and songful with birds.

My last gift to you will be a tear dropped into the depth of your youth; it will make your smile all the sweeter, and bemist your outlook on the pitiless mirth of day.

. . . . .

## IX

IF I were living in the royal town of Ujjain, when Kalidas was the King's poet, I should know some Malwa girl and fill my thoughts with the music of her name. She would glance at me through the slanting shadow of her eyelids, and allow her veil to catch in the jasmine as an excuse for lingering near me.

This very thing happened in some past whose track is lost under time's dead leaves.

The scholars fight to-day about dates that play hide-and-seek.

I do not break my heart dreaming over flown and vanished ages: but alas and alas again, that those Malwa girls have followed them!

To what heaven, I wonder, have they carried in their flower-baskets those days that tingled to the lyrics of the King's poet?

This morning, separation from those whom I was born too late to meet weighs on and saddens my heart.

Yet April carries the same flowers with which they decked their hair, and the same south breeze fluttered their veils as whispers over modern roses.

And, to tell the truth, joys are not lacking to this spring, though Kalidas sing no more; and I know, if he can watch me from the Poets' Paradise, he has reasons to be envious.

## X

BE not concerned about her heart, my heart: leave it in the dark.

What if her beauty be of the figure and her smile merely of the face? Let me take without question the simple meaning of her glances and be happy.

I care not if it be a web of delusion that her arms wind about me, for the web itself is rich and rare, and the deceit can be smiled at and forgotten.

Be not concerned about her heart, my heart: be content if the music is true, though the words are not to be believed; enjoy the grace that dances like a lily on the rippling, deceiving surface, whatever may lie beneath.

XI

NEITHER mother nor daughter are you, nor bride, Urvashi.[1] Woman you are, to ravish the soul of Paradise.

When weary-footed evening comes down to the folds whither the cattle have returned, you never trim the house-lamps nor walk to the bridal bed with a tremulous heart and a wavering smile on your lips, glad that the dark hours are so secret.

Like the dawn you are without veil, Urvashi, and without shame.

Who can imagine that aching overflow of splendour which created you!

You rose from the churned ocean on the first day of the first spring, with the cup of life in your right hand and poison in your left. The monster sea, lulled like an enchanted snake, laid down its thousand hoods at your feet.

Your unblemished radiance rose from the foam, white and naked as a jasmine.

Were you ever small, timid or in bud, Urvashi, O Youth everlasting?

Did you sleep, cradled in the deep blue night where the strange light of gems plays over coral, shells and moving creatures of dreamlike form, till day revealed your awful fullness of bloom?

[1] The dancing-girl of Paradise who rose from the sea.

Adored are you of all men in all ages, Urvashi, O endless wonder!

The world throbs with youthful pain at the glance of your eyes, the ascetic lays the fruit of his austerities at your feet, the songs of poets hum and swarm round the perfume of your presence. Your feet, as in careless joy they flit on, wound even the heart of the hollow wind with the tinkle of golden bells.

When you dance before the gods, flinging orbits of novel rhythm into space, Urvashi, the earth shivers, leaf and grass, and autumn fields heave and sway; the sea surges into a frenzy of rhyming waves; the stars drop into the sky—beads from the chain that leaps till it breaks on your breast; and the blood dances in men's hearts with sudden turmoil.

You are the first break on the crest of heaven's slumber, Urvashi, you thrill the air with unrest. The world bathes your limbs in her tears; with colour of her heart's blood are your feet red; lightly you poise on the wave-tossed lotus of desire, Urvashi; you play forever in that limitless mind wherein labours God's tumultuous dream.

XII

You, like a rivulet swift and sinuous, laugh and dance, and your steps sing as you trip along.

I, like a bank rugged and steep, stand speechless and stock-still and darkly gaze at you.

I, like a big, foolish storm, of a sudden come rushing on and try to rend my being and scatter it parcelled in a whirl of passion.

410

You, like the lightning's flash slender and keen, pierce the heart of the turbulent darkness, to disappear in a vivid streak of laughter.

·   ·   ·   ·   ·

## XIV

I AM glad you will not wait for me with that lingering pity in your look.

It is only the spell of the night and my farewell words, startled at their own tune of despair, which bring these tears to my eyes. But day will dawn, my eyes will dry and my heart; and there will be no time for weeping.

Who says it is hard to forget?

The mercy of death works at life's core, bringing it respite from its own foolish persistence.

The stormy sea is lulled at last in its rocking cradle; the forest fire falls to sleep on its bed of ashes.

You and I shall part, and the cleavage will be hidden under living grass and flowers that laugh in the sun.

·   ·   ·   ·   ·

## XVI

I FORGOT myself for a moment, and I came.

But raise your eyes, and let me know if there still linger some shadow of other days, like a pale cloud on the horizon that has been robbed of its rain.

For a moment bear with me if I forget myself.

The roses are still in bud; they do not yet know how we neglect to gather flowers this summer.

The morning star has the same palpitating hush; the early light is enmeshed in the branches that overbrow your window, as in those other days.

That times are changed I forget for a little, and have come.

I forget if you ever shamed me by looking away when I bared my heart.

I only remember the words that stranded on the tremor of your lips; I remember in your dark eyes sweeping shadows of passion, like the wings of a home-seeking bird in the dusk.

I forget that you do not remember, and I come.

## XVII

THE rain fell fast. The river rushed and hissed. It licked up and swallowed the island, while I waited alone on the lessening bank with my sheaves of corn in a heap.

From the shadows of the opposite shore the boat crosses with a woman at the helm.

I cry to her, "Come to my island coiled round with hungry water, and take away my year's harvest."

She comes, and takes all that I have to the last grain; I ask her to take me.

But she says, "No"—the boat is laden with my gift and no room is left for me.

・　・　・　・　・

## XIX

ON this side of the water there is no landing; the girls do not come here to fetch water; the land along its edge is shaggy with stunted shrubs; a noisy flock of *saliks* dig their nests in the steep bank under whose frown the fisher-boats find no shelter.

You sit there on the unfrequented grass, and the morning wears on. Tell me what you do on this bank so dry that it is agape with cracks?

She looks in my face and says, "Nothing, nothing whatsoever."

On this side of the river the bank is deserted, and no cattle come to water. Only some stray goats from the village browse the scanty grass all day, and the solitary water-hawk watches from an uprooted *peepal* aslant over the mud.

You sit there alone in the miserly shade of a *shimool*, and the morning wears on.

Tell me, for whom do you wait?

She looks in my face and says, "No one, no one at all!"

· · · · ·

## XXI

### I

"WHY these preparations without end?"—I said to Mind—"Is some one to come?"

Mind replied, "I am enormously busy gathering things and building towers. I have no time to answer such questions."

Meekly I went back to my work.

When things were grown to a pile, when seven wings of his palace were complete, I said to Mind, "Is it not enough?"

Mind began to say, "Not enough to contain——"
and then stopped.

"Contain what?" I asked.

Mind affected not to hear.

I suspected that Mind did not know, and with ceaseless work smothered the question.

His one refrain was, "I must have more."

"Why must you?"

"Because it is great."

"What is great?"

Mind remained silent. I pressed for an answer.

In contempt and anger, Mind said, "Why ask about
things that are not? Take notice of those that are hugely
before you,—the struggle and the fight, the army and
armaments, the bricks and mortar, and labourers without number."

I thought, "Possibly Mind is wise."

2

Days passed. More wings were added to his palace—
more lands to his domain.

The season of rains came to an end. The dark clouds
became white and thin, and in the rain-washed sky the
sunny hours hovered like butterflies over an unseen
flower. I was bewildered and asked everybody I met,
"What is that music in the breeze?"

A tramp walked the road whose dress was wild as his
manner; he said, "Hark to the music of the Coming!"

I cannot tell why I was convinced, but the words
broke from me, "We have not much longer to wait."

"It is close at hand," said the mad man.

I went to the office and boldly said to Mind, "Stop
all work!"

Mind asked, "Have you any news?"

"Yes," I answered. "News of the Coming." But I could not explain.

Mind shook his head and said, "There are neither banners nor pageantry!"

3

The night waned, the stars paled in the sky. Suddenly the touchstone of the morning light tinged everything with gold. A cry spread from mouth to mouth—

"Here is the herald!"

I bowed my head and asked, "Is he coming?"

The answer seemed to burst from all sides, "Yes."

Mind grew troubled and said, "The dome of my building is not yet finished, nothing is in order."

A voice came from the sky, "Pull down your building!"

"But why?" asked Mind.

"Because to-day is the day of the Coming, and your building is in the way."

4

The lofty building lies in the dust and all is scattered and broken.

Mind looked about. But what was there to see?

Only the morning star and the lily washed in dew.

And what else? A child running laughing from its mother's arms into the open light.

"Was it only for this that they said it was the day of the Coming?"

"Yes, this was why they said there was music in the air and light in the sky."

"And did they claim all the earth only for this?"

415

"Yes," came the answer. "Mind, you build walls to imprison yourself. Your servants toil to enslave themselves; but the whole earth and infinite space are for the child, for the New Life."

"What does that child bring you?"

"Hope for all the world and its joy."

Mind asked me, "Poet, do you understand?"

"I lay my work aside," I said, "for I must have time to understand."

## II

### I

ENDLESSLY varied art thou in the exuberant world, Lady of Manifold Magnificence. Thy path is strewn with lights, thy touch thrills into flowers; that trailing skirt of thine sweeps the whirl of a dance among the stars, and thy many-toned music is echoed from innumerable worlds through signs and colours.

Single and alone in the unfathomed stillness of the soul, art thou, Lady of Silence and Solitude, a vision thrilled with light, a lonely lotus blossoming on the stem of love.

•     •     •     •     •

### III

I REMEMBER the day.

The heavy shower of rain is slackening into fitful pauses, renewed gusts of wind startle it from a first lull.

I take up my instrument. Idly I touch the strings, till, without my knowing, the music borrows the mad cadence of that storm.

I see her figure as she steals from her work, stops at my door, and retreats with hesitating steps. She comes again, stands outside leaning against the wall, then slowly enters the room and sits down. With head bent, she plies her needle in silence; but soon stops her work, and looks out of the window through the rain at the blurred line of trees.

Only this—one hour of a rainy noon filled with shadows and song and silence.

IV

WHILE stepping into the carriage she turned her head and threw me a swift glance of farewell.

This was her last gift to me. But where can I keep it safe from the trampling hours?

Must evening sweep this gleam of anguish away, as it will the last flicker of fire from the sunset?

Ought it to be washed off by the rain, as treasured pollen is from heart-broken flowers?

Leave kingly glory and the wealth of the rich to death. But may not tears keep ever fresh the memory of a glance flung through a passionate moment?

"Give it to me to keep," said my song; "I never touch kings' glory or the wealth of the rich, but these small things are mine for ever."

.    .    .    .    .

VI

I WAS to go away; still she did not speak. But I felt, from a slight quiver, her yearning arms would say: "Ah, no, not yet."

417

I have often heard her pleading hands vocal in a touch, though they knew not what they said.

I have known those arms to stammer when, had they not, they would have become youth's garland round my neck.

Their little gestures return to remembrance in the covert of still hours; like truants they playfully reveal things she had kept secret from me.

VII

MY songs are like bees; they follow through the air some fragrant trace—some memory—of you, to hum around your shyness, eager for its hidden store.

When the freshness of dawn droops in the sun, when in the noon the air hangs low with heaviness and the forest is silent, my songs return home, their languid wings dusted with gold.

．　　．　　．　　．　　．

IX

I THINK I shall stop startled if ever we meet after our next birth, walking in the light of a far-away world.

I shall know those dark eyes then as morning stars, and yet feel that they have belonged to some un-remembered evening sky of a former life.

I shall know that the magic of your face is not all its own, but has stolen the passionate light that was in my eyes at some immemorial meeting, and then gathered from my love a mystery that has now forgotten its origin.

## X

LAY down your lute, my love, leave your arms free to embrace me.

Let your touch bring my overflowing heart to my body's utmost brink.

Do not bend your neck and turn away your face, but offer up a kiss to me, which has been like some perfume long closed in a bud.

Do not smother this moment under vain words, but let our hearts quake in a rush of silence sweeping all thoughts to the shoreless delight.

## XI

YOU have made me great with your love, though I am but one among the many, drifting in the common tide, rocking in the fluctuant favour of the world.

You have given me a seat where poets of all time bring their tribute, and lovers with deathless names greet one another across the ages.

Men hastily pass me in the market,—never noting how my body has grown precious with your caress, how I carry your kiss within, as the sun carries in its orb the fire of the divine touch and shines for ever.

## XII

LIKE a child that frets and pushes away its toys, my heart to-day shakes its head at every phrase I suggest, and says, "No, not this."

Yet words, in the agony of their vagueness, haunt my mind, like vagrant clouds hovering over hills, waiting for some chance wind to relieve them of their rain.

419

But leave these vain efforts, my soul, for the stillness will ripen its own music in the dark.

My life to-day is like a cloister during some penance, where the spring is afraid to stir or to whisper.

This is not the time, my love, for you to pass the gate; at the mere thought of your anklet bells tinkling down the path, the garden echoes are ashamed.

Know that to-morrow's songs are in bud to-day, and should they see you walk by they would strain to breaking their immature hearts.

## XIII

WHENCE do you bring this disquiet, my love?

Let my heart touch yours and kiss the pain out of your silence.

The night has thrown up from its depth this little hour, that love may build a new world within these shut doors, to be lighted by this solitary lamp.

We have for music but a single reed which our two pairs of lips must play on by turns—for crown, only one garland to bind my hair after I have put it on your forehead.

Tearing the veil from my breast I shall make our bed on the floor; and one kiss and one sleep of delight shall fill our small boundless world.

## XIV

ALL that I had I gave to you, keeping but the barest veil of reserve.

It is so thin that you secretly smile at it and I feel ashamed.

The gust of the spring breeze sweeps it away unawares, and the flutter of my own heart moves it as the waves move their foam.

My love, do not grieve if I keep this flimsy mist of distance round me.

This frail reserve of mine is no mere woman's coyness, but a slender stem on which the flower of my self-surrender bends towards you with reticent grace.

## XV

I HAVE donned this new robe to-day because my body feels like singing.

It is not enough that I am given to my love once and for ever, but out of that I must fashion new gifts every day; and shall I not seem a fresh offering, dressed in a new robe?

My heart, like the evening sky, has its endless passion for colour, and therefore I change my veils, which have now the green of the cool young grass and now that of the winter rice.

To-day my robe is tinted with the rain-rimmed blue of the sky. It brings to my limbs the colour of the boundless, the colour of the oversea hills; and it carries in its folds the delight of summer clouds flying in the wind.

## XVI

I THOUGHT I would write love's words in their own colour; but that lies deep in the heart, and tears are pale.

Would you know them, friend, if the words were colourless?

I thought I would sing love's words to their own tune, but that sounds only in my heart, and my eyes are silent.

Would you know them, friend, if there were no tune?

## XVII

IN the night the song came to me; but you were not there.

It found the words for which I had been seeking all day. Yes, in the stillness a moment after dark they throbbed into music, even as the stars then began to pulse with light; but you were not there. My hope was to sing it to you in the morning; but, try as I might, though the music came, the words hung back, when you were beside me.

## XVIII

THE night deepens and the dying flame flickers in the lamp.

I forgot to notice when the evening—like a village girl who has filled her pitcher at the river a last time for that day—closed the door on her cabin.

I was speaking to you, my love, with mind barely conscious of my voice—tell me, had it any meaning? Did it bring you any message from beyond life's borders?

For now, since my voice has ceased, I feel the night throbbing with thoughts that gaze in awe at the abyss of their dumbness.

## XIX

WHEN we two first met my heart rang out in music, "She who is eternally afar is beside you for ever."

That music is silent, because I have grown to believe that my love is only near, and have forgotten that she is also far, far away.

Music fills the infinite between two souls. This has been muffled by the mist of our daily habits.

On shy summer nights, when the breeze brings a vast murmur out of the silence, I sit up in my bed and mourn the great loss of her who is beside me. I ask myself, "When shall I have another chance to whisper to her words with the rhythm of eternity in them?"

Wake up, my song, from thy languor, rend this screen of the familiar, and fly to my beloved there, in the endless surprise of our first meeting!

. . . . .

## XXI

THE father came back from the funeral rites.

His boy of seven stood at the window, with eyes wide open and a golden amulet hanging from his neck, full of thoughts too difficult for his age.

His father took him in his arms and the boy asked him, "Where is mother?"

"In heaven," answered his father, pointing to the sky.

AT night the father groaned in slumber, weary with grief.

A lamp dimly burned near the bedroom door, and a lizard chased moths on the wall.

The boy woke up from sleep, felt with his hands the emptiness in the bed, and stole out to the open terrace.

The boy raised his eyes to the sky and long gazed in silence. His bewildered mind sent abroad into the night the question, "Where is heaven?"

No answer came: and the stars seemed like the burning tears of that ignorant darkness.

## XXII

SHE went away when the night was about to wane.

My mind tried to console me by saying, "All is vanity."

I felt angry and said, "That unopened letter with her name on it, and this palm-leaf fan bordered with red silk by her own hands, are they not real?"

The day passed, and my friend came and said to me, "Whatever is good is true, and can never perish."

"How do you know?" I asked impatiently; "was not this body good which is now lost to the world?"

As a fretful child hurting its own mother, I tried to wreck all the shelters that ever I had, in and about me, and cried, "This world is treacherous."

Suddenly I felt a voice saying—"Ungrateful!"

I looked out of the window, and a reproach seemed to come from the star-sprinkled night,—"You pour out into the void of my absence your faith in the truth that I came!"

## XXIII

THE river is grey and the air dazed with blown sand.

On a morning of dark disquiet, when the birds are mute and their nests shake in the gust, I sit alone and ask myself, "Where is she?"

The days have flown wherein we sat too near each other; we laughed and jested, and the awe of love's majesty found no words at our meetings.

I made myself small, and she trifled away every moment with pelting talk.

To-day I wish in vain that she were by me, in the gloom of the coming storm, to sit in the soul's solitude.

### XXIV

THE name she called me by, like a flourishing jasmine, covered the whole seventeen years of our love. With its sound mingled the quiver of the light through the leaves, the scent of the grass in the rainy night, and the sad silence of the last hour of many an idle day.

Not the work of God alone was he who answered to that name; she created him again for herself during those seventeen swift years.

Other years were to follow, but their vagrant days, no longer gathered within the fold of that name uttered in her voice, stray and are scattered.

They ask me, "Who should fold us?"

I find no answer and sit silent, and they cry to me while dispersing, "We seek a shepherdess!"

Whom should they seek?

That they do not know. And like derelict evening clouds they drift in the trackless dark, and are lost and forgotten.

### XXV

I FEEL that your brief days of love have not been left behind in those scanty years of your life.

I seek to know in what place, away from the slow-thieving dust, you keep them now. I find in my solitude some song of your evening that died, yet left a deathless echo; and the sighs of your unsatisfied hours I find nestled in the warm quiet of the autumn noon.

Your desires come from the hive of the past to haunt
my heart, and I sit still to listen to their wings.

·    ·    ·    ·    ·

## XXVII

I WAS walking along a path overgrown with grass, when
suddenly I heard from some one behind, "See if you
know me?"

I turned round and looked at her and said, "I cannot
remember your name."

She said, "I am that first great Sorrow whom you met
when you were young."

Her eyes looked like a morning whose dew is still in
the air.

I stood silent for some time till I said, "Have you
lost all the great burden of your tears?"

She smiled and said nothing. I felt that her tears had
had time to learn the language of smiles.

"Once you said," she whispered, "that you would
cherish your grief for ever."

I blushed and said, "Yes, but years have passed and I
forget."

Then I took her hand in mine and said, "But you
have changed."

"What was sorrow once has now become peace," she
said.

## XXVIII

OUR life sails on the uncrossed sea whose waves chase
each other in an eternal hide-and-seek.

It is the restless sea of change, feeding its foaming

flocks to lose them over and over again, beating its hands against the calm of the sky.

Love, in the centre of this circling war-dance of light and dark, yours is that green island, where the sun kisses the shy forest shade and silence is wooed by birds' singing.

.  .  .  .  .

## XXX

A PAINTER was selling pictures at the fair; followed by servants, there passed the son of a Minister who in youth had cheated this painter's father so that he had died of a broken heart.

The boy lingered before the pictures and chose one for himself. The painter flung a cloth over it and said he would not sell it.

After this the boy pined heart-sick till his father came and offered a large price. But the painter kept the picture unsold on his shop wall and grimly sat before it, saying to himself, "This is my revenge."

The sole form this painter's worship took was to trace an image of his god every morning.

And now he felt these pictures grow daily more different from those he used to paint.

This troubled him, and he sought in vain for an explanation till one day he started up from work in horror; the eyes of the god he had just drawn were those of the Minister, and so were the lips.

He tore up the picture, crying, "My revenge has returned on my head!"

## XXXI

THE General came before the silent and angry King and saluting him said: "The village is punished, the men are stricken to dust, and the women cower in their unlit homes afraid to weep aloud."

The High Priest stood up and blessed the King and cried: "God's mercy is ever upon you."

The Clown, when he heard this, burst out laughing and startled the Court. The King's frown darkened.

"The honour of the throne," said the Minister, "is upheld by the King's prowess and the blessing of Almighty God."

Louder laughed the Clown, and the King growled,— "Unseemly mirth!"

"God has showered many blessings upon your head," said the Clown; "the one he bestowed on me was the gift of laughter."

"This gift will cost you your life," said the King, gripping his sword with his right hand.

Yet the Clown stood up and laughed till he laughed no more.

A shadow of dread fell upon the Court, for they heard that laughter echoing in the depth of God's silence.

●　　　●　　　●　　　●　　　●

XXXIII

FIERCELY they rend in pieces the carpet woven during ages of prayer for the welcome of the world's best hope.

The great preparations of love lie a heap of shreds, and there is nothing on the ruined altar to remind the mad crowd that their god was to have come. In a fury of passion they seem to have burnt their future to cinders, and with it the season of their bloom.

The air is harsh with the cry, "Victory to the Brute!" The children look haggard and aged; they whisper to one another that time revolves but never advances, that we are goaded to run but have nothing to reach, that creation is like a blind man's groping.

I said to myself, "Cease thy singing. Song is for one who is to come, the struggle without an end is for things that are."

The road, that ever lies along like some one with ear to the ground listening for footsteps, to-day gleans no hint of coming guest, nothing of the house at its far end.

My lute said, "Trample me in the dust."

I looked at the dust by the roadside. There was a tiny flower among thorns. And I cried, "The world's hope is not dead!"

The sky stooped over the horizon to whisper to the earth, and a hush of expectation filled the air. I saw the palm leaves clapping their hands to the beat of inaudible music, and the moon exchanged glances with the glistening silence of the lake.

The road said to me, "Fear nothing!" and my lute said, "Lend me thy songs!"

### III

#### I

COME, Spring, reckless lover of the earth, make the forest's heart pant for utterance!

Come in gusts of disquiet where flowers break open and jostle the new leaves!

Burst, like a rebellion of light, through the night's vigil, through the lake's dark dumbness, through the dungeon under the dust, proclaiming freedom to the shackled seeds!

Like the laughter of lightning, like the shout of a storm, break into the midst of the noisy town; free stifled word and unconscious effort, reinforce our flagging fight, and conquer death!

## II

I HAVE looked on this picture in many a month of March when the mustard is in bloom—this lazy line of the water and the grey of the sand beyond, the rough path along the river-bank carrying the comradeship of the field into the heart of the village.

I have tried to capture in rhyme the idle whistle of the wind, the beat of the oar-strokes from a passing boat.

I have wondered in my mind how simply it stands before me, this great world: with what fond and familiar ease it fills my heart, this encounter with the Eternal Stranger.

## III

THE ferry-boat plies between the two villages facing each other across the narrow stream.

The water is neither wide nor deep—a mere break in the path that enhances the small adventures of daily life, like a break in the words of a song across which the tune gleefully streams.

While the towers of wealth rise high and crash to ruin, these villages talk to each other across the garrulous stream, and the ferry-boat plies between them, age after age, from seed-time to harvest.

.    .    .    .    .

## V

In Baby's world, the trees shake their leaves at him, murmuring verses in an ancient tongue that dates from before the age of meaning, and the moon feigns to be of his own age—the solitary baby of night.

In the world of the old, flowers dutifully blush at the make-believe of faery legends, and broken dolls confess that they are made of clay.

.    .    .    .    .

## VII

How often, great Earth, have I felt my being yearn to flow over you, sharing in the happiness of each green blade that raises its signal banner in answer to the beckoning blue of the sky!

I feel as if I had belonged to you ages before I was born. That is why, in the days when the autumn light shimmers on the mellowing ears of rice, I seem to remember a past when my mind was everywhere, and even to hear voices as of playfellows echoing from the remote and deeply veiled past.

When, in the evening, the cattle return to their folds, raising dust from the meadow paths, as the moon rises higher than the smoke ascending from the village huts, I feel sad as for some great separation that happened in the first morning of existence.

.    .    .    .    .

## IX

THE clouds thicken till the morning light seems like a bedraggled fringe to the rainy night.

A little girl stands at her window, still as a rainbow at the gate of a broken-down storm.

She is my neighbour, and has come upon the earth like some god's rebellious laughter. Her mother in anger calls her incorrigible; her father smiles and calls her mad.

She is like a runaway waterfall leaping over boulders, like the topmost bamboo twig rustling in the restless wind.

She stands at her window looking out into the sky.

Her sister comes to say, "Mother calls you." She shakes her head.

Her little brother with his toy boat comes and tries to pull her off to play; she snatches her hand from his. The boy persists and she gives him a slap on the back.

The first great voice was the voice of wind and water in the beginning of earth's creation.

That ancient cry of nature—her dumb call to unborn life—has reached this child's heart and leads it out alone beyond the fence of our times: so there she stands, possessed by eternity!

## X

THE kingfisher sits still on the prow of an empty boat, while in the shallow margin of the stream a buffalo lies tranquilly blissful, its eyes half closed to savour the luxury of cool mud.

Undismayed by the barking of the village cur, the cow browses on the bank, followed by a hopping group of *saliks* hunting moths.

I sit in the tamarind grove, where the cries of dumb life congregate—the cattle's lowing, the sparrows' chatter, the shrill scream of a kite overhead, the crickets' chirp, and the splash of a fish in the water.

I peep into the primeval nursery of life, where the mother Earth thrills at the first living clutch near her breast.

### XI

AT the sleepy village the noon was still like a sunny midnight when my holidays came to their end.

My little girl of four had followed me all the morning from room to room, watching my preparations in grave silence, till, wearied, she sat by the door-post strangely quiet, murmuring to herself, "Father must not go!"

This was the meal-hour, when sleep daily overcame her, but her mother had forgotten her and the child was too unhappy to complain.

At last, when I stretched out my arms to her to say farewell, she never moved, but sadly looking at me said, "Father, you must not go!"

And it amused me to tears to think how this little child dared to fight the giant world of necessity with no other resource than those few words, "Father, you must not go!"

### XII

TAKE your holiday, my boy; there are the blue sky and the bare field, the barn and the ruined temple under the ancient tamarind.

My holiday must be taken through yours, finding

light in the dance of your eyes, music in your noisy shouts.

To you autumn brings the true holiday freedom: to me it brings the impossibility of work; for lo! you burst into my room.

Yes, my holiday is an endless freedom for love to disturb me.

### XIII

IN the evening my little daughter heard a call from her companions below the window.

She timidly went down the dark stairs holding a lamp in her hand, shielding it behind her veil.

I was sitting on my terrace in the star-lit night of March, when at a sudden cry I ran to see.

Her lamp had gone out in the dark spiral staircase. I asked, "Child, why did you cry?"

From below she answered in distress, "Father, I have lost myself!"

When I came back to the terrace under the star-lit night of March, I looked at the sky, and it seemed that a child was walking there treasuring many lamps behind her veils.

If their light went out, she would suddenly stop and a cry would sound from sky to sky, "Father, I have lost myself!"

### XIV

THE evening stood bewildered among street-lamps, its gold tarnished by the city dust.

A woman, gaudily decked and painted, leant over the rail of her balcony, a living fire waiting for its moths.

Suddenly an eddy was formed in the road round a street-boy crushed under the wheels of a carriage, and the woman on the balcony fell to the floor screaming in agony, stricken with the grief of the great white-robed Mother who sits in the world's inner shrine.

## XV

I REMEMBER the scene on the barren heath—a girl sat alone on the grass before the gipsy camp, braiding her hair in the afternoon shade.

Her little dog jumped and barked at her busy hands, as though her employment had no importance.

In vain did she rebuke it, calling it "a pest," saying she was tired of its perpetual silliness.

She struck it on the nose with her reproving forefinger, which only seemed to delight it the more.

She looked menacingly grave for a few moments, to warn it of impending doom; and then, letting her hair fall, quickly snatched it up in her arms, laughed, and pressed it to her heart.

. . . . .

## XVII

IF the ragged villager, trudging home from the market, could suddenly be lifted to the crest of a distant age, men would stop in their work and shout and run to him in delight.

For they would no longer whittle down the man into the peasant, but find him full of the mystery and spirit of his age.

Even his poverty and pain would grow great, released

from the shallow insult of the present, and the paltry things in his basket would acquire pathetic dignity.

WITH the morning he came out to walk a road shaded by a file of deodars, that coiled the hill round like importunate love.

He held the first letter from his newly wedded wife in their village home, begging him to come to her, and come soon.

The touch of an absent hand haunted him as he walked, and the air seemed to take up the cry of the letter: "Love, my love, my sky is brimming with tears!"

He asked himself in wonder, "How do I deserve this?"

The sun suddenly appeared over the rim of the blue hills, and four girls from a foreign shore came with swift strides, talking loud and followed by a barking dog.

The two elder turned away to conceal their amusement at something strange in his insignificance, and the younger ones pushed each other, laughed aloud, and ran off in exuberant mirth.

He stopped and his head sank. Then he suddenly felt his letter, opened and read it again.

THE day came for the image from the temple to be drawn round the holy town in its chariot.

The Queen said to the King, "Let us go and attend the festival."

Only one man out of the whole household did not join in the pilgrimage. His work was to collect stalks of spear-grass to make brooms for the King's house.

The chief of the servants said in pity to him, "You may come with us."

He bowed his head, saying, "It cannot be."

The man dwelt by the road along which the King's followers had to pass. And when the Minister's elephant reached this spot, he called to him and said, "Come with us and see the God ride in his chariot!"

"I dare not seek God after the King's fashion," said the man.

"How should you ever have such luck again as to see the God in his chariot?" asked the Minister.

"When God himself comes to my door," answered the man.

The Minister laughed loud and said, "Fool! 'When God comes to your door!' yet a King must travel to see him!"

"Who except God visits the poor?" said the man.

XX

DAYS were drawing out as the winter ended, and, in the sun, my dog played in his wild way with the pet deer.

The crowd going to the market gathered by the fence, and laughed to see the love of these playmates struggle with languages so dissimilar.

The spring was in the air, and the young leaves fluttered like flames. A gleam danced in the deer's dark eyes when she started, bent her neck at the movement of her own shadow, or raised her ears to listen to some whisper in the wind.

The message comes floating with the errant breeze,

with the rustle and glimmer abroad in the April sky. It sings of the first ache of youth in the world, when the first flower broke from the bud, and love went forth seeking that which it knew not, leaving all it had known.

And one afternoon, when among the *amlak* trees the shadow grew grave and sweet with the furtive caress of light, the deer set off to run like a meteor in love with death.

It grew dark, and lamps were lighted in the house; the stars came out and night was upon the fields, but the deer never came back.

My dog ran up to me whining, questioning me with his piteous eyes which seemed to say, "I do not understand!"

But who does ever understand?

## XXI

OUR Lane is tortuous, as if, ages ago, she started in quest of her goal, vacillated right and left, and remained bewildered for ever.

Above in the air, between her buildings, hangs like a ribbon a strip torn out of space: she calls it her sister of the blue town.

She sees the sun only for a few moments at midday, and asks herself in wise doubt, "Is it real?"

In June rain sometimes shades her band of daylight as with pencil hatchings. The path grows slippery with mud, and umbrellas collide. Sudden jets of water from spouts overhead splash on her startled pavement. In her dismay, she takes it for the jest of an unmannerly scheme of creation.

The spring breeze, gone astray in her coil of contortions, stumbles like a drunken vagabond against angle and corner, filling the dusty air with scraps of paper and rag. "What fury of foolishness! Are the Gods gone mad?" she exclaims in indignation.

But the daily refuse from the houses on both sides—scales of fish mixed with ashes, vegetable peelings, rotten fruit, and dead rats—never rouses her to question, "Why should these things be?"

She accepts every stone of her paving. But from between their chinks sometimes a blade of grass peeps up. That baffles her. How can solid facts permit such intrusion?

On a morning when at the touch of autumn light her houses wake up into beauty from their foul dreams, she whispers to herself, "There is a limitless wonder somewhere beyond these buildings."

But the hours pass on; the households are astir; the maid strolls back from the market, swinging her right arm and with the left clasping the basket of provisions to her side; the air grows thick with the smell and smoke of kitchens. It again becomes clear to our Lane that the real and normal consist solely of herself, her houses, and their muck-heaps.

## XXII

THE house, lingering on after its wealth has vanished, stands by the wayside like a madman with a patched rag over his back.

Day after day scars it with spiteful scratches, and rainy months leave their fantastic signatures on its bared bricks.

In a deserted upper room one of a pair of doors has

fallen from rusty hinges; and the other, widowed, bangs day and night to the fitful gusts.

One night the sound of women wailing came from that house. They mourned the death of the last son of the family, a boy of eighteen, who earned his living by playing the part of the heroine in a travelling theatre.

A few days more and the house became silent, and all the doors were locked.

Only on the north side in the upper room that desolate door would neither drop off to its rest nor be shut, but swung to and fro in the wind like a self-torturing soul.

After a time children's voices echo once more through that house. Over the balcony-rail women's clothes are hung in the sun, a bird whistles from a covered cage, and a boy plays with his kite on the terrace.

A tenant has come to occupy a few rooms. He earns little and has many children. The tired mother beats them and they roll on the floor and shriek.

A maid-servant of forty drudges through the day, quarrels with her mistress, threatens to, but never leaves.

Every day some small repairs are done. Paper is pasted in place of missing panes; gaps in the railings are made good with split bamboo; an empty box keeps the boltless gate shut; old stains vaguely show through new whitewash on the walls.

The magnificence of wealth had found a fitting memorial in gaunt desolation; but, lacking sufficient means, they try to hide this with dubious devices, and its dignity is outraged.

They have overlooked the deserted room on the north side. And its forlorn door still bangs in the wind, like Despair beating her breast.

XXIII

In the depths of the forest the ascetic practised penance with fast-closed eyes; he intended to deserve Paradise.

But the girl who gathered twigs brought him fruits in her skirt, and water from the stream in cups made of leaves.

The days went on, and his penance grew harsher till the fruits remained untasted, the water untouched: and the girl who gathered twigs was sad.

The Lord of Paradise heard that a man had dared to aspire to be as the Gods. Time after time he had fought the Titans, who were his peers, and kept them out of his kingdom; yet he feared a man whose power was that of suffering.

But he knew the ways of mortals, and he planned a temptation to decoy this creature of dust away from his adventure.

A breath from Paradise kissed the limbs of the girl who gathered twigs, and her youth ached with a sudden rapture of beauty, and her thoughts hummed like the bees of a rifled hive.

The time came when the ascetic should leave the forest for a mountain cave, to complete the rigour of his penance.

When he opened his eyes in order to start on this journey, the girl appeared to him like a verse familiar, yet forgotten, and which an added melody made

441

strange. The ascetic rose from his seat and told her that it was time he left the forest.

"But why rob me of my chance to serve you?" she asked with tears in her eyes.

He sat down again, thought for long, and remained on where he was.

That night remorse kept the girl awake. She began to dread her power and hate her triumph, yet her mind tossed on the waves of turbulent delight.

In the morning she came and saluted the ascetic and asked his blessing, saying she must leave him.

He gazed on her face in silence, then said, "Go, and may your wish be fulfilled."

For years he sat alone till his penance was complete.

The Lord of the Immortals came down to tell him that he had won Paradise.

"I no longer need it," said he.

The God asked him what greater reward he desired.

"I want the girl who gathers twigs."

## XXIV

THEY said that Kabir, the weaver, was favoured of God, and the crowd flocked round him for medicine and miracles. But he was troubled; his low birth had hither-to endowed him with a most precious obscurity to sweeten with songs and with the presence of his God. He prayed that it might be restored.

Envious of the repute of this outcast, the priests leagued themselves with a harlot to disgrace him. Kabir came to the market to sell cloths from his loom; when the woman grasped his hand, blaming him for being faithless, and followed him to his house, saying she would not be forsaken, Kabir said to himself, "God answers prayers in his own way."

Soon the woman felt a shiver of fear and fell on her knees and cried, "Save me from my sin!" To which he said, "Open your life to God's light!"

Kabir worked at his loom and sang, and his songs washed the stains from that woman's heart, and by way of return found a home in her sweet voice.

One day the King, in a fit of caprice, sent a message to Kabir to come and sing before him. The weaver shook his head: but the messenger dared not leave his door till his master's errand was fulfilled.

The King and his courtiers started at the sight of Kabir when he entered the hall. For he was not alone, the woman followed him. Some smiled, some frowned, and the King's face darkened at the beggar's pride and shamelessness.

Kabir came back to his house disgraced, the woman fell at his feet crying, "Why accept such dishonour for my sake, master? Suffer me to go back to my infamy!"

Kabir said, "I dare not turn my God away when he comes branded with insult."

·　·　·　·　·

## XXVI

THE man had no useful work, only vagaries of various kinds.

Therefore it surprised him to find himself in Paradise after a life spent perfecting trifles.

Now the guide had taken him by mistake to the

wrong Paradise—one meant only for good, busy souls.

In this Paradise, our man saunters along the road only to obstruct the rush of business.

He stands aside from the path and is warned that he tramples on sown seed. Pushed, he starts up: hustled, he moves on.

A very busy girl comes to fetch water from the well. Her feet run on the pavement like rapid fingers over harp-strings. Hastily she ties a negligent knot with her hair, and loose locks on her forehead pry into the dark of her eyes.

The man says to her, "Would you lend me your pitcher?"

"My pitcher?" she asks, "to draw water?"

"No, to paint patterns on."

"I have no time to waste," the girl retorts in contempt.

Now a busy soul has no chance against one who is supremely idle.

Every day she meets him at the well, and every day he repeats the same request, till at last she yields.

Our man paints the pitcher with curious colours in a mysterious maze of lines.

The girl takes it up, turns it round and asks, "What does it mean?"

"It has no meaning," he answers.

The girl carries the pitcher home. She holds it up in different lights and tries to con its mystery.

At night she leaves her bed, lights a lamp, and gazes at it from all points of view.

This is the first time she has met with something without meaning.

On the next day the man is again near the well.
The girl asks, "What do you want?"
"To do more work for you."
"What work?" she enquires.
"Allow me to weave coloured strands into a ribbon to bind your hair."
"Is there any need?" she asks.
"None whatever," he allows.
The ribbon is made, and thenceforward she spends a great deal of time over her hair.
The even stretch of well-employed time in that Paradise begins to show irregular rents.
The elders are troubled; they meet in council.
The guide confesses his blunder, saying that he has brought the wrong man to the wrong place.
The wrong man is called. His turban, flaming with colour, shows plainly how great that blunder has been.
The chief of the elders says, "You must go back to the earth."
The man heaves a sigh of relief: "I am ready."
The girl with the ribbon round her hair chimes in: "I also!"
For the first time the chief of the elders is faced with a situation which has no sense in it.

## XXVII

IT is said that in the forest, near the meeting of river and lake, certain fairies live in disguise who are only recognized as fairies after they have flown away.
A Prince went to this forest, and when he came

where river met lake he saw a village girl sitting on the bank ruffling the water to make the lilies dance.

He asked her in a whisper, "Tell me, what fairy art thou?"

The girl laughed at the question and the hillsides echoed her mirth.

The Prince thought she was the laughing fairy of the waterfall.

News reached the King that the Prince had married a fairy: he sent horses and men and brought them to his house.

The Queen saw the bride and turned her face away in disgust, the Prince's sister flushed red with annoyance, and the maids asked if that was how fairies dressed.

The Prince whispered, "Hush! my fairy has come to our house in disguise."

On the day of the yearly festival the Queen said to her son, "Ask your bride not to shame us before our kinsfolk who are coming to see the fairy."

And the Prince said to his bride, "For my love's sake show thy true self to my people."

Long she sat silent, then nodded her promise while tears ran down her cheeks.

The full moon shone, the Prince, dressed in a wedding robe, entered his bride's room.

No one was there, nothing but a streak of moonlight from the window aslant the bed.

The kinsfolk crowded in with the King and the Queen, the Prince's sister stood by the door.

All asked, "Where is the fairy bride?"

The Prince answered, "She has vanished for ever to make herself known to you."

· · · · ·

## XXIX

WHEN like a flaming scimitar the hill stream has been sheathed in gloom by the evening, suddenly a flock of birds passes overhead, their loud-laughing wings hurling their flight like an arrow among stars.

It startles a passion for speed in the heart of all motionless things; the hills seem to feel in their bosom the anguish of storm-clouds, and trees long to break their rooted shackles.

For me the flight of these birds has rent a veil of stillness, and reveals an immense flutter in this deep silence.

I see these hills and forests fly across time to the unknown, and darkness thrill into fire as the stars wing by.

I feel in my own being the rush of the sea-crossing bird, cleaving a way beyond the limits of life and death, While the migrant world cries with a myriad voice, "Not here, but somewhere else, in the bosom of the Far-away."

## XXX

THE crowd listens in wonder to Kashi, the young singer, whose voice, like a sword in feats of skill, dances amidst hopeless tangles, cuts them to pieces, and exults.

Among the hearers sits old Rajah Pratap in weary endurance. For his own life had been nourished and encircled by Barajlal's songs, like a happy land which a river laces with beauty. His rainy evenings and the still hours of autumn days spoke to his heart through Baraj-

447

lal's voice, and his festive nights trimmed their lamps and tinkled their bells to those songs.

When Kashi stopped for rest, Pratap smilingly winked at Barajlal and spoke to him in a whisper, "Master, now let us hear music and not this new-fangled singing, which mimics frisky kittens hunting paralysed mice."

The old singer with his spotlessly white turban made a deep bow to the assembly and took his seat. His thin fingers struck the strings of his instrument, his eyes closed, and in timid hesitation his song began. The hall was large, his voice feeble, and Pratap shouted "Bravo!" with ostentation, but whispered in his ear, "Just a little louder, friend!"

The crowd was restless; some yawned, some dozed, some complained of the heat. The air of the hall hummed with many-toned inattention, and the song, like a frail boat, tossed upon it in vain till it sank under the hubbub.

Suddenly the old man, stricken at heart, forgot a passage, and his voice groped in agony, like a blind man at a fair for his lost leader. He tried to fill the gap with any strain that came. But the gap still yawned: and the tortured notes refused to serve the need, suddenly changed their tune, and broke into a sob. The master laid his head on his instrument, and in place of his forgotten music there broke from him the first cry of life that a child brings into the world.

Pratap touched him gently on his shoulder, and said, "Come away, our meeting is elsewhere. I know, my

friend, that truth is widowed without love, and beauty
dwells not with the many, nor in the moment."

### XXXI

IN the youth of the world, Himalaya, you sprang from
the rent breast of the earth, and hurled your burning
challenges to the sun, hill after hill. Then came the
mellow time when you said to yourself, "No more, no
further!" and your fiery heart, that raged for the freedom of clouds, found its limits, and stood still to salute
the limitless. After this check on your passion, beauty
was free to play upon your breast, and trust surrounded
you with the joy of flowers and birds.

You sit in your solitude like a great reader, on whose
lap lies open some ancient book with its countless pages
of stone. What story is written there, I wonder?—is it
the eternal wedding of the divine ascetic, Shiva, with
Bhavani, the divine love?—the drama of the Terrible
wooing the power of the Frail?

.    .    .    .    .

### XXXIII

MY eyes feel the deep peace of this sky, and there stirs
through me what a tree feels when it holds out its
leaves like cups to be filled with sunshine.
A thought rises in my mind, like the warm breath
from grass in the sun; it mingles with the gurgle of
lapping water and the sigh of weary wind in village
lanes,—the thought that I have lived along with the
whole life of this world and have given to it my own
love and sorrows.

.    .    .    .    .

GIVE me the supreme courage of love, this is my prayer
—the courage to speak, to do, to suffer at thy will, to
leave all things or be left alone. Strengthen me on
errands of danger, honour me with pain, and help me
climb to that difficult mood which sacrifices daily to
thee.

Give me the supreme confidence of love, this is my
prayer—the confidence that belongs to life in death, to
victory in defeat, to the power hidden in frailest beauty,
to that dignity in pain which accepts hurt but disdains
to return it.

## THIS EVIL DAY

AGE after age, hast Thou, O Lord, sent Thy messengers
into this pitiless world, who have left their word:
"Forgive all. Love all. Cleanse your hearts from the
blood-red stains of hatred."

Adorable are they, ever to be remembered; yet from
the outer door have I turned them away to-day—this
evil day—with unmeaning salutation.

Have I not seen secret malignance strike down the
helpless under the cover of hypocritical night?

Have I not heard the silenced voice of Justice weeping
in solitude at might's defiant outrages?

Have I not seen in what agony reckless youth,
running mad, has vainly shattered its life against in-
sensitive rocks?

Choked is my voice, mute are my songs to-day, and
darkly my world lies imprisoned in a dismal dream; and
I ask Thee, O Lord, in tears: "Hast Thou Thyself for-

given, hast even Thou loved those who are poisoning Thy air, and blotting out Thy light?"

## BORO-BUDUR [1]

THE sun shone on a far-away morning, while the forest murmured its hymn of praise to light; and the hills, veiled in vapour, dimly glimmered like earth's dream in purple.

The King sat alone in the coconut grove, his eyes drowned in a vision, his heart exultant with the rapturous hope of spreading the chant of adoration along the unending path of time:

"Let Buddha be my refuge."

His words found utterance in a deathless speech of delight, in an ecstasy of forms.

The island took it upon her heart; her hill raised it to the sky.

Age after age, the morning sun daily illumined its great meaning.

While the harvest was sown and reaped in the near-by fields by the stream, and life, with its chequered light, made pictured shadows on its epochs of changing screen, the prayer, once uttered in the quiet green of an ancient morning, ever rose in the midst of the hide-and-seek of tumultuous time:

"Let Buddha be my refuge."

The King, at the end of his days, is merged in the

[1] Boro-budur is the great Buddhist *Stupa* built on a hill-top in the island of Java.

shadow of a nameless night among the unremembered, leaving his salutation in an imperishable rhythm of stone which ever cries:

"Let Buddha be my refuge."

Generations of pilgrims came on the quest of an immortal voice for their worship; and this sculptured hymn, in a grand symphony of gestures, took up their lowly names and uttered for them:

"Let Buddha be my refuge."

The spirit of those words has been muffled in mist in this mocking age of unbelief, and the curious crowds gather here to gloat in the gluttony of an irreverent sight.

Man to-day has no peace,—his heart arid with pride. He clamours for an ever-increasing speed in a fury of chase for objects that ceaselessly run, but never reach a meaning.

And now is the time when he must come groping at last to the sacred silence, which stands still in the midst of surging centuries of noise, till he feels assured that in an immeasurable love dwells the final meaning of Freedom, whose prayer is:

"Let Buddha be my refuge."

## FULFILMENT

THE overflowing bounty of thy grace comes down from the heaven to seek my soul only, wherein it can contain itself.

The light that is rained from the sun and stars is fulfilled when it reaches my life.

The colour is like sleep that clings to the flower which waits for the touch of my mind to be awakened.

The love that tunes the strings of existence breaks out in music when my heart is won.


## THE SON OF MAN

FROM His eternal seat Christ comes down to this earth, where, ages ago, in the bitter cup of death He poured his deathless life for those who came to the call and those who remained away.

He looks about Him, and sees the weapons of evil that wounded His own age.

The arrogant spikes and spears, the slim, sly knives, the scimitar in diplomatic sheath, crooked and cruel, are hissing and raining sparks as they are sharpened on monster wheels.

But the most fearful of them all, at the hands of the slaughterers, are those on which has been engraved His own name, that are fashioned from the texts of His own words fused in the fire of hatred and hammered by hypocritical greed.

He presses His hand upon His heart; He feels that the age-long moment of His death has not yet ended, that new nails, turned out in countless numbers by those who are learned in cunning craftsmanship, pierce Him in every joint.

They had hurt Him once, standing at the shadow of their temple; they are born anew in crowds.

From before their sacred altar they shout to the soldiers, "Strike!"

And the Son of Man in agony cries, "My God, My God, why hast Thou forsaken Me?"

## RAIDAS, THE SWEEPER

RAIDAS, the sweeper, sat still, lost in the solitude of his soul, and some songs born of his silent vision found their way to the Rani's heart,—the Rani Jhali of Chitore.

Tears flowed from her eyes, her thoughts wandered away from her daily duties, till she met Raidas who guided her to God's presence.

The old Brahmin priest of the King's house rebuked her for her desecration of sacred law by offering homage as a disciple to an outcaste.

"Brahmin," the Rani answered, "while you were busy tying your purse-strings of custom ever tighter, love's gold slipped unnoticed to the earth, and my Master in his divine humility has picked it up from the dust.

"Revel in your pride of the unmeaning knots without number, harden your miserly heart, but I, a beggar woman, am glad to receive love's wealth, the gift of the lowly dust, from my Master, the sweeper."

## FREEDOM

FREEDOM from fear is the freedom I claim for you, my Motherland!—fear, the phantom demon, shaped by your own distorted dreams;

Freedom from the burden of ages, bending your head, breaking your back, blinding your eyes to the beckoning call of the future;

freedom from shackles of slumber wherewith you fasten yourself to night's stillness, mistrusting the star that speaks of truth's adventurous path;

Freedom from the anarchy of a destiny, whose sails are weakly yielded to blind uncertain winds, and the helm to a hand ever rigid and cold as Death;

Freedom from the insult of dwelling in a puppet's world, where movements are started through brainless wires, repeated through mindless habits; where figures wait with patient obedience for a master of show to be stirred into a moment's mimicry of life.

## THE NEW YEAR

LIKE fruit, shaken free by an impatient wind
    from the veils of its mother flower,
      thou comest, New Year, whirling in a frantic dance
        amid the stampede of the wind-lashed clouds
          and infuriate showers,
    while trampled by thy turbulence
      are scattered away the faded and the frail
      in an eddying agony of death.

Thou art no dreamer afloat on a languorous breeze,
    lingering among the hesitant whisper and hum
      of an uncertain season.
Thine is a majestic march, O terrible Stranger,
    thundering forth an ominous incantation,
      driving the days on to the perils of a pathless
      dark,
    where thou carriest a dumb signal in thy banner,
    a decree of destiny undeciphered.

# KRISHNAKALI

I CALL her my Krishna flower
 though they call her dark in the village.
I remember a cloud-laden day
 and a glance from her eyes,
  her veil trailing down at her feet,
   her braided hair loose on her back.
  Ah, you call her dark; let that be,
   her black gazelle eyes I have seen.


Her cows were lowing in the meadow,
 when the fading light grew grey.
With hurried steps she came out
 from her hut near the bamboo grove.
She raised her quick eyes to the sky,
 where the clouds were heavy with rain.
Ah, you call her dark! let that be,
 her black gazelle eyes I have seen.


  The East wind in fitful gusts
   ruffled the young shoots of rice.
  I stood at the boundary hedge
   with none else in the lonely land.
  If she espied me in secret or not
   She only knows and know I.
  Ah, you call her dark! let that be,
   her black gazelle eyes I have seen.


She is the surprise of cloud
 in the burning heart of May,
 a tender shadow on the forest
 in the stillness of sunset hour,

a mystery of dumb delight
   in the rain-loud night of June.
Ah, you call her dark! let that be,
   her black gazelle eyes I have seen.

     I call her my Krishna flower,
        let all others say what they like.
     In the rice-field of Maina village
        I felt the first glance of her eyes.
     She had not a veil on her face,
        not a moment of leisure for shyness.
     Ah, you call her dark! let that be,
        her black gazelle eyes I have seen.

## W. W. PEARSON

THY nature is to forget thyself;
   but we remember thee.
Thou shinest in self-concealment
   revealed by our love.

Thou lendest light from thine own soul
   to those that are obscure.
Thou seekest neither love nor fame;
   Love discovers thee.

## SANTINIKETAN SONG

SHE is our own, the darling of our hearts, Santiniketan.
   Our dreams are rocked in her arms.
Her face is a fresh wonder of love every time we see her,
   for she is our own, the darling of our hearts.

In the shadows of her trees we meet,
    in the freedom of her open sky.
Her mornings come and her evenings
    bringing down heaven's kisses,
    making us feel anew that she is our own, the darling
        of our hearts.

The stillness of her shades is stirred by the woodland
    whisper;
        her *amlaki* groves are aquiver with the rapture of
        leaves.
She dwells in us and around us, however far we may
    wander.
She weaves our hearts in a song, making us one in music,
        tuning our strings of love with her own fingers;
    and we ever remember that she is our own,
        the darling of our hearts.

# SACRIFICE
# AND OTHER PLAYS

# SANYASI, OR THE ASCETIC

"Lead us from the unreal to the real."

# SANYASI, OR THE ASCETIC

## I

*Sanyasi, outside the cave*

THE division of days and nights is not for me, nor that of months and years. For me, the stream of time has stopped, on whose waves dances the world, like straws and twigs. In this dark cave I am alone, merged in myself,—and the eternal night is still, like a mountain lake afraid of its own depth. Water oozes and drips from the cracks, and in the pools float the ancient frogs. I sit chanting the incantation of nothingness. The world's limits recede, line after line. —The stars, like sparks of fire, flown from the anvil of time, are extinct; and that joy is mine which comes to the God Shiva, when, after æons of dream, he wakes up to find himself alone in the heart of the infinite annihilation. I am free, I am the great solitary One. When I was thy slave, O Nature, thou didst set my heart against itself, and madest it carry the fierce war of suicide through its world. Desires, that have no other ends but to feed upon themselves and all that comes to their mouths, lashed me into fury. I ran about, madly chasing my shadow. Thou drovest me with thy lightning lashes of pleasure into the void of satiety. And the hungers, who are thy decoys, ever led me into the endless famine, where food turned into dust, and drink into vapour.

Till, when my world was spotted with tears and ashes, I took my oath that I would have revenge upon thee, interminable Appearance, mistress of endless disguises. I took shelter in the darkness,—the castle of the Infinite,—and fought the deceitful light, day after day, till it lost all its weapons and lay powerless at my feet. Now, when I am free of fear and desires, when the mist has vanished, and my reason shines pure and bright, let me go out into the kingdom of lies, and sit upon its heart, untouched and unmoved.

## II

*Sanyasi, by the roadside*

How small is this earth and confined, watched and followed by the persistent horizons! The trees, houses, and crowd of things are pressing upon my eyes. The light, like a cage, has shut out the dark eternity; and the hours hop and cry within its barriers, like prisoned birds. But why are these noisy men rushing on, and for what purpose? They seem always afraid of missing something,—the something that never comes to their hands.     [*The crowd passes*

(*Enter a Village Elder and Two Women*)

*First Woman.* O my, O my! You *do* make me laugh.

*Second Woman.* But who says you are old?

*Village Elder.* There are fools who judge men by their outside.

*First Woman.* How sad! We have been watching your outside from our infancy. It is just the same all through these years.

*Village Elder.* Like the morning sun.

*First Woman.* Yes, like the morning sun in its shining baldness.

*Village Elder.* Ladies, you are over-critical in your taste. You notice things that are unessential.

*Second Woman.* Leave off your chatter, Ananga. Let us hasten home, or my man will be angry.

*First Woman.* Good-bye, sir. Please judge us from our outside; we won't mind that.

*Village Elder.* Because you have no inside to speak of.

[*They go*

(*Enter Three Villagers*)

*First Villager.* Insult me? the scoundrel! He shall regret it.

*Second Villager.* He must be taught a thorough lesson.

*First Villager.* A lesson that will follow him to his grave.

*Third Villager.* Yes, brother, set your heart upon it. Never give him quarter.

*Second Villager.* He has grown too big.

*First Villager.* Big enough to burst at last.

*Third Villager.* The ants, when they begin to grow wings, perish.

*Second Villager.* But have you got a plan?

*First Villager.* Not one, but hundreds. I will drive my ploughshare over his household.—I will give him a donkey-ride through the town, with his cheeks painted white and black. I will make the world too hot for him, and——

[*They go*

(*Enter Two Students*)

*First Student.* I am sure Professor Madhab won in the debate.

*Second Student.* No, it was Professor Janardan.

*First Student.* Professor Madhab maintained his point to the last. He said that the subtle is the outcome of the gross.

*Second Student.* But Professor Janardan conclusively proved that the subtle is the origin of the gross.

*First Student.* Impossible.

*Second Student.* It is as clear as the daylight.

*First Student.* Seeds come from the tree.

*Second Student.* The tree comes from the seed.

*First Student.* Sanyasi, which of these is true? Which is the original, the subtle or the gross?

*Sanyasi.* Neither.

*Second Student.* Neither. Well, that sounds satisfactory.

*Sanyasi.* The origin is the end, and the end is the origin. It is a circle.—The distinction between the subtle and gross is in your ignorance.

*First Student.* Well, it sounds very simple—and I think this was what my master meant.

*Second Student.* Certainly this agrees more with what *my* master teaches. [*They go out*

*Sanyasi.* These birds are word-peckers. When they pick up some wriggling nonsense, which can fill their mouth, they are happy.

(*Enter Two Flower-Girls, singing*)

### Song

*The weary hours pass by.*
*The flowers that blossom in the light*
*Fade and drop in the shadow.*
*I thought I would weave a garland*
*In the cool of the morning for my love.*
*But the morning wears on,*
*The flowers are not gathered,*
*And my love is lost.*

*A Wayfarer.* Why such regret, my darlings? When the

garlands are ready, the necks will not be wanting.

*First Flower-Girl.* Nor the halter.

*Second Flower-Girl.* You *are* bold. Why do you come so close?

*Wayfarer.* You quarrel for nothing, my girl. I am far enough from you to allow an elephant to pass between us.

*Second Flower-Girl.* Indeed! Am I such a fright? I wouldn't have eaten you, if you had come.

[*They go out laughing*
(*Comes an old Beggar*)

*Beggar.* Kind sirs, have pity on me. May God prosper you! Give me one handful from your plenty.

(*Enters a Soldier*)

*Soldier.* Move away. Don't you see the Minister's son is coming? [*They go out*

*Sanyasi.* It is midday. The sun is growing strong. The sky looks like an overturned burning copper bowl. The earth breathes hot sighs, and the whirling sands dance by. What sights of man have I seen! Can I ever again shrink back into the smallness of these creatures, and become one of them? No, I am free. I have not this obstacle, this world round me. I live in a pure desolation.

(*Enter the girl Vasanti and a Woman*)

*Woman.* Girl, you are Raghu's daughter, aren't you? You should keep away from this road. Don't you know it goes to the temple?

*Vasanti.* I am on the farthest side, Lady.

*Woman.* But I thought my cloth-end touched you. I am taking my offerings to the goddess,—I hope they are not polluted.

*Vasanti.* I assure you, your cloth did not touch me.

467

(*The Woman goes.*) I am Vasanti, Raghu's daughter. May I come to you, father?

*Sanyasi.* Why not, child?

*Vasanti.* I am a pollution, as they call me.

*Sanyasi.* But they are all that,—a pollution. They roll in the dust of existence. Only he is pure who has washed away the world from his mind. But what have you done, daughter?

*Vasanti.* My father, who is dead, had defied their laws and their gods. He would not perform their rites.

*Sanyasi.* Why do you stand away from me?

*Vasanti.* Will you touch me?

*Sanyasi.* Yes, because nothing can touch me truly. I am ever away in the endless. You can sit here, if you wish.

*Vasanti* (*breaking into a sob*). Never tell me to leave you, when once you have taken me near you.

*Sanyasi.* Wipe away your tears, child. I am a Sanyasi. I have neither hatred nor attachment in my heart.—I never claim you as mine; therefore I can never discard you. You are to me as this blue sky is,—you are,—yet you are not.

*Vasanti.* Father, I am deserted by gods and men alike.

*Sanyasi.* So am I. I have deserted both gods and men.

*Vasanti.* You have no mother?

*Sanyasi.* No.

*Vasanti.* Nor father?

*Sanyasi.* No.

*Vasanti.* Nor any friend?

*Sanyasi.* No.

*Vasanti.* Then I shall be with you.—You won't leave me?

*Sanyasi.* I have done with leaving. You can stay near me, yet never coming near me.

*Vasanti.* I do not understand you, father. Tell me, is there no shelter for me in the whole world?

*Sanyasi.* Shelter? Don't you know this world is a bottomless chasm? The swarm of creatures, coming out from the hole of nothingness, seeks for shelter, and enters into the gaping mouth of this emptiness, and is lost. These are the ghosts of lies around you, who hold their market of illusions,—and the foods which they sell are shadows. They only deceive your hunger, but do not satisfy. Come away from here, child, come away.

*Vasanti.* But, father, they seem so happy in this world. Can we not watch them from the roadside?

*Sanyasi.* Alas, they do not understand. They cannot see that this world is death spread out to eternity.—It dies every moment, yet never comes to the end.—And we, the creatures of this world, live by feeding upon death.

*Vasanti.* Father, you frighten me.

(*Enters a Traveller*)

*Traveller.* Can I get a shelter near this place?

*Sanyasi.* Shelter there is nowhere, my son, but in the depth of one's self.—Seek that; hold to it fast, if you would be saved.

*Traveller.* But I am tired, and want shelter.

*Vasanti.* My hut is not far from here. Will you come?

*Traveller.* But who are you?

*Vasanti.* Must you know me? I am Raghu's daughter.

*Traveller.* God bless you, child, but I cannot stay.

[*Goes*

(*Men come bearing somebody on a bed*)

*First Bearer.* He is still asleep.

469

*Second Bearer.* How heavy the rascal is!

*A Traveller (outside their group).* Whom do you carry?

*Third Bearer.* Bindé, the weaver, was sleeping as one dead, and we have taken him away.

*Second Bearer.* But I am tired, brothers. Let us give him a shake, and waken him up.

*Bindé (wakes up).* Ee, a, u——

*Third Bearer.* What's that noise?

*Bindé.* I say. Who are you? Where am I being carried?
    (*They put down the bed from their shoulders*)

*Third Bearer.* Can't you keep quiet, like all decent dead people?

*Second Bearer.* The cheek of him! He must talk, even though he is dead.

*Third Bearer.* It would be more proper of you, if you kept still.

*Bindé.* I am sorry to disappoint you, gentlemen; you have made a mistake.—I was not dead, but fast asleep.

*Second Bearer.* I admire this fellow's impudence. Not only must he die, but argue.

*Third Bearer.* He won't confess the truth. Let us go, and finish the rites of the dead.

*Bindé.* I swear by your beard, my brother, I am as alive as any of you.        [*They take him away, laughing*

*Sanyasi.* The girl has fallen asleep, with her arm beneath her little head; I think I must leave her now, and go. But, coward, must you run away,—run away from this tiny thing? These are Nature's spiders' webs, they have danger merely for moths, and not for a Sanyasi like me.

*Vasanti (awaking with a start).* Have you left me, Master?—Have you gone away?

*Sanyasi.* Why should I go away from you? What fear have I? Afraid of a shadow?

*Vasanti.* Do you hear the noise in the road?

*Sanyasi.* But stillness is in my soul.

(*Enters a young Woman, followed by Men*)

*Woman.* Go now. Leave me. Don't talk to me of love.

*First Man.* Why, what has been my crime?

*Woman.* You men have hearts of stone.

*First Man.* Incredible. If our hearts were of stone, how could Cupid's darts make damage there?

*Other Man.* Bravo! Well said!

*Second Man.* Now, what is your answer to that, my dear?

*Woman.* Answer! You think you have said something very fine,—don't you? It is perfect rubbish.

*First Man.* I leave it to your judgment, gentlemen. What I said was this, that if our hearts be of stone, how can——

*Third Man.* Yes, yes, it has no answer at all.

*First Man.* Let me explain it to you. She said we men have hearts of stone, didn't she? Well, I said, in answer, if our hearts were truly of stone, how could Cupid's darts damage them? You understand?

*Second Man.* Brother, I have been selling molasses in the town for the last twenty-four years,—do you think I cannot understand what you say? [*They go out*

*Sanyasi.* What are you doing, my child?

*Vasanti.* I am looking at your broad palm, father. My hand is a little bird that finds its nest here. Your palm is great, like the great earth which holds all. These lines are the rivers, and these are hills.

[*Puts her cheek upon it*

*Sanyasi.* Your touch is soft, my daughter, like the touch of sleep. It seems to me this touch has something

471

of the great darkness, which touches one's soul with the wand of the eternal.—But, child, you are the moth of the daylight. You have your birds and flowers and fields—what can you find in me, who have my centre in the One and my circumference nowhere?

*Vasanti.* I do not want anything else. Your love is enough for me.

*Sanyasi.* The girl imagines I love her,—foolish heart. She is happy in that thought. Let her nourish it. For they have been brought up in illusions, and they must have illusions to console them.

*Vasanti.* Father, this creeper trailing on the grass, seeking some tree to twine itself round, is my creeper. I have tended it and watered it from the time when it had pushed up only two little leaves into the air, like an infant's cry. This creeper is me,—it has grown by the roadside, it can be so easily crushed. Do you see these beautiful little flowers, pale blue with white spots in their hearts?—these white spots are their dreams. Let me gently brush your forehead with these flowers. To me, things that are beautiful are the keys to all that I have not seen and not known.

*Sanyasi.* No, no, the beautiful is mere phantasy. To him who knows, the dust and the flower are the same. —But what languor is this that is creeping into my blood and drawing before my eyes a thin mist-veil of all the rainbow colours? Is it Nature herself weaving her dreams round me, clouding my senses? (*Suddenly he tears the creeper, and rises up.*) No more of this; for this is death. What game of yours is this with me, little girl? I am a Sanyasi, I have cut all my knots, I am free.—No, no, not those tears. I cannot bear them.—But where was hidden in my heart this snake, this anger, that hissed

472

out of its dark with its fang? No, they are not dead,—
they outlive starvation. These hell-creatures clatter
their skeletons and dance in my heart, when their mistress, the great witch, plays upon her magic flute.—
Weep not, child, come to me. You seem to me like a
cry of a lost world, like the song of a wandering star.
You bring to my mind something which is infinitely
more than this Nature,—more than the sun and stars.
It is as great as the darkness. I understand it not. I have
never known it, therefore I fear it. I must leave you.—
Go back whence you came,—the messenger of the
unknown.

*Vasanti.* Leave me not, father,—I have none else but
you.

*Sanyasi.* I must go, I thought that I had known,—
but I do not know. Yet I must know. I leave you, to
know who you are.

*Vasanti.* Father, if you leave me, I shall die.

*Sanyasi.* Let go my hand. Do not touch me. I must
be free.——                                   [*He runs away*


### III

*The Sanyasi is seen, sitting upon a boulder in a mountain path.*
  *A shepherd boy passes by, singing.*

#### SONG

> *Do not turn away your face, my love,*
> *The spring has bared open its breast.*
>   *The flowers breathe their secrets in the dark.*
> *The rustle of the forest leaves comes across the sky*
>   *Like the sobs of the night.*
> *Come, love, show me your face.*

*Sanyasi.* The gold of the evening is melting in the heart of the blue sea. The forest, on the hillside, is drinking the last cup of the daylight. On the left, the village huts are seen through the trees with their evening lamps lighted, like a veiled mother watching by her sleeping children. Nature, thou art my slave. Thou hast spread thy many-coloured carpet in the great hall where I sit alone, like a king, and watch thee dance with thy starry necklace twinkling on thy breast.

(*Shepherd girls pass by, singing*)

### SONG OF THE SHEPHERD GIRLS

*The music comes from across the dark river and calls me.*
  *I was in the house and happy.*
*But the flute sounded in the still air of night,*
  *And a pain pierced my heart.*
*Oh, tell me the way who know it,—*
  *Tell me the way to him.*
*I will go to him with my one little flower,*
  *And leave it at his feet,*
  *And tell him that his music is one with my love.*

  *[They go*

*Sanyasi.* I think such an evening had come to me only once before in all my births. Then its cup overbrimmed with love and music, and I sat with some one, the memory of whose face is in that setting star of the evening.—But where is my little girl, with her dark sad eyes, big with tears? Is she there, sitting outside her hut, watching that same star through the immense loneliness of the evening? But the star must set, the evening close her eyes in the night, and tears must cease and sobs be stilled in sleep. No, I will not go back. Let the world-dreams take their own shape. Let me not trouble its course and create new phantasies. I will see, and think, and know.

(*Enters a ragged Girl*)

*Girl.* Are you there, father?

*Sanyasi.* Come, child, sit by me. I wish I could own that call of yours. Some one did call me father, once, and the voice was somewhat like yours. The father answers now,—but where is that call?

*Girl.* Who are you?

*Sanyasi.* I am a Sanyasi. Tell me, child, what is your father?

*Girl.* He gathers sticks from the forest.

*Sanyasi.* And you have a mother?

*Girl.* No. She died when I was young.

*Sanyasi.* Do you love your father?

*Girl.* I love him more than anything else in the world. I have no one else but him.

*Sanyasi.* I understand you. Give me your little hand, —let me hold it in my palm,—in this big palm of mine.

*Girl.* Sanyasi, do you read palms? Can you read in my palm all that I am and shall be?

*Sanyasi.* I think I can read, but dimly know its meaning. One day I shall know it.

*Girl.* Now I must go to meet my father.

*Sanyasi.* Where?

*Girl.* Where the road goes into the forest. He will miss me, if he does not find me there.

*Sanyasi.* Bring your head near to me, child. Let me give you my kiss of blessing before you go.

[*Girl goes*

(*A Mother enters, with two children*)

*Mother.* How stout and chubby Misri's children are!

475

They are something to look at. But the more I feed you, the more you seem to grow thin every day.

*First Girl.* But why do you always blame us for that, mother? Can we help it?

*Mother.* Didn't I tell you to take plenty of rest? But you must always be running about.

*Second Girl.* But, mother, we run about on your errands.

*Mother.* How dare you answer me like that?

*Sanyasi.* Where are you going, daughter?

*Mother.* My salutation, father. We are going home.

*Sanyasi.* How many are you?

*Mother.* My mother-in-law, and my husband and two other children, besides these.

*Sanyasi.* How do you spend your days?

*Mother.* I hardly know how my days pass. My man goes to the field, and I have my house to look after. Then, in the evening, I sit to spin with my elder girls. (*To the girls.*) Go and salute the Sanyasi. Bless them, father.                                              [*They go*

(*Enter Two Men*)

*First Man.* Friend, go back from here. Do not come any farther.

*Second Man.* Yes, I know. Friends meet in this earth by chance, and the chance carries us on together some portion of the way, and then comes the moment when we must part.

*Second Friend.* Let us carry away with us the hope that we part to meet again.

*First Friend.* Our meetings and partings belong to all the movements of the world. Stars do not take special notice of us.

*Second Friend.* Let us salute those stars which *did*

throw us together. If for a moment, still it has been much.

*First Friend.* Look back for a minute before you go. Can you see that faint glimmer of the water in the dark, and those *casuarina* trees on the sandy bank? Our village is all one heap of dark shadows. You can only see the lights. Can you guess which of those lights are ours?

*Second Friend.* Yes, I think I can.

*First Friend.* That light is the last farewell look of our past days upon their parting guest. A little farther on, and there will remain one blot of darkness.

[*They go away*

*Sanyasi.* The night grows dark and desolate. It sits like a woman forsaken,—those stars are her tears turned into fire. O my child, the sorrow of your little heart has filled, for ever, all the nights of my life with its sadness. Your dear caressing hand has left its touch in this night air,—I feel it on my forehead,—it is damp with your tears. My darling, your sobs that pursued me, when I fled away, have clung to my heart. I shall carry them to my death.


IV

*Sanyasi, in the village path*

LET my vows of Sanyasi go. I break my staff and my alms-bowl. This stately ship, this world, which is crossing the sea of time,—let it take me up again, let me join once more the pilgrims. Oh, the fool, who wanted to seek safety in swimming alone, and gave up the light of the sun and stars, to pick his way with his glow-worm's lamp! The bird flies in the sky, not to fly

477

away into the emptiness, but to come back again to this great earth.—I am free. I am free from the bodiless chain of the Nay. I am free among things and forms and purpose. The finite is the true infinite, and love knows its truth. My girl, you are the spirit of all that is,—I can never leave you.

(*Enters a Village Elder*)

*Sanyasi.* Do you know, brother, where Raghu's daughter is?

*Elder.* She has left her village, and we are glad.

*Sanyasi.* Where has she gone?

*Elder.* Do you ask where? It is all one to her where she goes. [*Goes out*

*Sanyasi.* My darling has gone to seek a somewhere in the emptiness of nowhere. She must find me.

(*A crowd of Villagers enter*)

*First Man.* So our King's son is going to be married to-night.

*Second Man.* Can you tell me, when is the wedding hour?

*Third Man.* The wedding hour is only for the bride-groom and the bride. What have we got to do with it?

*A Woman.* But won't they give us cakes for the happy day?

*First Man.* Cakes? You *are* silly. My uncle lives in the town—I have heard from him that we shall have curds and parched rice.

*Second Man.* Grand!

*Fourth Man.* But we shall have a great deal more water than curds. You may be sure of that.

*First Man.* Moti, you are a dull fellow. Water in the curds at a prince's wedding!

*Fourth Man.* But we are not princes ourselves,

478

*Panchu.* For us, poor people, the curds have the trick of turning into water most parts.

*First Man.* Look there. That son of the charcoal-burner is still busy with his work. We mustn't allow that.

*Second Man.* We shall burn him into charcoal, if he does not come out.

*Sanyasi.* Do you know, any of you, where is Raghu's daughter?

*The Woman.* She has gone away.

*Sanyasi.* Where?

*Woman.* That we don't know.

*First Man.* But we are sure that she is not the bride for our prince.                    [*They laugh and go out*
                    (*Enters a Woman, with a child*)

*Woman.* My obeisance to you, father. Let my child touch your feet with his head. He is sick. Bless him, father.

*Sanyasi.* But, daughter, I am no longer a Sanyasi. Do not mock me with your salutation.

*Woman.* Then who are you? What are you doing?

*Sanyasi.* I am seeking.

*Woman.* Seeking whom?

*Sanyasi.* Seeking my lost world back.—Do you know Raghu's daughter? Where is she?

*Woman.* Raghu's daughter? She is dead.

*Sanyasi.* No, she cannot be dead. No! No!

*Woman.* But what is her death to you, Sanyasi?

*Sanyasi.* Not only to me; it would be death to all.

*Woman.* I do not understand you.

*Sanyasi.* She can never be dead.

# MALINI

# MALINI

## ACT I

### The Balcony of the Palace facing the street

*Malini.* The moment has come for me, and my life, like the dewdrop upon a lotus leaf, is trembling upon the heart of this great time. I shut my eyes and seem to hear the tumult of the sky, and there is an anguish in my heart, I know not for what.

*(Enters Queen)*

*Queen.* My child, what is this? Why do you forget to put on dresses that befit your beauty and youth? Where are your ornaments? My beautiful dawn, how can you absent the touch of gold from your limbs?

*Malini.* Mother, there are some who are born poor, even in a king's house. Wealth does not cling to those whose destiny it is to find riches in poverty.

*Queen.* That the child whose only language was the baby cry should talk to me in such riddles!—My heart quakes in fear when I listen to you. Where did you pick up your new creed, which goes against all our holy books? My child, they say that the Buddhist monks, from whom you take your lessons, practise black arts; that they cast their spells upon men's minds, confounding them with lies. But I ask you, is religion a thing that one has to find by seeking? Is it not like sunlight, given to you for all days? I am a simple woman. I do not understand men's creeds and dogmas. I only know that women's true objects of worship come to their own

483

arms, without asking, in the shape of their husbands and their children.

(Enters King)

*King.* My daughter, storm-clouds are gathering over the King's house. Go no farther along your perilous path. Pause, if only for a short time.

*Queen.* What dark words are these?

*King.* My foolish child, if you must bring your new creed into this land of the old, let it not come like a sudden flood threatening those who dwell on the bank. Keep your faith to your own self. Rake not up public hatred and mockery against it.

*Queen.* Do not chide my girl and teach her the crookedness of your diplomacy. If my child should choose her own teachers and pursue her own path, I do not know who can blame her.

*King.* Queen, my people are agitated, they clamour for my daughter's banishment.

*Queen.* Banishment? Of your own daughter?

*King.* The Brahmins, frightened at her heresy, have combined, and——

*Queen.* Heresy indeed! Are all truths confined only in their musty old books? Let them fling away their worm-eaten creeds, and come and take their lessons from this child. I tell you, King, she is not a common girl,—she is a pure flame of fire. Some divine spirit has taken birth in her. Do not despise her, lest some day you strike your forehead, and weep, and find her no more.

*Malini.* Father, grant to your people their request. The great moment has come. Banish me.

*King.* Why, child? What want do you feel in your father's house?

*Malini.* Listen to me, father. Those who cry for my

banishment, cry for me. Mother, I have no words in which to tell you what I have in my mind. Leave me without regret, like the tree that sheds its flowers unheeding. Let me go out to all men,—for the world has claimed me from the King's hands.

*King.* Child, I do not understand you.

*Malini.* Father, you are a King. Be strong and fulfil your mission.

*Queen.* Child, is there no place for you here, where you were born? Is the burden of the world waiting for your little shoulders?

*Malini.* I dream, while I am awake, that the wind is wild, and the water is troubled; the night is dark, and the boat is moored in the haven. Where is the captain, who shall take the wanderers home? I feel I know the path, and the boat will thrill with life at my touch, and speed on.

*Queen.* Do you hear, King? Whose words are these? Do they come from this little girl? Is she your daughter, and have I borne her?

*King.* Yes, even as the night bears the dawn,—the dawn that is not of the night, but of all the world.

*Queen.* King, have you nothing to keep her bound to your house,—this image of light?—My darling, your hair has come loose on your shoulders. Let me bind it up.—Do they talk of banishment, King? If this be a part of their creed, then let come the new religion, and let those Brahmins be taught afresh what is truth.

*King.* Queen, let us take away our child from this balcony. Do you see the crowd gathering in the street?

[*They all go out*

(*Enter a crowd of Brahmins, in the street, before the palace balcony. They shout*)

485

*Brahmins.* Banishment of the King's daughter!

*Kemankar.* Friends, keep your resolution firm. The woman, as an enemy, is to be dreaded more than all others. For reason is futile against her and forces are ashamed; man's power gladly surrenders itself to her powerlessness, and she takes her shelter in the strongholds of our own hearts.

*First Brahmin.* We must have audience with our King, to tell him that a snake has raised its poisonous hood from his own nest, and is aiming at the heart of our sacred religion.

*Supriya.* Religion? I *am* stupid. I do not understand you. Tell me, sir, is it your religion that claims the banishment of an innocent girl?

*First Brahmin.* You are a marplot, Supriya, you are ever a hindrance to all our enterprises.

*Second Brahmin.* We have united in defence of our faith, and you come like a subtle rift in the wall, like a thin smile on the compressed lips of contempt.

*Supriya.* You think that, by the force of numbers, you will determine truth, and drown reason by your united shouts?

*First Brahmin.* This is rank insolence, Supriya.

*Supriya.* The insolence is not mine but theirs who shape their scripture to fit their own narrow hearts.

*Second Brahmin.* Drive him out. He is none of us.

*First Brahmin.* We have all agreed upon the banishment of the Princess.—He who thinks differently, let him leave this assembly.

*Supriya.* Brahmins, it was a mistake on your part to elect me as one of your league. I am neither your shadow nor an echo of your texts. I never admit that truth sides with the shrillest voice, and I am ashamed to own as mine a creed that depends on force for its existence. (*To Kemankar.*) Dear friend, let me go.

*Kemankar.* No, I will not. I know you are firm in your action, only doubting when you debate. Keep silence, my friend; for the time is evil.

*Supriya.* Of all things the blind certitude of stupidity is the hardest to bear. To think of saving your religion by banishing a girl from her home! But let me know what is her offence? Does she not maintain that truth and love are the body and soul of religion? If so, is that not the essence of all creeds?

*Kemankar.* Religion is one in its essence, but different in its forms. The water is one, yet by its different banks it is bounded and preserved for different peoples. What if you have a well-spring of your own in your heart, spurn not your neighbours who must go for their draught of water to their ancestral pond with the green of its gradual slopes mellowed by ages and its ancient trees bearing eternal fruit.

*Supriya.* I shall follow you, my friend, as I have ever done in my life, and not argue.

(*Enters third Brahmin*)

*Third Brahmin.* I have good news. Our words have prevailed, and the King's army is about to take our side openly.

*Second Brahmin.* The army?—I do not quite like it.

*First Brahmin.* Nor do I. It smells of rebellion.

*Second Brahmin.* Kemankar, I am not for such extreme measures.

*First Brahmin.* Our faith will give us victory, not our arms. Let us make penance, and recite sacred verses. Let us call on the names of our guardian gods.

*Second Brahmin.* Come, Goddess, whose wrath is the

sole weapon of thy worshippers, deign to take form and crush even to dust the blind pride of unbelievers. Prove to us the strength of our faith, and lead us to victory.

*All.* We invoke thee, Mother, descend from thy heavenly heights and do thy work among mortals.

(*Enters Malini*)

*Malini.* I have come. (*They all bow to her, except Kemankar and Supriya, who stand aloof and watch.*)

*Second Brahmin.* Goddess.—Thou hast come at last, as a daughter of man, withdrawing all thy terrible power into the tender beauty of a girl. Whence hast thou come, Mother? What is thy wish?

*Malini.* I have come down to my exile at your call.

*Second Brahmin.* To exile from heaven, because thy children of earth have called thee?

*First Brahmin.* Forgive us, Mother. Utter ruin threatens this world and it cries aloud for thy help.

*Malini.* I will never desert you. I always knew that your doors were open for me. The cry went from you for my banishment and I woke up, amidst the wealth and pleasure of the King's house.

*Kemankar.* The Princess!

*All.* The King's daughter!

*Malini.* I am exiled from my home, so that I may make your home my own. Yet tell me truly, have you need of me? When I lived in seclusion, a lonely girl, did you call to me from the outer world? Was it no dream of mine?

*First Brahmin.* Mother, you have come, and taken your seat in the heart of our hearts.

*Malini.* I was born in a King's house, never once looking out from my window. I had heard that it was a sorrowing world,—the world out of my reach. But I did not know where it felt its pain. Teach me to find this out.

*First Brahmin.* Your sweet voice brings tears to our eyes.

*Malini.* The moon has just come out of those clouds. Great peace is in the sky. It seems to gather all the world in its arms, under the fold of one vast moonlight. There goes the road, losing itself among the solemn trees with their still shadows. There are the houses, and there the temple; the river bank in the distance looks dim and desolate. I seem to have come down, like a sudden shower from a cloud of dreams, into this world of men, by the roadside.

*First Brahmin.* You are the divine soul of this world.

*Second Brahmin.* Why did not our tongues burst in pain when they shouted for your banishment?

*First Brahmin.* Come, Brahmins, let us restore our Mother to her home.                                    [*They shout*
Victory to the Mother of the World! Victory to the Mother in the heart of the Man's daughter!

[*Malini goes, surrounded by them*
*Kemankar.* Let the illusion vanish. Where are you going, Supriya, like one walking in his sleep?

*Supriya.* Leave hold of me, let me go.

*Kemankar.* Control yourself. Will you, too, fly into the fire with the rest of the blinded swarm?

*Supriya.* Was it a dream, Kemankar?

*Kemankar.* It was nothing but a dream. Open your eyes, and wake up.

*Supriya.* Your hope of heaven is false, Kemankar. Vainly have I wandered in the wilderness of doctrines, —I never found peace. The God who belongs to the multitude and the God of the books are not my own God. These never answered my questions and never consoled me. But, at last, I have found the divine breathing and alive in the living world of men.

*Kemankar.* Alas, my friend, it is a fearful moment when a man's heart deceives him. Then blind desire becomes his gospel and fancy usurps the dread throne of his gods. Is yonder moon, lying asleep among soft fleecy clouds, the true emblem of everlasting reality? The naked day will come to-morrow, and the hungry crowd begin again to draw the sea of existence with their thousand nets. And then this moonlight night will hardly be remembered but as a thin film of unreality made of sleep and shadows and delusions. The magic web, woven of the elusive charms of a woman, is like that,—and can it take the place of highest truth? Can any creed, born of your fancy, satisfy the gaping thirst of the midday, when it is wide awake in its burning heat?

*Supriya.* Alas, I know not.

*Kemankar.* Then shake yourself up from your dreams, and look before you. The ancient house is on fire, whose nurslings are the ages. The spirits of our forefathers are hovering over the impending ruins, like crying birds over their perishing nests. Is this the time for vacillation, when the night is dark, the enemies knocking at the gate, the citizens asleep, and men drunken with delusions laying their hands upon their brothers' throats?

*Supriya.* I will stand by you.

*Kemankar.* I must go away from here.

*Supriya.* Where? And for what?

*Kemankar.* To foreign lands. I shall bring soldiers

from outside. For this conflagration cries for blood, to be quenched.

*Supriya.* But our own soldiers are ready.

*Kemankar.* Vain is all hope of help from them. They, like moths, are already leaping into the fire. Do you not hear how they are shouting like fools? The whole town has gone mad, and is lighting her festival lamps at the funeral pyre of her own sacred faith.

*Supriya.* If you must go, take me with you.

*Kemankar.* No. You remain here, to watch and keep me informed. But, friend, let not your heart be drawn away from me by the novelty of the falsehood.

*Supriya.* Falsehood is new, but our friendship is old. We have ever been together from our childhood. This is our first separation.

*Kemankar.* May it prove our last! In evil times the strongest bonds give way. Brothers strike brothers and friends turn against friends. I go out into the dark, and in the darkness of night I shall come back to the gate. Shall I find my friend watching for me, with the lamp lighted? I take away that hope with me.        [*They go*

(*Enter King, with the Prince, on the balcony*)

*King.* I fear I must decide to banish my daughter.

*Prince.* Yes, Sire, delay will be dangerous.

*King.* Gently, my son, gently. Never doubt that I will do my duty. Be sure I will banish her.

[*Prince goes*

(*Enters Queen*)

Tell me, King, where is she? Have you hidden her, even from me?

*King.* Whom?

*Queen.* My Malini.

*King.* What? Is she not in her room?

*Queen.* No, I cannot find her. Go with your soldiers and search for her through all the town, from house to house. The citizens have stolen her. Banish them all. Empty the whole town, till they return her.

*King.* I will bring her back,—even if my Kingdom goes to ruin.

(*The Brahmins and soldiers bring Malini, with torches lighted*)

*Queen.* My darling, my cruel child! I never keep my eyes off you,—how could you evade me, and go out?

*Second Brahmin.* Do not be angry with her, Queen. She came to our home to give us her blessings.

*First Brahmin.* Is she only yours? And does she not belong to us as well?

*Second Brahmin.* Our little mother, do not forget us. You are our star, to lead us across the pathless sea of life.

*Malini.* My door has been opened for you. These walls will nevermore separate us.

*Brahmins.* Blessed are we, and the land where we were born.  [*They go*

*Malini.* Mother, I have brought the outer world into your house. I seem to have lost the bounds of my body. I am one with the life of this world.

*Queen.* Yes, child. Now you shall never need to go out. Bring in the world to you, and to your mother.— It is close upon the second watch of the night. Sit here. Calm yourself. This flaming life in you is burning out all sleep from your eyes.

*Malini* (*embracing her mother*). Mother, I am tired. My body is trembling. So vast is this world.—Mother dear, sing me to sleep. Tears come to my eyes, and a sadness descends upon my heart.

## ACT II

*The Palace Garden. Malini and Supriya.*

*Malini.* What can I say to you? I do not know how to argue. I have not read your books.

*Supriya.* I am learned only among the fools of learning. I have left all arguments and books behind me. Lead me, Princess, and I shall follow you, as the shadow follows the lamp.

*Malini.* But, Brahmin, when you question me, I lose all my power and do not know how to answer you. It is a wonder to me to see that even you, who know everything, come to me with your questions.

*Supriya.* Not for knowledge I come to you. Let me forget all that I have ever known. Roads there are, without number, but the light is missing.

*Malini.* Alas, sir, the more you ask me, the more I feel my poverty. Where is that voice in me, which came down from heaven, like an unseen flash of lightning, into my heart? Why did you not come that day, but keep away in doubt? Now that I have met the world face to face my heart has grown timid, and I do not know how to hold the helm of the great ship that I must guide. I feel I am alone, and the world is large, and ways are many, and the light from the sky comes of a sudden to vanish the next moment. You who are wise and learned, will you help me?

*Supriya.* I shall deem myself fortunate, if you ask my help.

*Malini.* There are times when despair comes to choke all the life-currents; when suddenly, amidst crowds of men, my eyes turn upon myself and I am frightened. Will you befriend me in those moments of blankness,

493

and utter me one word of hope that will bring me back to life?

*Supriya.* I shall keep myself ready. I shall make my heart simple and pure, and my mind peaceful, to be able truly to serve you.

(*Enters Attendant*)

*Attendant.* The citizens have come, asking to see you.

*Malini.* Not to-day. Ask their pardon for me. I must have time to fill my exhausted mind, and have rest to get rid of weariness. (*Attendant goes.*) Tell me again about Kemankar, your friend. I long to know what your life has been and its trials.

*Supriya.* Kemankar is my friend, my brother, my master. His mind has been firm and strong, from early days, while my thoughts are always flickering with doubts. Yet he has ever kept me close to his heart, as the moon does its dark spots. But, however strong a ship may be, if it harbours a small hole in its bottom, it must sink.—That I would make you sink, Kemankar, was in the law of nature.

*Malini.* You made him sink?

*Supriya.* Yes, I did. The day when the rebellion slunk away in shame before the light in your face and the music in the air that touched you, Kemankar alone was unmoved. He left me behind him, and said that he must go to the foreign land to bring soldiers, and uproot the new creed from the sacred soil of Kashi.—You know what followed. You made me live again in a new land of birth. "Love for all life" was a mere word, waiting from the old time to be made real,—and I saw that truth in you in flesh. My heart cried for my friend, but he was away, out of my reach; then came his letter, in

494

which he wrote that he was coming with a foreign army at his back, to wash away the new faith in blood, and to punish you with death.—I could wait no longer. I showed the letter to the King.

*Malini.* Why did you forget yourself, Supriya? Why did fear overcome you? Have I not room enough in my house for him and his soldiers?

(*Enters King*)

*King.* Come to my arms, Supriya; I went at a fit time to surprise Kemankar and to capture him. An hour later, and a thunderbolt would have burst upon my house in my sleep. You are my friend, Supriya, come——

*Supriya.* God forgive me.

*King.* Do you not know that a King's love is not unsubstantial? I give you leave to ask for any reward that comes to your mind. Tell me, what do you want?

*Supriya.* Nothing, Sire, nothing. I shall live, begging from door to door.

*King.* Only ask me, and you shall have provinces worthy to tempt a king.

*Supriya.* They do not tempt me.

*King.* I understand you. I know towards what moon you raise your hands. Mad youth, be brave to ask even that which seems so impossible. Why are you silent? Do you remember the day when you prayed for my Malini's banishment? Will you repeat that prayer to me, to lead my daughter to exile from her father's house?— My daughter, do you know that you owe your life to this noble youth? And is it hard for you to pay off that debt with your——?

*Supriya.* For pity's sake, Sire, no more of this. Worshippers there are many who by lifelong devotion have gained the highest fulfilment of their desire. Could I be

495

counted one of them I should be happy. But to accept it from the King's hands as the reward of treachery? Lady mine, you have the plenitude and peace of your greatness; you know not the secret cravings of a poverty-stricken soul. I dare not ask from you an atom more than that pity of love which you have for every creature in the world.

*Malini.* Father, what is your punishment for the captive?

*King.* He shall die.

*Malini.* On my knees I beg from you his pardon.

*King.* But he is a rebel, my child.

*Supriya.* Do you judge him, King? He also judged you, when he came to punish you, not to rob your kingdom.

*Malini.* Spare him his life, father. Then only will you have the right to bestow on him your friendship, who has saved you from a great peril.

*King.* What do you say, Supriya? Shall I restore a friend to his friend's arms?

*Supriya.* That will be king-like in its grace.

*King.* It will come in its time, and you will find back your friend. But a King's generosity must not stop there. I must give you something which exceeds your hope,—yet not as a mere reward. You have won my heart, and my heart is ready to offer you its best treasure.—My child, where was this shyness in you before now? Your dawn had no tint of rose,—its light was white and dazzling. But to-day a tearful mist of tenderness sweetly tempers it for mortal eyes. (*To Supriya.*) Leave my feet, rise up and come to my heart. Happiness is pressing it like pain. Leave me now for a while. I want to be alone with my Malini. (*Supriya*

496

*goes.*) I feel I have found back my child once again,—not the bright star of the sky, but the sweet flower that blossoms on earthly soil. She is my daughter, the darling of my heart.

(*Enters Attendant*)

*Attendant.* The captive, Kemankar, is at the door.

*King.* Bring him in. Here comes he, with his eyes fixed, his proud head held high, a brooding shadow on his forehead, like a thunder-cloud motionless in a suspended storm.

*Malini.* The iron chain is shamed of itself upon those limbs. The insult to greatness is its own insult. He looks like a god defying his captivity.

(*Enters Kemankar in chains*)

*King.* What punishment do you expect from my hands?

*Kemankar.* Death.

*King.* But if I pardon you?

*Kemankar.* Then I shall have time again to complete the work I began.

*King.* You seem out of love with your life. Tell me your last wish, if you have any.

*Kemankar.* I want to see my friend, Supriya, before I die.

*King* (*to the attendant*). Ask Supriya to come.

*Malini.* There is a power in that face that frightens me. Father, do not let Supriya come.

*King.* Your fear is baseless, child.

(*Supriya enters, and walks towards Kemankar, with arms extended*)

*Kemankar.* No, no, not yet. First let us have our say, and then the greeting of love.—Come closer to me. You know I am poor in words,—and my time is short. My trial is over, but not yours. Tell me, why have you done this?

*Supriya.* Friend, you will not understand me. I had to keep my faith, even at the cost of my love.

*Kemankar.* I understand you, Supriya. I have seen that girl's face, glowing with an inner light, looking like a voice becoming visible. You offered, to the fire of those eyes, the faith in your fathers' creed, the faith in your country's good, and built up a new one on the foundation of a treason.

*Supriya.* Friend, you are right. My faith has come to me perfected in the form of that woman. Your sacred books were dumb to me. I have read, by the help of the light of those eyes, the ancient book of creation, and I have known that true faith is there, where there is man, where there is love. It comes from the mother in her devotion, and it goes back to her from her child. It descends in the gift of a giver and it appears in the heart of him who takes it. I accepted the bond of this faith which reveals the infinite in man when I set my eyes upon that face full of light and love and peace of hidden wisdom.

*Kemankar.* I also once set my eyes on that face, and for a moment dreamt that religion had come at last, in the form of a woman, to lead man's heart to heaven. For a moment, music broke out from the very ribs of my breast and all my life's hopes blossomed in their fulness. Yet did not I break through these meshes of illusion to wander in foreign lands? Did not I suffer humiliation from unworthy hands in patience, and bear the pain of separation from you, who have been my friend from my infancy? And what have you been doing meanwhile? You sat in the shade of the King's garden, and spent

498

your sweet leisure in idly weaving a lie to condone your infatuation and calling it a religion.

*Supriya.* My friend, is not this world wide enough to hold men whose natures are widely different? Those countless stars of the sky, do they fight for the mastery of the One? Cannot faiths hold their separate lights in peace for the separate worlds of minds that need them?

*Kemankar.* Words, mere words. To let falsehood and truth live side by side in amity, the infinite world is not wide enough. That the corn ripening for the food of man should make room for thorny weeds, love is not so hatefully all-loving. That one should be allowed to sap the sure ground of friendship with betrayal of trust, could tolerance be so traitorously wide as that? That one should die like a thief to defend his faith and the other live in honour and wealth who betrayed it—no, no, the world is not so stony-hard as to bear without pain such hideous contradictions in its bosom.

*Supriya (to Malini).* All these hurts and insults I accept in your name, my lady. Kemankar, you are paying your life for your faith,—I am paying more. It is your love, dearer than my life.

*Kemankar.* No more of this prating. All truths must be tested in death's court. My friend, do you remember our student days when we used to wrangle the whole night through, to come at last to our teacher, in the morning, to know in a moment which of us was right? Let that morning break now. Let us go there to that land of the final, and stand before death with all our questions, where the changing mist of doubts will vanish at a breath, and the mountain peaks of eternal truth will appear, and we two fools will look at each other and laugh.—Dear friend, bring before death that

499

which you deem your best and immortal.

*Supriya*. Friend, let it be as you wish.

*Kemankar*. Then come to my heart. You had wandered far from your comrade, in the infinite distance,—now, dear friend, come eternally close to me, and accept from one who loves you the gift of death. (*Strikes Supriya with his chains, and Supriya falls.*)

*Kemankar* (*embracing the dead body of Supriya*). Now call your executioner.

*King* (*rising up*). Where is my sword?

*Malini*. Father, forgive Kemankar!

# SACRIFICE

I DEDICATE THIS PLAY
TO THOSE HEROES WHO
BRAVELY STOOD FOR PEACE
WHEN HUMAN SACRIFICE
WAS CLAIMED FOR THE
GODDESS OF WAR

# SACRIFICE

*A temple in Tippera*

(*Enters Gunavati, the Queen*)

*Gunavati.* Have I offended thee, dread Mother? Thou grantest children to the beggar woman, who sells them to live, and to the adulteress, who kills them to save herself from infamy, and here am I, the Queen, with all the world lying at my feet, hankering in vain for the baby-touch at my bosom, to feel the stir of a dearer life within my life. What sin have I committed, Mother, to merit this,—to be banished from the mothers' heaven?

(*Enters Raghupati, the priest*)

O Master, have I ever been remiss in my worship? And my husband, is he not godlike in his purity? Then why has the Goddess who weaves the web of this world-illusion assigned my place in the barren waste of childlessness?

*Raghupati.* Our Mother is all caprice, she knows no law, our sorrows and joys are mere freaks of her mind. Have patience, daughter, to-day we shall offer special sacrifice in your name to please her.

*Gunavati.* Accept my grateful obeisance, father. My offerings are already on their way to the temple,—the red bunches of hibiscus and beasts of sacrifice.

[*They go out*

(*Enter Govinda, the King; Jaising, the servant of the temple; and Aparna, the beggar girl*)

*Jaising.* What is your wish, Sire?

503

*Govinda.* Is it true that this poor girl's pet goat has been brought by force to the temple to be killed? Will Mother accept such a gift with grace?

*Jaising.* King, how are we to know from whence the servants collect our daily offerings of worship? But, my child, why is this weeping? Is it worthy of you to shed tears for that which Mother herself has taken?

*Aparna.* Mother! I am his mother. If I return late to my hut, he refuses his grass, and bleats, with his eyes on the road. I take him up in my arms when I come, and share my food with him. He knows no other mother but me.

*Jaising.* Sire, could I make the goat live again, by giving up a portion of my life, gladly would I do it. But how can I restore that which Mother herself has taken?

*Aparna.* Mother has taken? It is a lie. Not mother, but demon.

*Jaising.* Oh, the blasphemy!

*Aparna.* Mother, art thou there to rob a poor girl of her love? Then where is the throne before which to condemn thee? Tell me, King.

*Govinda.* I am silent, my child. I have no answer.

*Aparna.* This blood-streak running down the steps is it his? Oh, my darling, when you trembled and cried for dear life, why did your call not reach my heart through the whole deaf world?

*Jaising* (*to the image*). I have served thee from my infancy, Mother Kali, yet I understand thee not. Does pity only belong to weak mortals, and not to gods? Come with me, my child, let me do for you what I can. Help must come from man when it is denied from gods.

[*Jaising and Aparna go out*

504

(*Enter Raghupati; Nakshatra, who is the King's brother; and the courtiers*)

*All.* Victory be to the King!

*Govinda.* Know you all, that I forbid shedding of blood in the temple from to-day for ever.

*Minister.* You forbid sacrifice to the Goddess?

*General Nayan Rai.* Forbid sacrifice?

*Nakshatra.* How terrible! Forbid sacrifice?

*Raghupati.* Is it a dream?

*Govinda.* No dream, father. It is awakening. Mother came to me, in a girl's disguise, and told me that blood she cannot suffer.

*Raghupati.* She has been drinking blood for ages. Whence comes this loathing all of a sudden?

*Govinda.* No, she never drank blood, she kept her face averted.

*Raghupati.* I warn you, think and consider. You have no power to alter laws laid down in scriptures.

*Govinda.* God's words are above all laws.

*Raghupati.* Do not add pride to your folly. Do you have the effrontery to say that *you* alone have heard God's words, and not I?

*Nakshatra.* It is strange that the King should have heard from gods and not the priest.

*Govinda.* God's words are ever ringing in the world, and he who is wilfully deaf cannot hear them.

*Raghupati.* Atheist! Apostate!

*Govinda.* Father, go to your morning service, and declare to all worshippers that from hence they will be punished with banishment who shed creatures' blood in their worship of the Mother of all creatures.

*Raghupati.* Is this your last word?

*Govinda.* Yes.

*Raghupati.* Then curse upon you! Do you, in your enormous pride, imagine that the Goddess, dwelling in your land, is your subject? Do you presume to bind her with your laws and rob her of her dues? You shall never do it. I declare it,—I who am her servant.          [*Goes*

*Nayan Rai.* Pardon me, Sire, but have you the right?

*Minister.* King, is it too late to revoke your order?

*Govinda.* We dare not delay to uproot sin from our realm.

*Minister.* Sin can never have such a long lease of life. Could they be sinful,—the rites that have grown old at the feet of the Goddess?

(*The King is silent*)

*Nakshatra.* Indeed they could not be.

*Minister.* Our ancestors have performed these rites with reverence; can you have the heart to insult them?

(*The King remains silent*)

*Nayan Rai.* That which has the sanction of ages, have you the right to remove it?

*Govinda.* No more doubts and disputes. Go and spread my order in all my lands.

*Minister.* But, Sire, the Queen has offered her sacrifice for this morning's worship; it is come near the temple gate.

*Govinda.* Send it back.          [*He goes*

*Minister.* What is this?

*Nakshatra.* Are we, then, to come down to the level of Buddhists, and treat animals as if they have their right to live? Preposterous!          [*They all go out*

(*Enters Raghupati,—Jaising following him with a jar of water to wash his feet*)

*Jaising.* Father.

*Raghupati.* Go!

*Jaising.* Here is some water.

*Raghupati.* No need of it!

*Jaising.* Your clothes.

*Raghupati.* Take them away!

*Jaising.* Have I done anything to offend you?

*Raghupati.* Leave me alone. The shadows of evil have thickened. The King's throne is raising its insolent head above the temple altar. Ye gods of these degenerate days, are ye ready to obey the King's laws with bowed heads, fawning upon him like his courtiers? Have only men and demons combined to usurp gods' dominions in this world, and is Heaven powerless to defend its honour? But there remain the Brahmins, though the gods be absent; and the King's throne will supply fuel to the sacrificial fire of their anger. My child, my mind is distracted.

*Jaising.* Whatever has happened, father?

*Raghupati.* I cannot find words to say. Ask the Mother Goddess who has been defied.

*Jaising.* Defied? By whom?

*Raghupati.* By King Govinda.

*Jaising.* King Govinda defied Mother Kali?

*Raghupati.* Defied you and me, all scriptures, all countries, all time, defied Mahākāli, the Goddess of the endless stream of time,—sitting upon that puny little throne of his.

*Jaising.* King Govinda?

*Raghupati.* Yes, yes, your King Govinda, the darling of your heart. Ungrateful! I have given all my love to bring you up, and yet King Govinda is dearer to you than I am.

*Jaising.* The child raises its arms to the full moon, sitting upon his father's lap. You are my father, and

507

my full moon is King Govinda. Then is it true, what I hear from people, that our King forbids all sacrifice in the temple? But in this we cannot obey him.

*Raghupati.* Banishment is for him who does not obey.

*Jaising.* It is no calamity to be banished from a land where Mother's worship remains incomplete. No, so long as I live, the service of the temple shall be fully performed. [*They go out*

(*Enter Gunavati and her attendant*)

*Gunavati.* What is it you say? The Queen's sacrifice turned away from the temple gate? Is there a man in this land who carries more than one head on his shoulders, that he could dare think of it? Who is that doomed creature?

*Attendant.* I am afraid to name him.

*Gunavati.* Afraid to name him, when I ask you? Whom do you fear more than me?

*Attendant.* Pardon me.

*Gunavati.* Only last evening Court minstrels came to sing my praise, Brahmins blessed me, the servants silently took their orders from my mouth. What can have happened in the meantime that things have become completely upset,—the Goddess refused her worship, and the Queen her authority? Was Tripura a dreamland? Give my salutation to the priest, and ask him to come. [*Attendant goes out*

(*Enters Govinda*)

*Gunavati.* Have you heard, King? My offerings have been sent back from Mother's temple.

*Govinda.* I know it.

*Gunavati.* You know it, and yet bear the insult?

*Govinda.* I beg to ask your pardon for the culprit.

*Gunavati.* I know, King, your heart is merciful, but

508

this is no mercy. It is feebleness. If your kindness hampers you, leave the punishment in my hand. Only, tell me, who is he?

*Govinda.* It is I, my Queen. My crime was in nothing else but having given you pain.

*Gunavati.* I do not understand you.

*Govinda.* From to-day shedding of blood in gods' temples is forbidden in my land.

*Gunavati.* Who forbids it?

*Govinda.* Mother herself.

*Gunavati.* Who heard it?

*Govinda.* I.

*Gunavati.* You! That makes me laugh. The Queen of all the world comes to the gate of Tripura's King with her petition.

*Govinda.* Not with her petition, but with her sorrow.

*Gunavati.* Your dominion is outside the temple limit. Do not send your commands there, where they are impertinent.

*Govinda.* The command is not mine, it is Mother's.

*Gunavati.* If you have no doubt in your decision, do not cross my faith. Let me perform my worship according to my light.

*Govinda.* I promised my Goddess to prevent sacrifice of life in her temple, and I must carry it out.

*Gunavati.* I also promised my Goddess the blood of three hundred kids and one hundred buffaloes, and I will carry it out. You may leave me now.

*Govinda.* As you wish.                    [*He goes out*
(*Enters Raghupati*)

*Gunavati.* My offerings have been turned back from the temple, father.

*Raghupati.* The worship offered by the most ragged of

all beggars is not less precious than yours, Queen. But the misfortune is that Mother has been deprived. The misfortune is that the King's pride is growing into a bloated monster, obstructing divine grace, fixing its angry red eyes upon all worshippers.

*Gunavati.* What will come of all this, father?

*Raghupati.* That is only known to her, who fashions this world with her dreams. But this is certain, that the throne which casts its shadow upon Mother's shrine will burst like a bubble, vanishing in the void.

*Gunavati.* Have mercy and save us, father.

*Raghupati.* Ha, ha! I am to save you,—you, the consort of a King who boasts of his kingdom in the earth and in heaven as well, before whom the gods and the Brahmins must—Oh, shame! Oh, the evil age, when the Brahmin's futile curse recoils upon himself, to sting him into madness.

(*About to tear his sacrificial thread*)

*Gunavati* (*preventing him*). Have mercy upon me.

*Raghupati.* Then give back to Brahmins what are theirs by right.

*Gunavati.* Yes, I will. Go, master, to your worship and nothing will hinder you.

*Raghupati.* Indeed your favour overwhelms me. At the merest glance of your eyes gods are saved from ignominy and the Brahmin is restored to his sacred offices. Thrive and grow fat and sleek till the dire day of judgment comes. [*Goes out*

(*Re-enters King Govinda*)

*Govinda.* My Queen, the shadow of your angry brows hides all light from my heart.

*Gunavati.* Go! Do not bring a curse upon this house.

510

*Govinda.* Woman's smile removes all curse from the house, her love is God's grace.

*Gunavati.* Go, and never show your face to me again.

*Govinda.* I shall come back, my Queen, when you remember me.

*Gunavati (clinging to the King's feet).* Pardon me, King. Have you become so hard that you forget to respect woman's pride? Do you not know, beloved, that thwarted love takes the disguise of anger?

*Govinda.* I would die, if I lost my trust in you. I know, my love, that clouds are for moments only, and the sun is for all days.

*Gunavati.* Yes, the clouds will pass by, God's thunder will return to his armoury, and the sun of all days will shine upon the traditions of all time. Yes, my King, order it so, that Brahmins be restored to their rights, the Goddess to her offerings, and the King's authority to its earthly limits.

*Govinda.* It is not the Brahmin's right to violate the eternal good. The creature's blood is not the offering for gods. And it is within the rights of the King and the peasant alike to maintain truth and righteousness.

*Gunavati.* I prostrate myself on the ground before you; I beg at your feet. The custom that comes through all ages is not the King's own. Like heaven's air, it belongs to all men. Yet your Queen begs it of you, with clasped hands, in the name of your people. Can you still remain silent, proud man, refusing entreaties of love in favour of duty which is doubtful? Then go, go, go from me.                                    [*They go*

(*Enter Raghupati, Jaising, and Nayan Rai*)

*Raghupati.* General, your devotion to Mother is well known.

511

*Nayan Rai*. It runs through generations of my ancestors.

*Raghupati*. Let this sacred love give you indomitable courage. Let it make your sword-blade mighty as God's thunder, and win its place above all powers and positions of this world.

*Nayan Rai*. The Brahmin's blessings will never be in vain.

*Raghupati*. Then I bid you collect your soldiers and strike Mother's enemy down to the dust.

*Nayan Rai*. Tell me, father, who is the enemy?

*Raghupati*. Govinda.

*Nayan Rai*. Our King?

*Raghupati*. Yes, attack him with all your force.

*Nayan Rai*. It is evil advice. Father, is this to try me?

*Raghupati*. Yes, it is to try you, to know for certain whose servant you are. Give up all hesitation. Know that the Goddess calls, and all earthly bonds must be severed.

*Nayan Rai*. I have no hesitation in my mind. I stand firm in my post, where my Goddess has placed me.

*Raghupati*. You are brave.

*Nayan Rai*. Am I the basest of Mother's servants, that the order should come for me to turn traitor? She herself stands upon the faith of man's heart. Can she ask me to break it? Then to-day comes to dust the King, and to-morrow the Goddess herself.

*Jaising*. Noble words!

*Raghupati*. The King, who has turned traitor to Mother, has lost all claims to your allegiance.

*Nayan Rai*. Drive me not, father, into a wilderness of debates. I know only one path,—the straight path of

512

faith and truth. This stupid servant of Mother shall never swerve from that highway of honour.

[*Goes out*

*Jaising.* Let us be strong in our faith as he is, Master. Why ask the aid of soldiers? We have the strength within ourselves for the task given to us from above. Open the temple gate wide, father. Sound the drum. Come, come, O citizens, to worship her who takes all fear away from our hearts. Come, Mother's children.

(*Citizens come*)

*First Citizen.* Come, come, we are called.

*All.* Victory to Mother!

(*They sing and dance*)

*The dread Mother dances naked in the battlefield,*
*Her lolling tongue burns like a red flame of fire,*
*Her dark tresses fly in the sky, sweeping away the sun and stars,*
*Red streams of blood run from her cloud-black limbs,*
*And the world trembles and cracks under her tread.*

*Jaising.* Do you see the beasts of sacrifice coming towards the temple, driven by the Queen's attendants?

(*They cry*)

Victory to Mother! Victory to our Queen!

*Raghupati.* Jaising, make haste and get ready for the worship.

*Jaising.* Everything is ready, father.

*Raghupati.* Send a man to call Prince Nakshatra in my name.

[*Jaising goes. Citizens sing and dance*

*Govinda.* Silence, Raghupati! Do you dare to disregard my order?

*Raghupati.* Yes, I do.

*Govinda.* Then you are not for my land.

*Raghupati.* No, my land is there, where the King's crown kisses the dust. No! Citizens! Let Mother's offerings be brought in here.

(*They beat drums*)

*Govinda.* Silence! (*To his attendants.*) Ask my General to come. Raghupati, you drive me to call soldiers to defend God's right. I feel the shame of it; for the force of arms only reveals man's weakness.

*Raghupati.* Sceptic, are you so certain in your mind that Brahmins have lost the ancient fire of their sacred wrath? No, its flame will burst out from my heart to burn your throne into ashes. If it does not, then I shall throw into the fire the scriptures, and my Brahmin pride, and all the arrant lies that fill our temple shrines in the guise of the divine.

(*Enter General Nayan Rai and Chandpal, who is the second in command of the army*)

*Govinda.* Stand here with your soldiers to prevent sacrifice of life in the temple.

*Nayan.* Pardon me, Sire. The King's servant is powerless in the temple of God.

*Govinda.* General, it is not for you to question my order. You are to carry out my words. Their merits and demerits belong only to me.

*Nayan.* I am your servant, my King, but I am a man above all. I have reason and my religion. I have my King,—and also my God.

*Govinda.* Then surrender your sword to Chandpal. He will protect the temple from pollution of blood.

*Nayan Rai.* Why to Chandpal? This sword was given to my forefathers by your royal ancestors. If you want it back, I will give it up to you. Be witness, my fathers, who are in the heroes' paradise,—the sword, that you

514

made sacred with your loyal faith and bravery, I surrender to my King. [*Goes out*

*Raghupati.* The Brahmin's curse has begun its work already.

(*Enters Jaising*)

*Jaising.* The beasts have been made ready for the sacrifice.

*Govinda.* Sacrifice?

*Jaising.* King, listen to my earnest entreaties. Do not stand in the way, hiding the Goddess, man as you are.

*Raghupati.* Shame, Jaising! Rise up and ask my pardon. I am your Master. Your place is at my feet, not the King's. Fool! Do you ask King's sanction to do God's service? Leave alone the worship and the sacrifice. Let us wait and see how his pride prevails in the end. Come away. [*They go out*

(*Enters Aparna*)

*Aparna.* Where is Jaising? He is not here, but only you,—the image whom nothing can move. You rob us of all our best without uttering a word. We pine for love, and die beggars for want of it. Yet it comes to you unasked, though you need it not. Like a grave, you hoard it under your miserly stone, keeping it from the use of the yearning world. Jaising, what happiness do you find from her? What can she speak to you? O my heart, my famished heart!

(*Enters Raghupati*)

*Raghupati.* Who are you?

*Aparna.* I am a beggar girl. Where is Jaising?

*Raghupati.* Leave this place at once. I know you are haunting this temple to steal Jaising's heart from the Goddess.

*Aparna.* Has the Goddess anything to fear from me?
I fear her. [*She goes out*

(*Enter Jaising and Prince Nakshatra*)

*Nakshatra.* Why have you called me?

*Raghupati.* Last night the Goddess told me in a
dream that you shall become king within a week.

*Nakshatra.* Ha, ha, this is news indeed.

*Raghupati.* Yes, you shall be king.

*Nakshatra.* I cannot believe it.

*Raghupati.* You doubt my words?

*Nakshatra.* I do not want to doubt them. But suppose,
by chance, it never comes to pass.

*Raghupati.* No, it shall be true.

*Nakshatra.* But, tell me, how can it ever become
true?

*Raghupati.* The Goddess thirsts for King's blood.

*Nakshatra.* King's blood?

*Raghupati.* You must offer it to her before you can be
king.

*Nakshatra.* I know not where to get it.

*Raghupati.* There is King Govinda.—Jaising, keep
still.—Do you understand? Kill him in secret. Bring his
blood, while warm, to the altar.—Jaising, leave this
place if you cannot remain still,—

*Nakshatra.* But he is my brother, and I love him.

*Raghupati.* Your sacrifice will be all the more precious.

*Nakshatra.* But, father, I am content to remain as I
am. I do not want the kingdom.

*Raghupati.* There is no escape for you, because the
Goddess commands it. She is thirsting for blood from
the King's house. If your brother is to live, then you
must die.

*Nakshatra.* Have pity on me, father.

516

*Raghupati.* You shall never be free in life, or in death, until her bidding is done.

*Nakshatra.* Advise me, then, how to do it.

*Raghupati.* Wait in silence. I will tell you what to do when the time comes. And now, go.   [*Nakshatra goes*

*Jaising.* What is it that I heard? Merciful Mother, is it your bidding? To ask brother to kill brother? Master, how could you say that it was Mother's own wish?

*Raghupati.* There was no other means but this to serve my Goddess.

*Jaising.* Means? Why means? Mother, have you not your own sword to wield with your own hand? Must your wish burrow underground, like a thief, to steal in secret? Oh, the sin!

*Raghupati.* What do you know about sin?

*Jaising.* What I have learnt from you.

*Raghupati.* Then come and learn your lesson once again from me. Sin has no meaning in reality. To kill is but to kill,—it is neither sin nor anything else. Do you not know that the dust of this earth is made of countless killings? Old Time is ever writing the chronicle of the transient life of creatures in letters of blood. Killing is in the wilderness, in the habitations of man, in birds' nests, in insects' holes, in the sea, in the sky; there is killing for life, for sport, for nothing whatever. The world is ceaselessly killing; and the great Goddess Kali, the spirit of ever-changing time, is standing with her thirsty tongue hanging down from her mouth, with her cup in hand, into which is running the red life-blood of the world, like juice from the crushed cluster of grapes.

*Jaising.* Stop, Master. Is, then, love a falsehood and mercy a mockery, and the one thing true, from beginning of time, the lust for destruction? Would it not have

517

destroyed itself long ago? You are playing with my heart, my Master. Look there, she is gazing at me with her sweet mocking smile. My bloodthirsty Mother, wilt thou accept my blood? Shall I plunge this knife into my breast and make an end to my life, as thy child, for evermore? The life-blood flowing in these veins, is it so delicious to thee? O my Mother, my bloodthirsty Mother!—Master, did you call me? I know you wanted my heart to break its bounds in pain overflowing my Mother's feet. This is the true sacrifice. But King's blood! The Mother, who is thirsting for our love, you accuse of bloodthirstiness!

*Raghupati.* Then let the sacrifice be stopped in the temple.

*Jaising.* Yes, let it be stopped.—No, no, Master, you know what is right and what is wrong. The heart's laws are not the laws of scripture. Eyes cannot see with their own light,—the light must come from the outside. Pardon me, Master, pardon my ignorance. Tell me, father, is it true that the Goddess seeks King's blood?

*Raghupati.* Alas, child, have you lost your faith in me?

*Jaising.* My world stands upon my faith in you. If the Goddess must have King's blood, let me bring it to her. I will never allow a brother to kill his brother.

*Raghupati.* But there can be no evil in carrying out God's wishes.

*Jaising.* No, it must be good, and I will earn the merit of it.

*Raghupati.* But, my boy, I have reared you from your childhood, and you have grown close to my heart. I can never bear to lose you, by any chance.

*Jaising.* I will not let your love for me be soiled with sin. Release Prince Nakshatra from his promise.

*Raghupati.* I shall think, and decide to-morrow.

[*He goes*

*Jaising.* Deeds are better, however cruel they may be, than the hell of thinking and doubting. You are right, my Master; truth is in your words. To kill is no sin, to kill brother is no sin, to kill king is no sin.—Where do you go, my brothers? To the fair at Nishipur? There the women are to dance? Oh, this world is pleasant! And the dancing limbs of the girls are beautiful. In what careless merriment the crowds flew through the roads, making the sky ring with their laughter and song. I will follow them.

(*Enters Raghupati*)

*Raghupati.* Jaising.

*Jaising.* I do not know you. I drift with the crowd. Why ask me to stop? Go your own way.

*Raghupati.* Jaising.

*Jaising.* The road is straight before me. With an alms-bowl in hand and the beggar girl as my sweetheart I shall walk on. Who says that the world's ways are difficult? Anyhow we reach the end,—the end where all laws and rules are no more, where the errors and hurts of life are forgotten, where is rest, eternal rest. What is the use of scriptures, and the teacher and his instructions?—My Master, my father, what wild words are these of mine? I was living in a dream. There stands the temple, cruel and immovable as truth. What was your order, my teacher? I have not forgotten it. (*Bringing out the knife.*) I am sharpening your words in my mind, till they become one with this knife in keenness. Have you any other order to give me?

*Raghupati.* My boy, my darling, how can I tell you how deep is my love for you?

519

*Jaising.* No, Master, do not tell me of love. Let me think only of duty. Love, like the green grass, and the trees, and life's music, is only for the surface of the world. It comes and vanishes like a dream. But underneath is duty, like the rude layers of stone, like a huge load that nothing can move.                    [*They go out*

(*Enter Govinda and Chandpal*)

*Chandpal.* Sire, I warn you to be careful.

*Govinda.* Why? What do you mean?

*Chandpal.* I have overheard a conspiracy to take away your life.

*Govinda.* Who wants my life?

*Chandpal.* I am afraid to tell you, lest the news becomes to you more deadly than the knife itself. It was Prince Nakshatra, who——

*Govinda.* Nakshatra?

*Chandpal.* He has promised to Raghupati to bring your blood to the Goddess.

*Govinda.* To the Goddess? Then I cannot blame him. For a man loses his humanity when it concerns his gods. You go to your work and leave me alone.

                    [*Chandpal goes out*

(*Addressing the image.*) Accept these flowers, Goddess, and let your creatures live in peace. Mother, those who are weak in this world are so helpless, and those who are strong are so cruel. Greed is pitiless, ignorance blind, and pride takes no heed when it crushes the small under its foot. Mother, do not raise your sword and lick your lips for blood; do not set brother against brother, and woman against man. If it is your desire to strike me by the hand of one I love, then let it be fulfilled. For the sin has to ripen to its ugliest limits before it can burst and die a hideous death; and when King's blood is shed

520

by a brother's hand, then lust for blood will disclose its demon face, leaving its disguise as a goddess. If such be your wish I bow my head to it.

(*Jaising rushes in*)

*Jaising.* Tell me, Goddess, dost thou truly want King's blood? Ask it in thine own voice, and thou shalt have it.

*A voice.* I want King's blood.

*Jaising.* King, say your last prayer, for your time has come.

*Govinda.* What makes you say it, Jaising?

*Jaising.* Did you not hear what the Goddess said?

*Govinda.* It was not the Goddess. I heard the familiar voice of Raghupati.

*Jaising.* The voice of Raghupati? No, no! Drive me not from doubt to doubt. It is all the same, whether the voice comes from the Goddess, or from my Master.—

(*He unsheathes his knife, and then throws it away*)

Listen to the cry of thy children, Mother. Let there be only flowers, the beautiful flowers for thy offerings,— no more blood. They are red even as blood,—these bunches of hibiscus. They have come out of the heart-burst of the earth, pained at the slaughter of her children. Accept this. Thou must accept this. I defy thy anger. Blood thou shalt never have. Redden thine eyes. Raise thy sword. Bring thy furies of destruction. I do not fear thee.—King, leave this temple to its Goddess, and go to your men.     [*Govinda goes*

Alas, alas, in a moment I gave up all that I had, my Master, my Goddess.

(*Raghupati comes*)

*Raghupati.* I have heard all. Traitor, you have betrayed your master.

521

*Jaising.* Punish me, father.

*Raghupati.* What punishment will you have?

*Jaising.* Punish me with my life.

*Raghupati.* No, that is nothing. Take your oath touching the feet of the Goddess.

*Jaising.* I touch her feet.

*Raghupati.* Say, I will bring kingly blood to the altar of the Goddess before it is midnight.

*Jaising.* I will bring kingly blood to the altar of the Goddess before it is midnight.         [*They go out*

(*Enters Gunavati*)

*Gunavati.* I failed. I had hoped that, if I remained hard and cold for some days, he would surrender. Such faith I had in my power, vain woman that I am. I showed my sullen anger, and remained away from him; but it was fruitless. Woman's anger is like a diamond's glitter; it only shines, but cannot burn. I would it were like thunder, bursting upon the King's house, startling him up from his sleep, and dashing his pride to the ground.

(*Enters the boy Druva*)

*Gunavati.* Where are you going?

*Druva.* I am called by the King.         [*Goes out*

*Gunavati.* There goes the darling of the King's heart. He has robbed my unborn children of their father's love, usurped their right to the first place in the King's breast. O Mother Kali, your creation is infinite and full of wonders, only send a child to my arms in merest whim, a tiny little warm living flesh to fill my lap, and I shall offer you whatever you wish. (*Enters Nakshatra.*) Prince Nakshatra, why do you turn back? I am a mere woman, weak and without weapon; am I so fearful?

*Nakshatra.* No, do not call me.

522

*Gunavati.* Why? What harm is in that?

*Nakshatra.* I do not want to be a king.

*Gunavati.* But why are you so excited?

*Nakshatra.* May the King live long, and may I die as I am,—a prince.

*Gunavati.* Die as quick as you can; have I ever said anything against it?

*Nakshatra.* Then tell me what you want of me.

*Gunavati.* The thief that steals the crown is awaiting you,—remove him. Do you understand?

*Nakshatra.* Yes, except who the thief is.

*Gunavati.* That boy, Druva. Do you not see how he is growing in the King's lap, till one day he reaches the crown?

*Nakshatra.* Yes, I have often thought of it. I have seen my brother putting his crown on the boy's head in play.

*Gunavati.* Playing with the crown is a dangerous game. If you do not remove the player, he will make a game of you.

*Nakshatra.* Yes, I like it not.

*Gunavati.* Offer him to Kali. Have you not heard that Mother is thirsting for blood?

*Nakshatra.* But, sister, this is not my business.

*Gunavati.* Fool, can you feel yourself safe, so long as Mother is not appeased? Blood she must have; save your own, if you can.

*Nakshatra.* But she wants King's blood.

*Gunavati.* Who told you that?

*Nakshatra.* I know it from one to whom the Goddess herself sends her dreams.

*Gunavati.* Then that boy must die for the King. His blood is more precious to your brother than his own,

523

and the King can only be saved by paying the price, which is more than his life.

*Nakshatra.* I understand.

*Gunavati.* Then lose no time. Run after him. He is not gone far. But remember. Offer him in my name.

*Nakshatra.* Yes, I will.

*Gunavati.* The Queen's offerings have been turned back from Mother's gate. Pray to her that she may forgive me.                                         [*They go out*

(*Enters Jaising*)

*Jaising.* Goddess, is there any little thing that yet remains out of the wreck of thee? If there be but a faintest spark of thy light in the remotest of the stars of evening, answer my cry, though thy voice be the feeblest. Say to me, "Child, here I am."—No, she is nowhere. She is naught. But take pity upon Jaising, O Illusion, and for him become true. Art thou so irredeemably false, that not even my love can send the slightest tremor of life through thy nothingness? O fool, for whom have you upturned your cup of life, emptying it to the last drop?—for this unanswering void,—truthless, merciless, and motherless?

(*Enters Aparna*)

Aparna, they drive you away from the temple; yet you come back over and over again. For you are true, and truth cannot be banished. We enshrine falsehood in our temple, with all devotion; yet she is never there. Leave me not, Aparna. Sit here by my side. Why are you so sad, my darling? Do you miss some god, who is god no longer? But is there any need of God in this little world of ours? Let us be fearlessly godless and come closer to each other. They want our blood. And for this they have come down to the dust of our earth,

524

leaving their magnificence of heaven. For in their heaven there are no men, no creatures, who can suffer. No, my girl, there is no Goddess.

*Aparna.* Then leave this temple, and come away with me.

*Jaising.* Leave this temple? Yes, I will leave. Alas, Aparna, I must leave. Yet I cannot leave it, before I have paid my last dues to the—— But let that be. Come closer to me, my love. Whisper something to my ears which will overflow this life with sweetness, flooding death itself.

*Aparna.* Words do not flow when the heart is full.

*Jaising.* Then lean your head on my breast. Let the silence of two eternities, life and death, touch each other. But no more of this. I must go.

*Aparna.* Jaising, do not be cruel. Can you not feel what I have suffered?

*Jaising.* Am I cruel? Is this your last word to me? Cruel as that block of stone, whom I called Goddess? Aparna, my beloved, if you were the Goddess, you would know what fire is this that burns my heart. But you *are* my Goddess. Do you know how I know it?

*Aparna.* Tell me.

*Jaising.* You bring to me your sacrifice every moment, as a mother does to her child. God must be all sacrifice, pouring out his life in all creation.

*Aparna.* Jaising, come, let us leave this temple and go away together.

*Jaising.* Save me, Aparna, have mercy upon me and leave me. I have only one object in my life. Do not usurp its place. [*Rushes out*

*Aparna.* Again and again I have suffered. But my strength is gone. My heart breaks. [*She goes out*

525

*(Enter Raghupati and Prince Nakshatra)*

*Raghupati.* Prince, where have you kept the boy?

*Nakshatra.* He is in the room where the vessels for worship are kept. He has cried himself to sleep. I think I shall never be able to bear it when he wakes up again.

*Raghupati.* Jaising was of the same age when he came to me. And I remember how he cried till he slept at the feet of the Goddess,—the temple lamp dimly shining on his tear-stained child-face. It was a stormy evening like this.

*Nakshatra.* Father, delay not. I wish to finish it all while he is sleeping. His cry pierces my heart like a knife.

*Raghupati.* I will drug him to sleep if he wakes up.

*Nakshatra.* The King will soon find it out, if you are not quick. For, in the evening, he leaves the care of his kingdom to come to this boy.

*Raghupati.* Have more faith in the Goddess. The victim is now in her own hands and it shall never escape.

*Nakshatra.* But Chandpal is so watchful.

*Raghupati.* Not more so than our Mother.

*Nakshatra.* I thought I saw a shadow pass by.

*Raghupati.* The shadow of your own fear.

*Nakshatra.* Do we not hear the sound of a cry?

*Raghupati.* The sound of your own heart. Shake off your despondency, Prince. Let us drink this wine duly consecrated. So long as the purpose remains in the mind it looms large and fearful. In action it becomes small. The vapour is dark and diffused. It dissolves into water-drops, that are small and sparkling. Prince, it is nothing. It takes only a moment,—not more than it does to snuff a candle. That life's light will die in a flash, like lightning in the stormy night of July, leaving its thunderbolt for ever deep in the King's pride. But, Prince, why are you so silent?

*Nakshatra.* I think we should not be too rash. Leave this work till to-morrow night.

*Raghupati.* To-night is as good as to-morrow night, perhaps better.

*Nakshatra.* Listen to the sound of footsteps.

*Raghupati.* I do not hear it.

*Nakshatra.* See there,—the light.

*Raghupati.* The King comes. I fear we have delayed too long.

(*King comes with attendants*)

*Govinda.* Make them prisoners. (*To Raghupati.*) Have you anything to say?

*Raghupati.* Nothing.

*Govinda.* Do you admit your crime?

*Raghupati.* Crime? Yes, my crime was that, in my weakness, I delayed in carrying out Mother's service. The punishment comes from the Goddess. You are merely her instrument.

*Govinda.* According to my law, my soldiers shall escort you to exile, Raghupati, where you shall spend eight years of your life.

*Raghupati.* King, I never bent my knees to any mortal in my life. I am a Brahmin. Your caste is lower than mine. Yet, in all humility, I pray to you, give me only one day's time.

*Govinda.* I grant it.

*Raghupati (mockingly).* You are the King of all kings. Your majesty and mercy are alike immeasurable. Whereas I am a mere worm, hiding in the dust. [*He goes out*

527

*Govinda.* Nakshatra, admit your guilt.

*Nakshatra.* I am guilty, Sire, and I dare not ask for your pardon.

*Govinda.* Prince, I know you are tender of heart. Tell me, who beguiled you with evil counsel?

*Nakshatra.* I will not take other names, King. My guilt is my own. You have pardoned your foolish brother more than once, and once more he begs to be pardoned.

*Govinda.* Nakshatra, leave my feet. The judge is still more bound by his laws than his prisoner.

*Attendants.* Sire, remember that he is your brother, and pardon him.

*Govinda.* Let me remember that I am a king. Nakshatra shall remain in exile for eight years, in the house we have built, by the sacred river, outside the limits of Tripura. (*Taking Nakshatra's hands.*) The punishment is not yours only, brother, but also mine,— the more so because I cannot share it bodily. The vacancy that you leave in the palace will prick my heart every day with a thousand needles. May the gods be more friendly to you, while you are away from us.

[*They all go out*

(*Enter Raghupati and Jaising*)

*Raghupati.* My pride wallows in the mire. I have shamed my Brahminhood. I am no longer your master, my child. Yesterday I had the authority to command you. To-day I can only beg your favour. That light is extinct in me, which gave me the right to defy King's power. The earthen lamp can be replenished and lighted again and again, but the star once extinguished is lost for ever. I am that lost star. Life's days are mere tinsel, most trifling of God's gifts, and I had to beg for one of those days from the King with bent knees. Let that one day be not in vain. Let its infamous black brows be red with King's blood before it dies. Why do you not speak, my boy? Though I forsake my place as your master, yet have I not the right to claim your obedience as your father,—I who am more than a father to you, because father to an orphan? But that man is the most miserable of all beggars who has to beg for love. You are still silent, my child? Then let my knees bend to you, who were smaller than my knees when you first came to my arms.

*Jaising.* Father, do not torture the heart that is already broken. If the Goddess thirsts for kingly blood, I will bring it to her before to-night. I will pay all my debts, yes, every farthing. Keep ready for my return. I will delay not.                                    [*Goes out*

(*Storm outside*)

*Raghupati.* She is awake at last, the Terrible. Her curses go shrieking through the town. The hungry Furies are shaking the cracking branches of the world-tree with all their might, for the stars to break and drop. My Mother, why didst thou keep thine own people in doubt and dishonour so long? Leave it not for thy servant to raise thy sword. Let thy mighty arm do its own work!—I hear steps.

(*Enters Aparna*)

*Aparna.* Where is Jaising?

*Raghupati.* Away, evil omen. (*Aparna goes out.*) But if Jaising never comes back? No, he will not break his promise. Victory to thee, Great Kali, the giver of all success!—But if he meet with obstruction? If he be caught and lose his life at the guards' hands?—Victory to thee, watchful Goddess, Mother invincible! Do not

529

allow thy repute to be lost, and thine enemies to laugh at thee. If thy children must lose their pride and faith in their Mother, and bow down their heads in shame before the rebels, who then will remain in this orphaned world to carry thy banner?—I hear his steps. But so soon? Is he coming back foiled in his purpose? No, that cannot be. Thy miracle needs not time, O Mistress of all time, terrible with thy necklace of human skulls.

*(Jaising rushes in)*

Jaising, where is the blood?

*Jaising.* It is with me. Let go my hands. Let me offer it myself *(entering the temple).* Must thou have kingly blood, Great Mother, who nourishest the world at thy breast with life?—I am of the royal caste, a Kshatriya. My ancestors have sat upon thrones, and there are rulers of men in my mother's line. I have kingly blood in my veins. Take it, and quench thy thirst for ever.

*(Stabs himself, and falls)*

*Raghupati.* Jaising! O cruel, ungrateful! You have done the blackest crime. You kill your father!—Jaising, forgive me, my darling. Come back to my heart, my heart's one treasure! Let me die in your place.

*(Enters Aparna)*

*Aparna.* It will madden me. Where is Jaising? Where is he?

*Raghupati.* Come, Aparna, come, my child, call him with all your love. Call him back to life. Take him to you, away from me, only let him live.

*(Aparna enters the temple and swoons)*

*(Beating his forehead on the temple floor.)* Give him, give him, give him!—Give him back to me! *(Stands up addressing the image.)* Look how she stands there, the silly stone,—deaf, dumb, blind,—the whole sorrowing

world weeping at her door,—the noblest hearts wrecking themselves at her stony feet! Give me back my Jaising! Oh, it is all in vain. Our bitterest cries wander in emptiness,—the emptiness that we vainly try to fill with these stony images of delusion. Away with them! Away with these our impotent dreams, that harden into stones, burdening our world!

(*He throws away the image, and comes out into the courtyard. Enters Gunavati*)

*Gunavati.* Victory to thee, great Goddess!—But where is the Goddess?

*Raghupati.* Goddess there is none.

*Gunavati.* Bring her back, father. I have brought her my offerings. I have come at last, to appease her anger with my own heart's blood. Let her know that the Queen is true to her promise. Have pity on me, and bring back the Goddess only for this night. Tell me,— where is she?

*Raghupati.* She is nowhere,—neither above nor below.

*Gunavati.* Master, was not the Goddess here in the temple?

*Raghupati.* Goddess?—If there were any true Goddess anywhere in the world, could she bear this thing to usurp her name?

*Gunavati.* Do not torture me. Tell me truly. Is there no Goddess?

*Raghupati.* No, there is none.

*Gunavati.* Then who was here?

*Raghupati.* Nothing, nothing.

(*Aparna comes out from the temple*)

*Aparna.* Father!

*Raghupati.* My sweet child! "Father,"—did you say? Do you rebuke me with that name? My son, whom I have killed, has left that one dear call behind him in your sweet voice.

*Aparna.* Father, leave this temple. Let us go away from here.

(*Enters the King*)

*Govinda.* Where is the Goddess?

*Raghupati.* The Goddess is nowhere.

*Govinda.* But what blood-stream is this?

*Raghupati.* King, Jaising, who loved you so dearly, has killed himself.

*Govinda.* Killed himself? Why?

*Raghupati.* To kill the falsehood that sucks the life-blood of man.

*Govinda.* Jaising is great. He has conquered death. My flowers are for him.

*Gunavati.* My King!

*Govinda.* Yes, my love.

*Gunavati.* The Goddess is no more.

*Govinda.* She has burst her cruel prison of stone, and come back to the woman's heart.

*Aparna.* Father, come away.

*Raghupati.* Come, child. Come, Mother. I have found thee. Thou art the last gift of Jaising.

# THE KING AND THE QUEEN

TO

MRS. ARTHUR SEYMOUR

# THE KING AND THE QUEEN

## ACT I

*The Palace Garden. King Vikram and Queen Sumitra.*

*Vikram.* Why have you delayed in coming to me for so long, my love?

*Sumitra.* Do you not know, my King, that I am utterly yours, wherever I am? It was your house, and its service, that kept me away from your presence, but not from you.

*Vikram.* Leave the house, and its service, alone. My heart cannot spare you for my world, I am jealous of its claims.

*Sumitra.* No, King, I have my place in your heart, as your beloved, and in your world, as your Queen.

*Vikram.* Alas, my darling, where have vanished those days of unalloyed joy when we first met in love; when our world awoke not,—only the flush of the early dawn of our union broke through our hearts in overflowing silence? You had sweet shyness in your eyelids, like a dew-drop on the tip of a flower-petal, and the smile flickered on your lips like a timid evening lamp in the breeze. I remember the eager embrace of your love, when the morning broke and we had to part, and your unwilling steps, heavy with languor, that took you away from me. Where were the house, and its service, and the cares of your world?

*Sumitra.* But then we were scarcely more than a boy

535

and a girl; and to-day we are the King and the Queen.

*Vikram.* The King and the Queen? Mere names. We are more than that; we are lovers.

*Sumitra.* You are my King, my husband, and I am content to follow your steps. Do not shame me by putting me before your kingship.

*Vikram.* Do you not want my love?

*Sumitra.* Love me truly by not making your love extravagant; for truth can afford to be simple.

*Vikram.* I do not understand woman's heart.

*Sumitra.* King, if you thriftlessly squander your all upon me, then I shall be deprived.

*Vikram.* No more vain words, Queen. The birds' nests are silent with love. Let lips keep guard upon lips, and allow not words to clamour.

           *(Enters Attendant)*

*Attendant.* The Minister begs audience, to discuss a grave matter of state.

*Vikram.* No, not now.          *[Attendant goes*

*Sumitra.* Sire, ask him to come.

*Vikram.* The state and its matter can wait. But sweet leisure comes rarely. It is frail, like a flower. Respite from duty is a part of duty.

*Sumitra.* Sire, I beg of you, attend to your work.

*Vikram.* Again, cruel woman! Do you imagine that I always follow you to win your unwilling favour, drop by drop? I leave you and go.     *[He goes*

    *(Enter Devadatta, the King's Brahmin friend)*

*Sumitra.* Tell me, sir, what is that noise outside the gate?

*Devadatta.* That noise? Command me, and with the help of soldiers I shall drive away that noise, ragged and hungry.

*Sumitra.* Do not mock me. Tell me what has happened.

*Devadatta.* Nothing. It is merely hunger,—the vulgar hunger of poverty. The famished horde of barbarians is rudely clamouring, making the drowsy cuckoos in your royal garden start up in fear.

*Sumitra.* Tell me, father, who are hungry?

*Devadatta.* It is their ill-fate. The King's poor subjects have been practising long to live upon half a meal a day, but they have not yet become experts in complete starvation. It is amazing.

*Sumitra.* But, father, the land is smiling with ripe corn. Why should the King's subjects die of hunger?

*Devadatta.* The corn is his whose is the land,—it is not for the poor. They, like intruding dogs at the King's feast, crouch in the corner for their crumbs, or kicks.

*Sumitra.* Does it mean that there is no King in this land?

*Devadatta.* Not one, but hundreds.

*Sumitra.* Are not the King's officers watchful?

*Devadatta.* Who can blame your officers? They came penniless from the alien land. Is it to bless the King's subjects with their empty hands?

*Sumitra.* From the alien land? Are they my relatives?

*Devadatta.* Yes, Queen.

*Sumitra.* What about Jaisen?

*Devadatta.* He rules the province of Singarh with such scrupulous care that all the rubbish, in the shape of food and raiment, has been cleared away; only the skin and bones remain.

*Sumitra.* And Shila?

*Devadatta.* He keeps his eyes upon the trade; he

relieves all merchants of their excessive profits, taking the burden upon his own broad shoulders.

*Sumitra.* And Ajit?

*Devadatta.* He lives in Vijaykote. He smiles sweetly, strokes the land on its back with his caressing hand, and whatever comes to his touch gathers with care.

*Sumitra.* What shame is this! I must remove this refuse from my father's land and save my people. Leave me now, the King comes. (*Enters the King.*) I am the mother of my people. I cannot bear their cry. Save them, King.

*Vikram.* What do you want me to do?

*Sumitra.* Turn those out from your kingdom who are oppressing the land.

*Vikram.* Do you know who they are?

*Sumitra.* Yes, I know.

*Vikram.* They are your own cousins.

*Sumitra.* They are not a whit more my own than my people. They are robbers, who, under the cover of your throne, seek for their victims.

*Vikram.* They are Jaisen, Shila, Ajit.

*Sumitra.* My country must be rid of them.

*Vikram.* They will not move without a fight.

*Sumitra.* Then fight them, Sire.

*Vikram.* Fight? But let me conquer *you* first, and then I shall have time to conquer my enemies.

*Sumitra.* Allow me, King, as your Queen. I will save your subjects myself. [*Goes*

*Vikram.* This is how you make my heart distraught. You sit alone upon your peak of greatness, where I do not reach you. You go to attend your own God, and I go seeking you in vain.

(*Enters Devadatta*)

538

*Devadatta.* Where is the Queen, Sire? Why are you alone?

*Vikram.* Brahmin, this is all your conspiracy. You come here to talk of the state news to the Queen?

*Devadatta.* The state is shouting its own news loud enough to reach the Queen's ears. It has come to that pass when it takes no heed lest your rest be broken. Do not be afraid of me, King. I have come to ask my Brahmin's dues from the Queen. For my wife is out of humour, her larder is empty, and in the house there are a number of empty stomachs.                    [*He goes*

*Vikram.* I wish all happiness to my people. Why should there be suffering and injustice? Why should the strong cast his vulture's eyes upon the poor man's comforts, pitifully small? (*Enters Minister.*) Banish all the foreign robbers from my kingdom this moment. I must not hear the cry of the oppressed for a day longer.

*Minister.* But, King, the evil that has been slowly growing for long, you cannot uproot in a day.

*Vikram.* Strike at its root with vigour, and fell it with your axe in a day,—the tree that has taken a hundred years to grow.

*Minister.* But we want arms and soldiers.

*Vikram.* Where is my general?

*Minister.* He himself is a foreigner.

*Vikram.* Then invite the hungry people. Open my treasure; stop this cry with food; send them away with money.—And if they want to have my kingdom, let them do so in peace, and be happy.                    [*He goes*

(*Enter Sumitra and Devadatta*)

*Minister.* Queen, my humble salutation to you.

*Sumitra.* We cannot allow misery to go unchecked in our land.

*Minister.* What are your commands, Queen?

*Sumitra.* Call immediately, in my name, all our chiefs who are foreigners.

*Minister.* I have done so already. I have taken upon myself to invite them into the capital, in the King's name, without asking for his sanction, for fear of refusal.

*Sumitra.* When did you send your messengers?

*Minister.* It will soon be a month hence. I am expecting their answers every moment. But I am afraid they will not respond.

*Sumitra.* Not respond to the King's call?

*Devadatta.* The King has become a piece of wild rumour, which they can believe, or not, as they like.

*Sumitra.* Keep your soldiers ready, Minister, for these people. They shall have to answer to me, as my relatives.                                   [*The Minister goes*

*Devadatta.* Queen, they will not come.

*Sumitra.* Then the King shall fight them.

*Devadatta.* The King will not fight.

*Sumitra.* Then I will.

*Devadatta.* You!

*Sumitra.* I will go to my brother Kumarsen, Kashmir's King, and with his help fight these rebels, who are a disgrace to Kashmir. Father, help me to escape from this kingdom, and do your duty, if things come to the worst.

*Devadatta.* I salute thee, Mother of the people.

[*He goes*

(*Enters Vikram*)

*Vikram.* Why do you go away, Queen? My hungry desire is revealed to you in its naked poverty. Do you therefore go away from me in derision?

540

*Sumitra.* I feel shamed to share alone your heart, which is for all men.

*Vikram.* Is it absolutely true, Queen, that you stand on your giddy height, and I grovel in the dust? No. I know my power. There is an unconquerable force in my nature, which I have turned into love for you.

*Sumitra.* Hate me, King, hate me. Forget me. I shall bear it bravely,—but do not wreck your manhood against a woman's charms.

*Vikram.* So much love, yet such neglect? Your very indifference, like a cruel knife, cuts into my bosom, laying bare the warm bleeding love,—and then, to fling it into the dust!

*Sumitra.* I throw myself at your feet, my beloved. Have you not forgiven your Queen, again and again, for wrongs done? Then why is this wrath, Sire, when I am blameless?

*Vikram.* Rise up, my love. Come to my heart. Shut my life from all else for a moment, with your encircling arms, rounding it into a world completely your own.

*A voice from outside.* Queen.

*Sumitra.* It is Devadatta.—Yes, father, what is the message?

### (Enters Devadatta)

*Devadatta.* They have defied the King's call,—the foreign governors of the provinces,—and they are preparing for rebellion.

*Sumitra.* Do you hear, King?

*Vikram.* Brahmin, the palace garden is not the council-house.

*Devadatta.* Sire, we rarely meet our King in the council-house, because it is not the palace garden.

*Sumitra.* The miserable dogs, grown fat upon the

King's table-sweepings, dare dream of barking against their master? King, is it time for debating in the council-chamber? Is not the course clear before you? Go with your soldiers and crush these miscreants.

*Vikram.* But our general himself is a foreigner.

*Sumitra.* Go yourself.

*Vikram.* Am I your misfortune, Queen,—a bad dream, a thorn in your flesh? No, I will never move a step from here. I will offer them terms of peace. Who is it that has caused this mischief? The Brahmin and the woman conspired to wake up the sleeping snake from its hole. Those who are too feeble to protect themselves are the most thoughtless in causing disasters to others.

*Sumitra.* Oh, the unfortunate land, and the unfortunate woman who is the Queen of this land!

*Vikram.* Where are you going?

*Sumitra.* I am going to leave you.

*Vikram.* Leave me?

*Sumitra.* Yes. I am going to fight the rebels.

*Vikram.* Woman, you mock me.

*Sumitra.* I take my farewell.

*Vikram.* You dare not leave me.

*Queen.* I dare not stay by your side when I weaken you.

*Vikram.* Go, proud woman. I will never ask you to turn back,—but claim no help from me.          [*Sumitra goes*

*Devadatta.* King, you allow her to go alone?

*Vikram.* She is not going. I do not believe her words.

*Devadatta.* I think she is in earnest.

*Vikram.* It is her woman's wiles. She threatens me, while she wants to spur me into action; and I despise her methods. She must not think that she can play with my love. She shall regret it. Oh, my friend, must I learn my lesson at last, that love is not for the King,—

and learn it from that woman, whom I love like my doom? Devadatta, you have grown with me from infancy,—can you not forget, for a moment, that I am a king, and feel that I have a man's heart that knows pain?

*Devadatta.* My heart is yours, my friend, which is not only ready to receive your love, but your anger.

*Vikram.* But why do you invite the snake into my nest?

*Devadatta.* Your house was on fire,—I merely brought the news, and wakened you up. Am I to blame for that?

*Vikram.* What is the use of waking? When all are mere dreams, let me choose my own little dream, if I can, and then die. Fifty years hence, who will remember the joys and sorrows of this moment? Go, Devadatta, leave me to my kingly loneliness of pain.

(*Enters a Courtier who is a foreigner*)

*Courtier.* We ask justice from your hands, King,— we who came to this land with the Queen.

*Vikram.* Justice for what?

*Courtier.* It has come to our ears that false accusations against us are brought before you, for no other cause than that we are foreigners.

*Vikram.* Who knows if they are not true? But so long as I trust you, can you not remain silent? Have I ever insulted you with the least suspicion—the suspicions that are bred like maggots in the rotten hearts of cowards? Treason I do not fear. I can crush it under my feet. But I fear to nourish littleness in my own mind.— You can leave me now.                    [*The Courtier goes*

(*Enter Minister and Devadatta*)

*Minister.* Sire, the Queen has left the palace, riding on her horse.

*Vikram.* What do you say? Left my palace?

*Minister.* Yes, King.

*Vikram.* Why did you not stop her?

*Minister.* She left in secret.

*Vikram.* Who brought you the news?

*Minister.* The priest. He saw her riding before the palace temple.

*Vikram.* Send for him.

*Minister.* But, Sire, she cannot be far. She has only just left. You can yet bring her back.

*Vikram.* Bringing her back is not important. The great fact is that she left me.—Left me! And all the King's soldiers and forts, and prisons and iron chains, could not keep fast this little heart of a woman.

*Minister.* Alas, King, Calumny, like a flood-burst, when the dyke is broken, will rush in from all sides.

*Vikram.* Calumny! Let the people's tongues rot with their own poison.

*Devadatta.* In the days of eclipse, men dare look at the midday sun through their broken pieces of glass, blackened with soot. Great Queen, your name will be soiled, tossed from mouth to mouth, but your light will ever shine far above all soiling.

*Vikram.* Bring the priest to me. (*Minister goes.*) I can yet go to seek her, and bring her back. But is this my eternal task? That she should always avoid me, and I should ever run after the fugitive heart? Take your flight, woman, day and night, homeless, loveless, without rest and peace. (*Enters Priest.*) Go, go, I have heard enough, I do not want to know more. (*The Priest is about to go.*) Come back.—Tell me, did she come down to the temple to pray with tears in her eyes?

*Priest.* No, Sire. Only, for a moment, she checked her horse and turned her face to the temple, bowing her head low,—then rode away fast as lightning. I cannot say if she had tears in her eyes. The light from the temple was dim.

*Vikram.* Tears in her eyes? You could not even imagine such enormity? Enough. You may go. (*The Priest goes.*) My God, you know that all the wrong that I have done to her was that I loved her. I was willing to lose my heaven and my kingdom for her love. But they have not betrayed me, only she has.

(*Enters Minister*)

*Minister.* Sire, I have sent messengers on horseback in pursuit of her.

*Vikram.* Call them back. The dream has fled away. Where can your messengers find it? Get ready my army. I will go to war myself, and crush the rebellion.

*Minister.* As you command.          [*Goes away*

*Vikram.* Devadatta, why do you sit silent and sad? The thief has fled, leaving the booty behind, and now I pick up my freedom. This is a moment of rejoicing to me. False, false friend, false are my words. Cruel pain pierces my heart.

*Devadatta.* You shall have no time for pain, or for love, now,—your life will become one stream of purpose, and carry your kingly heart to its great conquest.

*Vikram.* But I am not yet completely freed in my heart. I still believe she will soon come back to me, when she finds that the world is not her lover, and that man's heart is the only world for a woman. She will know what she has spurned, when she misses it; and my time will come when, her pride gone, she comes back and jealously begins to woo me.

(*Enters Attendant*)

*Attendant.* A letter from the Queen.

[*Gives the letter, and goes*

545

*Vikram.* She relents already. (*Reads the letter.*) Only this. Just two lines, to say that she is going to her brother in Kashmir, to ask him to help her to quell the rebellion in my kingdom. This is insult! Help from Kashmir!

*Devadatta.* Lose no time in forestalling her,—and let that be your revenge.

*Vikram.* My revenge? You shall know it.


## ACT II

*Tent in Kashmir. Vikram and the General.*

*General.* Pardon me, King, if I dare offer you advice in the interest of your kingdom.

*Vikram.* Speak to me.

*General.* The rebellion in our land has been quelled. The rebels themselves are fighting on your side. Why waste our strength and time in Kashmir when your presence in your own capital is so urgently needed?

*Vikram.* The fight here is not over yet.

*General.* But Kumarsen, the Queen's brother, is already punished for his sister's temerity. His army is routed, he is hiding for his life. His uncle, Chandrasen, is only too eager to be seated upon the vacant throne. Make him the king, and leave this unfortunate country to peace.

*Vikram.* It is not for punishment that I stay here; it is for fight. The fight has become like a picture to a painter. I must add bold lines, blend strong colours, and perfect it every day. My mind grows more and more immersed in it, as it blossoms into forms; and I leave it with a sigh when it is finished. The destruction is

546

merely its materials, out of which it takes its shape. It is beautiful as red bunches of *palash* that break out like a drunken fury, yet every one of its flowers delicately perfect.

*General.* But, Sire, this cannot go on for ever. You have other duties. The Minister has been sending me message after message, entreating me to help you to see how this war is ruining your country.

*Vikram.* I cannot see anything else in the world but what is growing under my masterly hands. Oh, the music of swords! Oh, the great battles, that clasp your breast tight like hard embraces of love! Go, General, you have other works to do,—your advices flash out best on the points of your swords. (*General goes.*) This is deliverance. The bondage has fled of itself, leaving the prisoner free. Revenge is stronger than the thin wine of love. Revenge is freedom,—freedom from the coils of cloying sweetness.

(Enters General)

*General.* I can espy a carriage coming towards our tent, perhaps bringing an envoy of peace. It has no escort of armed soldiers.

*Vikram.* Peace must follow the war. The time for it has not yet come.

*General.* Let us hear the messenger first, and then,——

*Vikram.* And then continue the war.

(Enters a Soldier)

*Soldier.* The Queen has come asking for your audience.

*Vikram.* What do you say?

*Soldier.* The Queen has come.

*Vikram.* Which Queen?

*Soldier.* Our Queen, Sumitra.

547

*Vikram.* Go, General, see who has come.

[*The General and the Soldier go*

*Vikram.* This is the third time that she has come, vainly attempting to coax me away, since I have carried war into Kashmir. But these are no dreams—these battles. To wake up suddenly, and then find again the same palace gardens, the flowers, the Queen, the long days made of sighs and small favours! No, a thousand times, no. She has come to make me captive, to take me as her trophy from the war-field into her palace hall. She may as well try to capture the thunderstorms.

(*Enters General*)

*General.* Yes, Sire, it is our own Queen who wants to see you. It breaks my heart that I cannot allow her to come freely into your presence.

*Vikram.* This is neither the time nor the place to see a woman.

*General.* But, Sire!

*Vikram.* No, no. Tell my guards to keep a strict watch at my tent door,—not for enemies, but for women.

[*General goes*

(*Enters Shankar*)

*Shankar.* I am Shankar,—King Kumarsen's servant. You have kept me captive in your tent.

*Vikram.* Yes, I know you.

*Shankar.* Your Queen waits outside your tent.

*Vikram.* She will have to wait for me farther away.

*Shankar.* It makes me blush to say that she has come humbly to ask your pardon; or, if that is impossible, to accept her punishment from your hand. For she owns that she alone was to blame,—and she asks you, in the name of all that is sacred, to spare her brother's country and her brother.

548

*Vikram.* But you must know, old man, it is war,—and this war is with her brother, and not herself. I have no time to discuss the rights and wrongs of the question with a woman. But, being a man, you ought to know that when once a war is started, rightly or wrongly, it is our man's pride that must carry it on to the end.

*Shankar.* But do you know, Sire, you are carrying on this war with a woman, and she is your Queen? Our King is merely espousing her cause, being her brother. I ask you, is it king-like, or man-like, to magnify a domestic quarrel into a war, carrying it from country to country?

*Vikram.* I warn you, old man, your tongue is becoming dangerous. You may tell the Queen, in my name, that when her brother, Kumarsen, owns his defeat and surrenders himself into our hands, the question of pardoning will then be discussed.

*Shankar.* That is as impossible as for the morning sun to kiss the dust of the western horizon. My King will never surrender himself alive into your hands, and his sister will never suffer it.

*Vikram.* Then the war must continue. But do you not think that bravery ceases to be bravery at a certain point, and becomes mere foolhardiness? Your King can never escape me. I have surrounded him on all sides, and he knows it.

*Shankar.* Yes, he knows it, and also knows that there is a great gap.

*Vikram.* What do you mean?

*Shankar.* I mean death,—the triumphal gate through which he will escape you, if I know him right. And there waits his revenge.  *[He goes*

(*Enters Attendant*)

549

*Attendant.* Sire, Chandrasen, and his wife Revati, Kumarsen's uncle and aunt, have come to see you.

*Vikram.* Ask them in. [*Attendant goes*

(*Enter Chandrasen and Revati*)

My obeisance to you both.

*Chandrasen.* May you live long!

*Revati.* May you be victorious!

*Chandrasen.* What punishment have you decided for him?

*Vikram.* If he surrenders I shall pardon him.

*Revati.* Only this, and nothing more? If tame pardon comes at the end, then why is there such preparation? Kings are not overgrown children, and war is no mere child's play.

*Vikram.* To rob was not my purpose, but to restore my honour. The head that bears the crown cannot bear insult.

*Chandrasen.* My son, forgive him. For he is mature neither in age nor in wisdom. You may deprive him of his right to the throne, or banish him, but spare him his life.

*Vikram.* I never wished to take his life.

*Revati.* Then why such an army and arms? You kill the soldiers, who have done you no harm, and spare him who is guilty?

*Vikram.* I do not understand you.

*Chandrasen.* It is nothing. She is angry with Kumarsen for having brought our country into trouble, and for giving you just cause for anger, who are so nearly related to us.

*Vikram.* Justice will be meted out to him when he is captured.

*Revati.* I have come to ask you never to suspect that we are hiding him. It is the people. Burn their crops and their villages,—drive them with hunger, and then they will bring him out.

*Chandrasen.* Gently, wife, gently! Come to the palace, son, the reception of Kashmir awaits you there.

*Vikram.* You go there now, and I shall follow you. (*They go out.*) Oh, the red flame of hell-fire! The greed and hatred in a woman's heart! Did I catch a glimpse of my own face in her face, I wonder? Are there lines like those on my forehead, the burnt tracks made by a hidden fire? Have my lips grown as thin and curved at both ends as hers, like some murderer's knife? No, my passion is for war,—it is neither for greed nor for cruelty; its fire is like love's fire, that knows no restraint, that counts no cost, that burns itself, and all that it touches, either into a flame, or to ashes.

(*Enters Attendant*)

*Attendant.* The Brahmin, Devadatta, has come, awaiting your pleasure.

*Vikram.* Devadatta has come? Bring him in,—No, no, stop. Let me think,—I know him. He has come to turn me back from the battle-field. Brahmin, you undermined the river banks, and now, when the water overflows, you piously pray that it may irrigate your fields, and then tamely go back. Will it not wash away your houses, and ruin the country? The joy of the terrible is blind,—its term of life is short, and it must gather its plunder in fearful haste, like a mad elephant uprooting the lotus from the pond. Wise counsels will come, in their turn, when the great force is spent.—No, I must not see the Brahmin.          [*Attendant goes*

(*Enters Amaru, the chieftain of Trichur hills*)

*Amaru.* Sire, I have come at your bidding, and I own you as my King.

*Vikram.* You are the chief of this place?

*Amaru.* Yes. I am the chief of Trichur. You are the King of many kings, and I am your servant. I have a daughter, whose name is Ila. She is young and comely. Do not think me vain when I say that she is worthy to be your spouse. She is waiting outside. Permit me, King, and I shall send her to you as the best greeting of this land of flowers.                    [*He goes out*

(*Enters Ila with her Attendant*)

*Vikram.* Ah! She comes, as a surprise of dawn, when the moment before it seemed like a dark night. Come, maiden, you have made the battle-field forget itself. Kashmir has shot her best arrow, at last, to pierce the heart of the war-god. You make me feel that my eyes had been wandering among the wilderness of things, to find at last their fulfilment. But why do you stand so silent, with your eyes on the ground? I can almost see a trembling of pain in your limbs, whose intensity makes it invisible.

*Ila (kneeling).* I have heard that you are a great King. Be pleased to grant me my prayer.

*Vikram.* Rise up, fair maiden. This earth is not worthy to be touched by your feet. Why do you kneel in the dust? There is nothing that I cannot grant you.

*Ila.* My father has given me to you. I beg myself back from your hands. You have wealth untold, and territories unlimited,—go and leave me behind in the dust; there is nothing that you can want.

*Vikram.* Is there, indeed, nothing that I can want? How shall I show you my heart? Where is its wealth? Where are its territories? It is empty. Had I no kingdom, but only you——

*Ila.* Then first take my life,—as you take that of the

wild deer of the forest, piercing her heart with your arrows,——

*Vikram.* But why, child,—why such contempt for me? Am I so utterly unworthy of you? I have won kingdoms with the might of my arms. Can I not hope to beg your heart for me?

*Ila.* But my heart is not mine. I have given it to one who left me months ago, promising to come back and meet me in the shade of our ancient forest. Days pass, and I wait, and the silence of the forest grows wistful. If he find me not, when he comes back! If he go away for ever, and the forest shadows keep their ancient watch for the love-meeting that remains eternally unfulfilled! King, do not take me away,—leave me for him who has left me to find me again.

*Vikram.* What a fortunate man is he! But I warn you, girl, gods are jealous of our love. Listen to my secret. There was a time when I despised the whole world, and only loved. I woke up from my dream, and found that the world was there,—only my love burst as a bubble. What is his name, for whom you wait?

*Ila.* He is Kashmir's King. His name is Kumarsen.

*Vikram.* Kumarsen!

*Ila.* Do you know him? He is known to all. Kashmir has given its heart to him.

*Vikram.* Kumarsen? Kashmir's King?

*Ila.* Yes. He must be your friend.

*Vikram.* But do you not know that the sun of his fortune has set? Give up all hope of him. He is like a hunted animal, running and hiding from one hole to another. The poorest beggar in these hills is happier than he.

*Ila.* I hardly understand you, King.

*Vikram.* You women sit in the seclusion of your hearts and only love. You do not know how the roaring torrent of the world passes by, and we men are carried away in its waves in all directions. With your sad, big eyes, filled with tears, you sit and watch, clinging to flimsy hope. But learn to despair, my child.

*Ila.* Tell me the truth, King. Do not deceive me. I am so very little and so trivial. But I am all his own. Where,—in what homeless wilds,—is my lover roaming? I will go to seek him,—I, who never have been out of my house. Show me the way,——

*Vikram.* His enemy's soldiers are after him,—he is doomed.

*Ila.* But are you not his friend? Will you not save him? A king is in danger, and will you suffer it as a King? Are you not honour-bound to succour him? I know that all the world loved him. But where are they, in his time of misfortune? Sire, you are great in power, but what is your power for if you do not help the great? Can you keep yourself aloof? Then show me the way,—I will offer my life for him,—the one, weak woman.

*Vikram.* Love him, love him with all you have—Love him, who is the King of your precious heart. I have lost my love's heaven myself,—but let me have the happiness to make you happy. I will not covet your love.— The withered branch cannot hope to blossom with borrowed flowers. Trust me. I am your friend. I will bring him to you.

*Ila.* Noble King! I owe you my life and my heaven of happiness.

*Vikram.* Go, and be ready with your bridal dress. I will change the tune of my music. (*Ila goes.*) This war is

554

growing tiresome. But peace is insipid. Homeless fugitive, you are more fortunate than I am. Woman's love, like heaven's watchful eyes, follows you wherever you go in this world, making your defeat a triumph and misfortune splendid, like sunset clouds.

*(Enters Devadatta)*

*Devadatta.* Save me from my pursuers.

*Vikram.* Who are they?

*Devadatta.* They are your guards, King. They kept me under strict watch for this everlasting half-hour. I talked to them of art and letters; they were amused. They thought I was playing the fool to please them. Then I began to recite to them the best lyrics of Kalidas,—and it soothed this pair of yokels to sleep. In perfect disgust, I left their tent to come to you.

*Vikram.* These guards should be punished for their want of taste in going off to sleep when the prisoner recited Kalidas.

*Devadatta.* We shall think of the punishment later on. In the meanwhile, we must leave this miserable war and go back home. Once I used to think that only they died of love's separation who were the favoured of fortune, delicately nurtured. But since I left home to come here, I have discovered that even a poor Brahmin is not too small to fall a victim to angered love.

*Vikram.* Love and death are not too careful in their choice of victims. They are impartial. Yes, friend, let us go back home. Only I have one thing to do before I leave this place. Try to find out, from the chief of Trichur, Kumarsen's hiding-place. Tell him, when you find him, that I am no longer his enemy. And, friend, if somebody else is there with him,—if you meet her,——

*Devadatta.* Yes, yes, I know. She is ever in our thoughts, yet she is beyond our words. She who is noble, her sorrow has to be great.

*Vikram.* Friend, you have come to me like the first sudden breeze of spring. Now my flowers will follow, with all the memories of the past happy years.

[*Devadatta goes*

*(Enters Chandrasen)*

I have glad tidings for you. I have pardoned Kumarsen.

*Chandrasen.* You may have pardoned him,—but now that I represent Kashmir, he must await his country's judgment at my hands. He shall have his punishment from me.

*Vikram.* What punishment?

*Chandrasen.* He shall be deprived of his throne.

*Vikram.* Impossible! His throne I will restore to him.

*Chandrasen.* What right have you in Kashmir's throne?

*Vikram.* The right of the victorious. This throne is now mine, and I will give it to him.

*Chandrasen.* You give it to him! Do I not know proud Kumarsen, from his infancy? Do you think he will accept his father's throne as a gift from you? He can bear your vengeance, but not your generosity.

*(Enters a Messenger)*

*Messenger.* The news has reached us that Kumarsen is coming in a closed carriage to surrender himself.

[*Goes out*

*Chandrasen.* Incredible! The lion comes to beg his chains! Is life so precious?

*Vikram.* But why does he come in a closed carriage?

*Chandrasen.* How can he show himself? The eyes of the crowd in the streets will pierce him, like arrows, to the quick. King, put out the lamp, when he comes, receive him in darkness. Do not let him suffer the insult of the light.

(*Enters Devadatta*)

*Devadatta.* I hear that the King, Kumarsen, is coming to see you of his own will.

*Vikram.* I will receive him with solemn rituals,— with you as our priest. Ask my general to employ his soldiers to make preparation for a wedding festival.

(*Enter the Brahmin Elders*)

*All.* Victory be to you!

*First Elder.* We hear that you have invited our King, to restore him to his throne,—Therefore we have come to bless you for

(*Enters Shankar*)

the joy that you have given to Kashmir.

[*They bless him, and the King bows to them. The Brahmins go out.*

*Shankar* (*to Chandrasen*). Sire, is it true that Kumarsen is coming to surrender himself to his enemies?

*Chandrasen.* Yes, it is true.

*Shankar.* Worse than a thousand lies. Oh, my beloved King, I am your old servant, I have suffered pain that only God knows, yet never complained. But how can I bear this? That you should travel through all the roads of Kashmir to enter your cage of prison? Why did not your servant die before this day?

(*Enters a Soldier*)

*Soldier.* The carriage is at the door.

*Vikram.* Have they no instruments at hand,—flutes and drums? Let them strike a glad tune. (*Coming near the*

557

*door.*) I welcome you, my kingly friend, with all my heart.

(*Enters Sumitra, with a covered tray in her hands*)

*Vikram.* Sumitra! My Queen!

*Sumitra.* King Vikram, day and night you sought him in hills and forests, spreading devastation, neglecting your people and your honour, and to-day he sends through me to you his coveted head,—the head upon which death sits even more majestic than his crown.

*Vikram.* My Queen!

*Sumitra.* Sire, no longer your Queen; for merciful death has claimed me.

(*Falls and dies*)

*Shankar.* My King, my Master, my darling boy, you have done well. You have come to your eternal throne. God has allowed me to live for so long to witness this glory. And now, my days are done, and your servant will follow you.

(*Enters Ila, dressed in a bridal dress*)

*Ila.* King, I hear the bridal music. Where is my lover? I am ready.

# KARNA AND KUNTI

# KARNA AND KUNTI

*The Pandava Queen Kunti before marriage had a son, Karna, who, in manhood, became the commander of the Kaurava host. To hide her shame she abandoned him at birth, and a charioteer, Adhiratha, brought him up as his son.*

*Karna.* I am Karna, the son of the charioteer, Adhiratha, and I sit here by the bank of holy Ganges to worship the setting sun. Tell me who you are.

*Kunti.* I am the woman who first made you acquainted with that light you are worshipping.

*Karna.* I do not understand: but your eyes melt my heart as the kiss of the morning sun melts the snow on a mountain-top, and your voice rouses a blind sadness within me of which the cause may well lie beyond the reach of my earliest memory. Tell me, strange woman, what mystery binds my birth to you?

*Kunti.* Patience, my son. I will answer when the lids of darkness come down over the prying eyes of day. In the meanwhile, know that I am Kunti.

*Karna.* Kunti! The mother of Arjuna?

*Kunti.* Yes, indeed, the mother of Arjuna, your antagonist. But do not, therefore, hate me. I still remember the day of the trial of arms in Hastina when you, an unknown boy, boldly stepped into the arena, like the first ray of dawn among the stars of night. Ah! who was that unhappy woman whose eyes kissed your bare, slim body through tears that blessed you, where she sat among the women of the royal household behind

561

the arras? Why, the mother of Arjuna! Then the Brahmin, master of arms, stepped forth and said, "No youth of mean birth may challenge Arjuna to a trial of strength." You stood speechless, like a thunder-cloud at sunset flashing with an agony of suppressed light. But who was the woman whose heart caught fire from your shame and anger, and flared up in silence? The mother of Arjuna! Praised be Duryodhana, who perceived your worth, and then and there crowned you King of Anga, thus winning the Kauravas a champion. Overwhelmed at this good fortune, Adhiratha, the charioteer, broke through the crowd; you instantly rushed to him and laid your crown at his feet amid the jeering laughter of the Pandavas and their friends. But there was one woman of the Pandava house whose heart glowed with joy at the heroic pride of such humility;—even the mother of Arjuna!

*Karna.* But what brings you here alone, Mother of kings?

*Kunti.* I have a boon to crave.

*Karna.* Command me, and whatever manhood and my honour as a Kshatriya permit shall be offered at your feet.

*Kunti.* I have come to take you.

*Karna.* Where?

*Kunti.* To my breast thirsting for your love, my son.

*Karna.* Fortunate mother of five brave kings, where can you find place for me, a small chieftain of lowly descent?

*Kunti.* Your place is before all my other sons.

*Karna.* But what right have I to take it?

*Kunti.* Your own God-given right to your mother's love.

*Karna.* The gloom of evening spreads over the earth, silence rests on the water, and your voice leads me back to some primal world of infancy lost in twilit consciousness. However, whether this be dream, or fragment of forgotten reality, come near and place your right hand on my forehead. Rumour runs that I was deserted by my mother. Many a night she has come to me in my slumber, but when I cried, "Open your veil, show me your face!" her figure always vanished. Has this same dream come this evening while I wake? See, yonder the lamps are lighted in your son's tents across the river; and on this side behold the tent-domes of my Kauravas, like the suspended waves of a spell-arrested storm at sea. Before the din of to-morrow's battle, in the awful hush of this field where it must be fought, why should the voice of the mother of my opponent, Arjuna, bring me a message of forgotten motherhood? and why should my name take such music from her tongue as to draw my heart out to him and his brothers?

*Kunti.* Then delay not, my son, come with me!

*Karna.* Yes, I will come and never ask question, never doubt. My soul responds to your call; and the struggle for victory and fame and the rage of hatred have suddenly become untrue to me, as the delirious dream of a night in the serenity of the dawn. Tell me whither you mean to lead?

*Kunti.* To the other bank of the river, where those lamps burn across the ghastly pallor of the sands.

*Karna.* Am I there to find my lost mother for ever?

*Kunti.* O my son!

*Karna.* Then why did you banish me—a castaway uprooted from my ancestral soil, adrift in a homeless current of indignity? Why set a bottomless chasm between Arjuna and myself, turning the natural attachment of kinship to the dread attraction of hate? You remain speechless. Your shame permeates the vast darkness and sends invisible shivers through my limbs. Leave my question unanswered! Never explain to me what made you rob your son of his mother's love! Only tell me why you have come to-day to call me back to the ruins of a heaven wrecked by your own hands?

*Kunti.* I am dogged by a curse more deadly than your reproaches: for, though surrounded by five sons, my heart shrivels like that of a woman deprived of her children. Through the great rent that yawned for my deserted first-born, all my life's pleasures have run to waste. On that accursed day when I belied my motherhood you could not utter a word; to-day your recreant mother implores you for generous words. Let your forgiveness burn her heart like fire and consume its sin.

*Karna.* Mother, accept my tears!

*Kunti.* I did not come with the hope of winning you back to my arms, but with that of restoring your rights to you. Come and receive, as a king's son, your due among your brothers.

*Karna.* I am more truly the son of a charioteer, and do not covet the glory of greater parentage.

*Kunti.* Be that as it may, come and win back the kingdom which is yours by right!

*Karna.* Must you, who once refused me a mother's love, tempt me with a kingdom? The quick bond of kindred which you severed at its root is dead, and can never grow again. Shame were mine should I hasten to call the mother of kings mother, and abandon *my* mother in the charioteer's house!

*Kunti.* You are great, my son! How God's punish-

564

ment invisibly grows from a tiny seed to a giant life! The helpless babe disowned by his mother comes back a man through the dark maze of events to smite his brothers!

*Karna.* Mother, have no fear! I know for certain that victory awaits the Pandavas. Peaceful and still though this night be, my heart is full of the music of a hopeless venture and baffled end. Ask me not to leave those who are doomed to defeat. Let the Pandavas win the throne, since they must: I remain with the desperate and forlorn. On the night of my birth you left me naked and unnamed to disgrace: leave me once again without pity to the calm expectation of defeat and death!

# INDEX OF FIRST LINES